SOLDIER TO SOLDIER
HEART TO HEART

SOLDIER TO SOLDIER
HEART TO HEART

A DOCTOR'S STORIES FROM A MILITARY CAMP

ADEL GOBRAN HANNA, M.D.

Copyright © 2011 and 2014 by Adel Gobran Hanna, M.D. All rights reserved. No part of this publication may be reproduced, stored in a retrieval system, or transmitted in any way by any means—electronic, mechanical, photocopy, recording, or otherwise—without the prior permission of the copyright holder, except as provided by USA copyright law.

Published by Alpha & Omega Healing Arts, New Albany, OH.
Unless otherwise noted, all Scripture references are taken from the *Holy Bible, New International Version®, NIV®*. Copyright © 1973, 1978, 1984 by Biblica, Inc.™ Used by permission of Zondervan. All rights reserved worldwide. www.zondervan.com

Scripture references marked KJV are taken from the *King James Version* of the Bible.

Scripture references marked NKJV are taken from the *New King James Version*. Copyright © 1982 by Thomas Nelson, Inc. Used by permission. All rights reserved.

Scripture references marked AB are taken from *The Amplified Bible*, Old Testament. Copyright © 1954, 1958, 1987, by The Lockman Foundation. Used by permission.

Second Edition
ISBN : 978-0-9960576-0-8
ISBN : 978-0-9960576-1-5 (e-book)
Library of Congress Catalog Card Number: 2014938967
www.hopeforsoldiers.org

This book is particularly dedicated to the memory of my loving dad, Gobran Hanna Khouri, who believed in me and sent me to America to be a doctor. He died before he could see his dream become a reality.

To all my past and present patients who honored me with their trust, especially those whose heart-changing stories are in the pages of this book.

Soldier to Soldier, Heart to Heart is my heartfelt, God-inspired contribution to all our soldiers and veterans and to my new home: America, land of my dreams.

CONTENTS

Author's Note ix

Acknowledgments. xi

Introduction. xvii

Chapter One: Abortion 1
Chapter Two: Anger. 7

Chapter Three: Anxiety............................13
Chapter Four: Compassion..........................23
Chapter Five: Courage 29
Chapter Six: Death and Healing the Grief..........33
Chapter Seven: Deception and True Freedom.........37
Chapter Eight: Life-Changing Decisions............47
Chapter Nine: Daddy's Love........................55
Chapter Ten: Divorce and Child Custody Wars.......59
Chapter Eleven: Fear..............................69
Chapter Twelve: Focusing for Survival.............83
Chapter Thirteen: God, Spirituality, and New Beginnings......89
Chapter Fourteen: Healing Childhood Wounds.......113
Chapter Fifteen: Humor in Wartime................119
Chapter Sixteen: Leadership......................125
Chapter Seventeen: Mama's Love...................137
Chapter Eighteen: Marriage and War...............145
Chapter Nineteen: Music and Healing..............161
Chapter Twenty: Patriotism.......................173
Chapter Twenty-One: PTSD, Light at the End of the Tunnel....177
Chapter Twenty-Two: Race and Prejudice...........195
Chapter Twenty-Three: Rape.......................209
Chapter Twenty-Four: Romance.....................215
Chapter Twenty-Five: Shining Like a Diamond......221
Chapter Twenty-Six: Soldiers' Survival Skills....245
Chapter Twenty-Seven: Surviving Words that Kill..253
Chapter Twenty-Eight: Thank You, Soldier.........261

Conclusion: The Liberty of Redemption............265

Resources for Your Spiritual Pilgrimage 271

AUTHOR'S NOTE

ALL THE STORIES here are true. In order to protect the soldiers' identities and confidentiality, minor details such as states of origin and all the names and ranks were changed.

Advice and recommendations offered here are not meant to replace your medical provider's individual evaluation, diagnosis, and treatment.

This book is not endorsed in any way by the military. Yet it is my hope that the reader will not only grow spiritually in the knowledge of God, but also find a renewed sense of patriotism, admiration, and respect for America, our soldiers, and the military.

ACKNOWLEDGMENTS

FINISHING THIS BOOK was a journey like no other in my life. It was like taking a long, hard, and risky hike though uncharted terrains—mountains, deep valleys, turbulent rivers, obstacles, human and natural hurdles, occasional calm waters, through lack and plenty, oftentimes alone except for the ever present company of the Almighty.

As I began to see the light at the end of the tunnel, I remembered how it felt when I first received my acceptance letter to start my freshman year at an undergraduate university in Indiana, leaving the comfort of my childhood home overseas to start a new, frightening, and exciting journey of my life in the USA.

At that university I began to write my thoughts and feelings about this amazing country, America, the land of my dreams, in the college newspaper, and I have never stopped writing since then.

I also remembered the joy of reading my letter of acceptance to medical school and the exuberance of receiving my MD degree after years of hard, lonely, sleepless nights—two divine miracles in their own right.

Yet to me, the road I traveled to finish this book was the mother of all the difficult journeys of my life, and the day I held the completed manuscript tightly in my arms was the mother of all memories.

All previous challenges overcome with God's help and providence seem now like small races and mini-battles compared to the long, arduous marathon and full-fledged war of completing this God-inspired and God-orchestrated finished product: *Soldier to Soldier, Heart to Heart*, a doctor's stories from a military camp.

Above all things and everyone else, thank You, Jesus: to God be the glory. He began this work in me, and I pray that it will ultimately be about God, for His glory, and from His Father's heart to ours.

Thank you, Mom, Anna (Tikabou). Your sacrificial love has always encouraged me to run the race that God has ordained for me and to accomplish all my dreams.

You've never stopped loving and encouraging me even when there was nothing but setbacks and endless obstacles on my path. By your godly, God-fearing walk in life, you've shown me more of Christ by example than thousands of eloquent words said by many others about Him. This book is dedicated to you.

Thank you Dad, Gobran. To me you're one of the clouds of witnesses watching and cheering me and the rest of our family. You always believed in me and invested your life to see me one day become a doctor in America. This book is in your memory, Dad.

Tatiana, my lovely wife, what a journey! Thank you for your love, compassion, caring, and encouragement. Your encouraging words can't be matched. God's Word is always the ultimate wisdom in this life. "Though one may be overpowered, two can defend themselves. A cord of three strands is not quickly broken" (Eccl. 4:12). "As for me and my house we will serve the Lord" (Josh. 24:15).

Thank you, AJ, Andre, my wonderful, smart, warmhearted children (my tigers). Remember, true joy, peace, and strength can only come from God! I'm so proud of you. Ana, my lively, and very talented child who is growing daily in the amazing joy, beauty, and infinite wisdom of the fear of God, and of surrender and obedience to His Word. Thank you for the Logo! And Abby, my little, innocent princess and God's gift to me who will one day grow like her sister to be God's Proverbs 31 woman. You are all blessings in my life and I'm proud of you. Your little hands typed for me, and your innocent, encouraging hearts delighted me when I needed a

ACKNOWLEDGMENTS

smile. You're all God's special gift to me, and I pray that this book will encourage you to know God intimately, to believe in His better ways for you, and to obey Him all the days of your lives. Hold on tightly to your humility as you put your God-given talents to practice and as you accomplish daily His purposes for you. I love you and am proud of each one of you.

Joseph, Anwar, Iman, Hani (Nabil), and Farid—thank you from the bottom of my heart. Each one of you has different God-given gifts, but all of you have in common the amazing gift of listening, caring, and counseling. You were and still are bright and shining lights at my life's finest or darkest moments.

Thank you, soldiers, for your sacrifices. We are all indebted to you. Words can't describe my heartfelt appreciation to our fallen soldiers and to every mother, father, brother, sister, family member, friend, or significant other who lost a loved one.

Thank you, Huda, for typing some stories; it really made a difference. Haddas, Muna, Almaz, Amina, Izgaharia, Alganesh, Samhar, Hala, Alfatih, Abraham, Amoney, Kay, Doctors Blake and DiCarlo, Ashley, Sue, Cindy, Laura, Val, Nate, Jake, Amanda, Nora, John, Kassie, and Kristin, thank you for your caring and encouragement. Andy, Abel, Perry III, Saria, Demaris, and Alex, God has a plan for you. Never give up. Joan, you have blessed me with your listening ears and the many times I saw how deeply you care about your family and those around you. Thank you all my family members and dear friends. God bless you all!

Thanks to the great medics and active duty soldiers at the camp's TMC (Troop Medical Clinic), whose skills to help me do my doctor's duty I desperately needed and were always provided.

Thanks to Dr. Cherrica, Debra, Selvie, and Ruth—four wonderful women of God who care and pray continually, and to each and every Columbus, Ohio, area medical drug company representative who cared enough to bless this book with encouragement.

I have also been greatly blessed by Lisa's encouraging smiles, kind words, prayers, and listening ears, by David at Vineyard Columbus for his gentle, encouraging spirit, by Ihab and Hala, and by the mean, tasty Northern Lite lattes and Columbus, Ohio, area lighthearted, uplifting encouragement of friendly, upbeat Jenna, and also Justin, Kim, and Nick at the good old Caribou Coffee.

Allen V., at the CMDA (Christian Medical & Dental Associations) you have been a blessing to me throughout the years. Your prayers have always reminded me that God loves me and remains in control of my life no matter what I go through.

Dr. David Stevens and the rest of the Christian Medical & Dental Associations, with its leadership and mission statement, have blessed me and countless others beyond measure. I thank you and the dedicated shepherds and spiritual mentors I have listed at the end of this book. You have been Christlike and bright beacons of light in a hard and dark world.

Thank you to all those who nurtured my medical career and mentored me, Doctors First, and Currant, and a host of other doctors during my medical school, residency, and practice years, including the excellent physicians at the HealthEast care system.

Thank you!

AFRC-TVA-OP

MEMORANDUM FOR: ADEL HANNA, MD

SUBJECT: Letter of Appreciation

1. This letter recognizes your outstanding contribution to the redeployment of Soldiers from the 80th Division (IT), Richmond, VA during July and August 2006.

2. During this stressful process, your caring, compassion and positive attitude were an inspiration to our Soldiers and their families. You actively participated as a member of the healthcare or case management team, lending your unique talents and expertise to ensure that each Soldier's individual needs were met. Whether you were directly involved in the care of Soldiers or you provided invaluable administrative support, you significantly contributed to their successful transition back from the theater.

3. You are to be commended for your attention to detail, commitment to excellence and willingness to do what ever you personally could to "take care of Soldiers". We applaud your exceptional efforts and extend our gratitude and appreciation for a job well done!

4. A copy of this letter will be placed in your permanent personnel file.

DISTRIBUTION:

1 – Indiv Conc
1 – Unit Files

INTRODUCTION

AS SOLDIERS WALKED briskly in the early morning hours towards the Troop Medical Clinic (TMC), the waiting room gradually filled. "Sick call" at the military camp was about to start. To the young men and women who filled the chairs of the waiting area with its nineteen-inch TV with a broken antenna, those short morning hours offered them a welcome temporary break from the daily grind of training for war. The vigorous physical and emotional demands of their extensive combat training made this early morning pilgrimage to the TMC a chance for many to rest and reflect on their lives.

They were from nearly every state in the Union and various US territories. Young and old, men and women—all are far away from the comfort zones of their civilian lives, heading to faraway nations with names some could hardly pronounce—Iraq, Afghanistan, Kuwait, and Kosovo. They were all heading into the unknown, into the most dangerous, life-changing mission of their young lives.

Some came from the warm climates of Florida, Texas, Alabama, and Guam and bravely marched on the snow-filled rugged terrain of the camp, battling the winter chills, hypothermia, and frostbites. Others, from the freezing temperatures of Minnesota, Wisconsin, and the Dakotas, risked heat exhaustion as they marched wearing their body armor, heavy gear, and holding tightly to their M16s and Kevlar as the merciless summer temperatures soared to the hundreds.

They ventured to the Troop Medical Clinic to see me and a team of medics and medical providers, seeking help not only for their burns, bruises, bumps, cuts, abscesses, ingrown toenails, colds, frostbites, and heat exhaustion, but to be listened to and find rest for their inner wounds and restless emotions. Each of the soldiers had a story to tell. Each story made me think, laugh, reflect, and tear up as one soldier after another poured out his or her heart and shared with me about the childhood homes left behind, dreams, setbacks, fears, tears, God, spirituality, life, and death.

Each story was different from the others, yet all had a common human thread that binds us all together—our deep need for healing, love, security, acceptance, forgiveness, and the desire to start anew. Faced with the daunting task ahead and the newness of their surroundings, each began to remember, think, hope, and gradually change. The old self-absorption and self-focus was now eclipsed by new realities—readiness to fight and die for America, freedom, a life of serving others, a quest for God, and a renewed thirst for spirituality.

It was with God's divine orchestration that I found myself like an instrument playing God's great composition; a great symphony with divine, compassionate melodies of His love, acceptance, and embrace of every soldier and his or her life's story.

Ultimately, their stories will inspire you and make you reflect and grow as we all begin to realize that their stories are not only theirs but they are ours as well, and not only from one soldier to another, but from the depth of God's heart of love to their hearts and to ours.

CHAPTER 1

ABORTION

Abortion

He sends forth his word and heals them and rescues them from the pit and destruction.
—Ps. 107:20 AB

Help! I'm still bleeding

I WAS QUITE surprised to see twenty-four-year-old Private Madison, just two weeks shy of her deployment to Afghanistan, breaking down in tears as she entered the exam room for her medical visit.

During her last two visits she had been full of cheer and bubbly in contrast to the grim look, sobbing, and ceaseless tears that flowed from her eyes as she made her way to the examination table.

"I can't stop bleeding. I need help…I need help, doctor," she said, crying.

I figured out that something was awfully wrong. She must be bleeding vaginally, from a very heavy period, I thought.

"I'm so sorry, Dr. Hanna—I didn't tell you last visit that I had an abortion two weeks before my deployment. I was three weeks pregnant. The doctor who performed it told me some tissue was still inside and will come out on its own. But the bleeding has not stopped since then. I feel so terrible. I'm so ashamed," she said, drying her flowing tears.

I had no idea. I had never encountered a situation like Madison's before. I knew I needed divine wisdom to listen and speak words of comfort and healing to her broken heart. For the next few minutes, I listened as she talked with eyes filled with tears about her ordeal—a boyfriend who had left it to her to make the decision, a guilt-ridden conscience, and her overwhelming sense of shame that she had let God, her mom, twin sister, and her Baptist church down. Having the abortion and keeping it a secret from everyone, including her mother and twin sister caused great emotional turmoil.

I embarked quickly on the medical exam and arranged for an immediate referral to a gynecologist. I knew her bleeding and physical discomfort would soon be over, but the journey of her emotional healing had just begun. I felt it was the right time to offer her all the help she needed for this journey. We began to talk.

"Madison, you seemed so happy the last time I saw you. I had no idea you were going through that. I'm glad you decided to talk," I said.

As she continued to sob, I reached quietly to the keyboard of my computer and Googled "post abortion recovery groups" in the area. I asked her permission to call the numbers on the screen and got her a phone counseling appointment the next day with one of the support group centers.

She thanked me and talked about her deep sense of pain for "failing God, my church, and my family." Her tender tears touched my heart, and I found myself telling her about God's love and forgiveness and the importance of forgiving herself.

"Madison, can I pray with you?" I asked.

"Yes, please." She nodded.

As she closed her misty eyes, I began to pray for God's forgiveness, love, comfort, and peace to her tired and weary heart. I could see her eyes tightly shut as I uttered the last word of my prayer, "Amen," that she softly repeated after me.

She dried her tears after the short prayer, thanked me, and gave me a big hug, promising to see the camp's behavioral health services, contact a few support groups, and return the next day for a follow-up visit.

For the rest of the day, I searched for and contacted a few more resources, including a kind, compassionate woman who had gone through an abortion of her own in the past and patiently shared with me by phone the detailed steps of the healing process that she had to undergo after her ordeal.

Madison returned for her follow-up appointment in two days as expected, her pretty face beaming with a smile

"I just came from the chaplain's office. I feel so much better. I'm no longer bleeding," she said, cheerfully, and began to ask me multiple questions as soon as she sat on the exam table.

"Dr. Hanna, how long do you think the grief will last? What do you think? Should I tell Mom and my twin sister? How will I ever get over what I feel inside?"

I tried to answer her barrage of questions to the best of my ability, but I knew my best effort would be no match for the words of a lady who had once walked in Madison's shoes.

"Madison, I talked yesterday with a caring woman who had an abortion before becoming a committed Christian and of course I never mentioned your name," I said. "She told me about her own painful experience, the overwhelming guilt she felt, and how she started to heal. She said so many important things about the healing walk that you will go through and I wrote all of them down. Is it okay to read the list of things she told me?" I said, digging in my pocket for the folded piece of paper.

"Thanks for taking the time to talk to her. I do want to hear what she had to say," she quickly answered.

For the next few minutes, I read Madison the exact words of one compassionate heart to a wounded soul she had never met.

"This is what she told me to tell you: 'The most important thing for me was to find out why I chose to terminate the pregnancy. I knew that I was bound to do it again if I had not learned to deal with and resolve the personal and emotional reasons in my life that led me to do it in the first place.

"I eventually decided to go to a pregnancy center that counsels women who have had abortions. Some of the women I met there finally came to the center after having more than one abortion, like this woman who had had seven abortions. She had so many unresolved issues in her life, and she finally realized that she needed to deal with the reasons that forced her to do it over and over again.

"At the pregnancy center, I talked and cried with many of the women who had gone through it. We cried again and again, held hands, asked God for forgiveness, and asked our babies who died for their forgiveness. Then on the last day of our meeting and counseling we all walked together outside the building. It was a clear, sunny day, and each one of us held a balloon in memory of our babies, who are now safe in God's arms in heaven. As we held tightly to them, the pregnancy center counselor told us it was okay to let go of our balloons, representing our babies, and release them to God until we meet them again in heaven. As we let go of the balloons and they flew farther and farther, higher and higher, we were reminded that we can now release our babies to God.

"She needs to receive God's forgiveness when she asks for it, and to let go of her baby and release her, like that balloon, into God's hands until she meets her baby again."

As I read the last sentence, tears started flowing from Madison's tender eyes. The words of a total stranger, who had once walked the same path, had touched and comforted her heart.

ABORTION

"That was the best thing. That was the best thing," she said, her eyes filled with tears.

Madison came to see me for one more visit after her return from a four-day pass, one day before her departure to Afghanistan. She was no longer crying. She looked very refreshed from her visit to her devout Christian family, who had comforted her with unconditional love, choosing not to condemn her.

"I'm leaving with my unit tomorrow. I'm doing well. Thanks for being there for me," she said, giving me one last hug. She had a peaceful smile on her face.

As she stepped out of the exam room, I couldn't help but reflect on the words that I'd once read to her from the folded piece of paper in my pocket. Maybe she had come to that place of rest, to that clear, sunny day in her life where she was finally able to release her beautiful balloon to go farther and farther, higher and higher to heaven, to God's open hands, until she meets her baby again.

> For you created my inmost being; *you knit me together in my mother's womb*. I praise you because I am fearfully and wonderfully made; your works are wonderful, I know that full well. My frame was not hidden from you when I was made in the secret place. When I was woven together in the depths of the earth, *your eyes saw my unformed body*. All the days ordained for me were written in your book before one of them came to be.
> —Ps. 139:13-16, emphasis added

CHAPTER 2

ANGER

Anger: Photo provided by Camp Atterbury Public Affairs

A gentle answer turns away wrath, but
a harsh word stirs up anger.
—Prov. 15:1

Be angry, and do not sin: do not let the
sun go down on your wrath.
—Eph. 4:26 NKJV

A raging heart

I DIDN'T KNOW what to expect when I entered the exam room where Private Melissa stood impatiently waiting for me. Her reputation of being an angry, disgruntled soldier followed her. The medics warned me before entering the room about her hot temper.

"I'm just not the type who likes to talk, doc. I'm tired of talking. That's all I did in Iraq, Germany, Walter Reed, and now Fort Knox—" she blurted out soon after I walked in.

I briefly looked at her chart and the "cold symptoms" complaint listed by the medic.

"So, Melissa, what brings you in to this humble dwelling today?" I asked, expecting to hear some coughing, wheezing, congestion complaints.

"I just about lost it in Iraq. The army sent me first to Germany. I wanted to go back to Iraq, but they won't let me and sent me here instead," she said angrily.

It was clear to me by now that what was bothering her was way more than her "cold" complaint. Soon after my medical exam and treatment plan, I placed the stethoscope down and offered my "I'm all ears" statement.

"First, I get told that I have ADD. I've gotten so used to bottling my feelings down and exploding in anger when I can't take it anymore. I don't want to go over those painful memories over and over again, doctor; I don't want to be judged," she said in a calmer voice.

It seemed to me like she wanted to talk about her "bottled emotions" but was afraid of being judged and of a "professional" looking down at her.

"It's always good to open your heart, Melissa, to someone you trust and feel comfortable with. I promise you one thing; I won't judge you. You can talk about anything that bothers you."

That was all it took and for the next half hour she talked freely and passionately about her life—her childhood, hurts, hopes, and dreams—her dad the pastor, whom she missed a lot, the sister she loved, and an ex-fiancé whom she had "beat so hard" in one of her anger fits.

The tension in her life between her deep-rooted anger and inner quest for love became clearer to me as she continued to speak.

"People don't understand how much a child remembers. I still remember it like it happened yesterday—the day Mom left Dad. I saw Dad cry for the first time in my life. Seeing Daddy cry was so unusual. I've never seen him cry except one time at my grandma's funeral."

It was easy for me to tell from her facial expressions how deeply engraved in her was the memory of that day.

"He cried so hard when she left him and took me and my sister away to Nebraska," she repeated.

Melissa, who was given the choice of "staying with Dad or leaving with Mom," chose to leave with her mother because she didn't want her sister to be alone.

"I felt so bad for Daddy. I felt so bad for him."

Years after the day that nearly shattered her world, Melissa remembered the deep pain she felt when her mom decided to only send her sister to live with her dad and how desperately she yearned to go with her to live with her father.

"When he came to pick up Sarah, my sister, I felt so confused and hurt. All I could think about was, 'What about me? Why does she get to go with Dad without me?'"

Her words made me think about the pain she must have felt during that second separation from him and her sister and about her dad who must have endured so much in pursuit of his daughters. Unfortunately, shortly after his divorce he resigned from the pulpit because he felt his denomination would not let him be the church's pastor. Melissa shared with me the injustice he was subjected to by her mom while she spoke fondly of her dad.

"He never said anything bad about Mom. She lied about him not paying child support and many other things. He just showed up one day and brought with him all the cancelled child support checks that mom had already cashed, but still he wouldn't say anything about all the nasty things she had told us about him. She is not a happy person. It's best that they are no longer together. He is now happy with his new wife," she said.

I couldn't help but notice how Melissa's new calm demeanor stood in vast contrast to her initial anger—a very welcome change. Her dad's positive influence in her life was obvious to me. She proudly shared with me a story about her dad and stepmom that left a positive mark on her heart.

"My stepmom was upset with me and wouldn't stop yelling until Dad stepped in and saw me crying. He gave her a very angry look and said, 'Julie. Shut up and sit down!' That was amazing! I just kept thinking, *Yah, yah, yah. This is my daddy. This is my daddy*," she said, her voice overflowing with the sense of honor and pride she felt at that moment.

Her early childhood was filled with regular church attendance with her sister, both "falling asleep on the pews" during her dad's sermons, and many "exciting tent revival nights" with visiting pastors that she enjoyed so much.

I listened to her spiritual journey as a child and a young adolescent. I began to wonder what could've transpired in her life leading to her forced removal by the army from her post in Iraq.

"My psychiatrist once asked me why I decided not to go back to church. I told him, 'Because I feel guilty.' I did many bad things that I don't feel sorry about. I just feel a lot of guilt about going back to church. I know God is trying to get hold of me," she said, her tears beginning to flow.

As tears filled her eyes, I began to wonder about the vastness and depth of her inner struggle. On one hand, she struggled with the guilt of sinning and straying from God; like roaring waves, her guilt seemed to block her return to the close relationship with God she once enjoyed. On the other hand, her tears seemed to reflect a deep soul yearning for the very love and forgiveness of the God she had heard her preacher daddy loudly proclaim from his pulpit.

It was at that moment I could clearly see a close relationship with God had always been important to her. The key to her inner peace might very well be in restoring her relationship with Him.

A patient once told me about a phrase she had heard in AA meetings, "You are only as sick as your secrets." I wondered about Melissa's "secrets" and how deeply buried they were.

"Melissa, do you know the story of the prodigal son in the Bible?" I asked.

"I know about it. Can you remind me of it?" she asked softly, her eyes piercing mine.

For the next few minutes, I told her my rendition of a story told by Jesus two thousand years ago about a young man who had deeply insulted and hurt his father, who represents God in the story.

"The son asked for his inheritance money then left the family home with cash in hand, looking for fun and sensual pleasures. But soon enough, after he wasted all his inheritance money on prostitutes and all sorts of indulgencies, his friends left him, and he was all alone."

I could see how intensely she paid attention to every word I said, and so I continued the rest of the story. I told her about how an unexpected famine hit the area, not much different from when we all face life's sudden, unexpected turn of events, just when we think everything is cool and we're in full control.

"The poor young man had no money to pay for food and could only find a job taking care of smelly pigs. He dreamed of eating their food but even that he couldn't do. In a culture which viewed pigs as filthy and unholy, that was to him 'hitting rock bottom.' It was in that pit of life that he finally realized how foolish he was and how much he had wronged his dad. Ultimately, it was an empty stomach growling from hunger, loss of peace, loneliness, and a depressing, messed-up life that drove him back to the road to his father's home. Not much different from when we are driven to God in tears of repentance when we can no longer tolerate our physical, emotional, and spiritual misery; when we reach our 'rock bottom' and our soul hungers and thirsts for peace, love, security, and worth."

Melissa was totally gripped by the story and so I continued.

"So anyway, the son decided to head back home with one hope—to be allowed to stay not in his rich dad's mansion but in his servants' quarters. Little did he know his dad was waiting for him every day on the very road he once took to walk away from home. His father missed him and yearned day and night for his return, the way God waits for us like a loving dad for our return home from a life of sin and transgression away from Him.

"When the father, who represents God, saw his son walking on that lonely road to get back home, he ran with open arms towards him, embraced him, and restored him totally to the family by placing the family ring and robe on him, and then topped it all with a big banquet, a party, on his behalf. To him, his 'prodigal son' was his precious son who was '…once lost but is now found, dead but is now alive.'

"Jesus wanted all of us who hear this story to know that God is this loving Father Who welcomes us back home like the "prodigal son" was welcomed with great joy and celebration when he came in repentance, asking for forgiveness. When we take the wrong road in life and stray away, there remains the light of God's love leading us to the road back home," I concluded.

"I've never heard the prodigal son story told that way. I remember Dad talking before about it," she said as tears welled in her eyes.

"He must be praying for you."

"Daddy once told me that he is always praying for me," she said as she wiped her tears. "God meant for me to be here today. I feel He is calling me back to Him."

She left the exam room after giving me a hug and telling me with a peaceful smile on her face that she felt ready now to "go to chapel and meet with the chaplain," whom she had heard was "a good man."

Her story made me ponder and reflect on the journey she has thus far traveled. The one thing I will never forget was the sight of Melissa's heart—darkened, hardened, and broken by pain and the turbulent, unpredictable waves of life—for a moment softened as she began to hope again.

"Dr. Hanna, Dad will love to meet you. You're an answer to his prayers," she said, smiling, as she stepped out of the exam room for the last time.

> My son, the father said, you are always with me, and everything I have is yours. But we had to celebrate and be glad, because this brother of yours was dead and is alive again; he was lost and is found.
> —Luke 15:31-32

> My dear brothers, take note of this: Everyone should be quick to listen, slow to speak, and slow to become angry, for man's anger does not bring about the righteousness life that God desires.
> —James 1:19-20

CHAPTER 3

ANXIETY

Anxiety: Photo provided by Camp Atterbury Public Affairs

I am the Lord; the God of all mankind.
Is anything too hard for me?
—Jer. 32:27

Home front anxieties

"SO! HOW DO you feel about leaving to go to Afghanistan next week? Do you feel scared?" I asked twenty-five-year-old private Nancy after the medical exam. I was expecting to hear some of her worries and fears about the deployment but then she surprised me.

"Not really. I volunteered to go this time," she said. "I handled my last deployment pretty well until I broke up with my boyfriend, you know. It was much easier handling the stress of being blown up by an IED than staying in that relationship and then finally breaking up with him," she said.

The concept that the war front with its blood, bullets, and IEDs (Improvised Explosive Devices) was better tolerated than a relationship full of turmoil and strife was a new one to me. To Nancy and many other soldiers I've talked to, the "war" of rejection, abuse, and disappointment they often battle against in their daily lives is comparatively harder than the deadly explosions of mortar attacks. A pretty convincing argument, I figured, for some of us dealing with such relationships, to run to safety before becoming a casualty of a home front war.

For the next few minutes, I listened to Nancy as she shared with me the memories of her parents' divorce, which caused her a lot of anxiety, and her worries about her stepdad's pending cardiac bypass surgery.

"It's much harder to deal with these emotions than going to combat," she said and began to talk to me about her understanding of God, spirituality, and her hope of one day conquering her fears and worries.

I could tell her frustration with being a hostage of her own fears and her deep desire to get over her iceberg of negative thinking and the toxic emotions they have produced in her life. As I listened to her, I could see how her emotions had for so long hindered her from living her life to the fullest and how fear had silenced her.

In the course of taking care of my military patients, I have shared with many soldiers before her what I've come to call the TEA story—three letters I put together to help my patients understand the intimate relationship between Thoughts, Emotions, and Actions. It made a lot of sense to me and to those who had heard it before and it felt appropriate to share with Nancy as well.

"Nancy, every single thought that crosses your mind that you begin to believe in and think about will produce in your heart and mind an emotion, either negative or positive. It will in turn fire you up and lead you to do something either good or bad. And so if your mind is full of negative, unhealthy thoughts, you will be plagued by the negative, destructive emotions of fear, guilt, anger, depression, low self-esteem, feeling a sense of high from controlling and abusing others, and many of the other toxic emotions these thoughts produce. These emotions will in turn influence you to choose negative actions and behaviors that can be extremely harmful and destructive to yourself and others and will be regretted one day.

On the other hand, if we think about encouraging, loving, and positive thoughts, then our emotions will be calm, positive, and sweet and our actions will be positive, loving, and full of self-discipline and self-control. In essence, we all become what we think. I guess it's safe to say it's all in the "thoughts."

"Thank you, doctor, that makes a lot of sense. Can you please give me the names of some of the books I can read about what you just talked about?" she asked.

It was time for her to catch up with her combat training, but I had one more question to ask before she left.

"Nancy, now that you have broken up with your boyfriend, what are your plans?"

"I plan to finish college when I get back," she said. "Maybe I'll be a doctor or a preacher. But for now, I'm thinking about the new soldiers in my unit. Some have never been to combat. I want to help them," she said as she opened the door.

I couldn't help but think about how her noble "thought" of caring for her new soldier friends had led her to the joyful "emotion" found in giving, which in turn motivated her to take "action" and volunteer to help them make it safely through their deployment—the TEA story lived one thought at a time.

Cast all your anxiety on him because he cares for you.
—1 Peter 5:7

The hidden battle with fear

The mind controlled by the Spirit is life and peace.
—Rom. 8:6

Courage is not the lack of fear. It is acting in spite of it.
—Mark Twain

After a quick glance at Private First Class Sally's anxiety/antidepressant medications, I wondered about her emotional well-being.

"So how are you doing, Sally? What's in your heart?" I asked the twenty-five-year-old blonde soldier as I gazed at her strikingly blue eyes.

That was all it took for her to open up her heart and begin talking to me about her fears, dreams, and hopes. She talked about her dream of making "something good out of my life" that led her to join the army where she can advance her knowledge, get education, and serve her country in Iraq.

"I didn't want to end up being a store clerk the rest of my life," she explained.

Yet, even as she marched courageously towards her goal, a deep-rooted battle with anxiety and fear began to rage within her and surface. But that didn't stop her from marching forward in pursuit of her dreams. For the next few minutes, she remembered early events in her life that launched her journey of fear and worry.

"I was about five years old when my parents separated and then divorced. Mom was so difficult to live with. She didn't treat Dad right. I couldn't get along with her. I hated the way she treated him."

At the military camp, training and preparation for her unit's anticipated departure to Iraq was at its fullest. As the training intensified, Sally's anxieties began to surface and erupt as she faced its daily rigors and demands.

"Sometimes it's so hard to deal with our drill sergeant yelling or someone pulling rank at me. I'm starting to lose my temper easily. Other soldiers in my unit suggested I come and talk to you."

As I listened, a wave of compassion, respect, and admiration for this wounded warrior swept me. Ultimately, I figured, it wasn't her unit buddies who had brought her to see me but a deep passionate desire "to make something good out of my life" that had ushered her into my exam room. Sally was determined to win her inner emotional battles, even as she prepared for the physical battles awaiting her in Iraq.

For the rest of the visit, I listened quietly to more of her painful childhood experiences that she wanted to talk about, more of her fears, anger, guilt, dreams, life passion, family, and her pride and honor of being a US soldier. As I paid full attention to her words, I could see the real Sally emerging—not only her external existence as a blue-eyed beauty—but a formidable, passionate, and lovely inner being held captive for years in a dark cell of negative thoughts and emotions of worry, fear, and anger. Yet despite the old echoes of these fears and other emotions, I could see in her deep blue eyes a fiery zeal to break free from her bondage and live her dream of "getting the most out of" her life.

Suddenly, it dawned on me that the more she dwelt on her old painful, negative thoughts, the more she seemed overwhelmed by the fear and anxiety that these thoughts brought to her and the more they took her away from focusing on her hopes and dreams. And so for the next few minutes, I spoke these words that I hoped would bring her comfort.

"Sally, think of these old, stinking thoughts as a thief who is always trying to enter your home to rob it. Would you give this thief the key to your home and invite him in at any time? Of course not! So why do we all—some of us more than others—allow some mean, no-good thoughts that create in us fear, depression, and anger to come into our precious homes—our minds and hearts? We all need to have a daily closed-door policy toward these stinking thoughts and only allow in the ones that make us feel peace and love and bring smiles to our faces. You know, if we are not careful, we tend to nurse and rock these old negative thoughts to sleep as if they are a little precious baby. That's crazy, right? But that's what we end up doing when we carry them with us everywhere.

"Sally, don't you feel like inviting these thoughts out of your mind like unwelcome guests and keeping the door of your heart and mind forever closed to them? What I mean is no more focusing on them or taking regular daily trips and excursions into the painful past. These constant rendezvouses down a sad memory lane will only trigger those thoughts in your mind and open the door of your life again and again to the destructive anxiety and depression they cause. So no more peaking back into the past, all right? No more focusing on it. I hope I'm not confusing you?" I asked as I looked at her to judge her interest in what I was talking about.

"No, not at all. That makes sense. I'm listening," she said, smiling, and signaled for me to continue.

"You know, this stuff I'm talking about is actually mentioned in the Bible. There is one verse in the New Testament that goes like this: "Whatever is true, whatever is noble, whatever is right, whatever is pure, whatever is lovely, whatever is admirable—if anything is excellent or praiseworthy—think about such things" (Phil. 4:8).

Another verse also reminds me not to look back into the abyss of the past but to look ahead. "But one thing I do: Forgetting what is behind and straining toward what is ahead." (Phil. 3:13).

I noticed a big, enthusiastic smile on her face as I continued to share what seemed to be a very interesting topic to her. "You know what; tomorrow doesn't belong to us. It's really not ours to worry about. What I mean is it is God's prerogative whether He decides to let us have another day on this planet or not! Our future (with its amazing blessings and great promises) is His. It's in God's good hands. We should not live in daily worry because of the things that can possibly go wrong in our futures. Instead we need to be focused every day on our life purpose.

"One more thing, Sally, it's best to never look back. Occasionally we might very briefly glance and remember how God helped us in difficult situations in the past when life seemed so messy, dark, and hopeless. This will help us not to repeat our mistakes and will remind us that God, Who saved us before, will help us again. What I mean is living the rest of our lives carrying the old heavy baggage of the past: fear, anger, bitterness, and the guilt of years past will make us miss the great things and blessings that God plans for us to have in the future. We will also miss the love and joy that comes when we have a close relationship with Him and with people who care about us.

"You know, Sally, we have no option but to trust our future, which is full of unknowns, to God, and to live each day with passion as if it's our last day. Does that make sense? I hope I'm not confusing you," I asked as I noticed her full attention to my words.

"Not at all! This is good!" she said as she took comfort in their meaning.

Talking to Sally made me think about how impossible it is to live my day-to-day life to the fullest and with peace and great passion if my eyes are focused towards the future through dark lenses of worry. I can't live peacefully, purposely, or joyfully today if I am worrying about my future. I must see my future with eyes of faith, believing in the great plans that God has prepared for me. The words I found in the Old Testament book of Jeremiah 29:11 often remind me of God's personal care for my future and have been a light to my feet at some of my darkest hours. "'For I know the plans I have for you,' declares the lord, 'plans to prosper you and not to harm you, plans to give you hope and a future.'"

There is indeed a deep sense of power that comes when you and I know that we have a great future planned for us. That thought keeps our hope alive no matter how hard things are today. It energizes us, and brings a smile to our faces when we face our daily life challenges and hurdles. We live life fully and confidently when we know that our future is well preserved, assured, and destined to be great because God is its planner. You and I have a future! A great one! Our worries will fade and begin to vanish when we believe, and as we see our future through the lens of hope, our visions and dreams become alive, and we become more focused on the race of life that is ours to run today. We must believe if we are to live.

It was time for her to join her unit. She gave me a big hug and thanked me repeatedly, saying how much she felt encouraged. The rest of her training went very well, and she returned a few more times to see me and for "one more good-bye hug" before her departure to the combat zone. Her drill sergeant's yelling routine and others pulling rank on her no longer bothered her and thankfully ceased to be the focus of her attention.

Two thousand years ago, Jesus Christ walked the face of this earth. As God Who decided to take a human walk on earth, He felt and experienced our deepest human emotions of suffering, love, and tears. To the many anxious hearts who were so overwhelmed with inner soul pain, negative thinking, and worries, like Sally and so many of us today, He brought a message of love and peace. As He encouraged and cheered up many weary souls and broken hearts loaded with guilt, shame, and low self-esteem, many came to find for the first time a purpose for their lives and inner peace and rest in the midst of their life storms. Two thousand years ago, Jesus taught them, as He is teaching all of us today, how to be free from their destructive emotions by trusting in His divine love, forgiveness, and providence. Jesus wanted them to know that in the midst of all their life's turbulent waters and deeply felt needs, He hears their cries and ours, and He will take care of every need, big or small, as we seek Him first and have faith in His promises.

> Do not worry about tomorrow, for tomorrow will worry about itself. Each day has enough trouble of its own.
> —Matt. 6:34

> A cheerful heart is good medicine, but a crushed spirit dries up the bones.
> —Prov. 17:22

When money worries are worse than war

> Give us today our daily bread.
> —Matt. 6:11

Sgt. Jack looked very anxious and gloomy as I wrapped up his final demobilizing medical exam. The exam, the final hurdle before going back home, should've been a happy event for Jack. I wondered about the source of his stress.

"You look worried, Jack. Are you glad to go back home?" I asked as I prepared myself to hear potentially disturbing wartime memories that he might have experienced.

"What worries me, Doc, is not what happened in Iraq. I'm worried about finding a job, a home, money for college, and what to expect when I get back home. This is what worries me," he said, tensely.

ANXIETY

"Tell me, Jack, how different are these fears from those you experienced in Iraq when IEDS exploded under your Humvee and insurgents' bullets were firing at you?"

"I think the fear of not finding a job or money for rent is worse. Over there I was afraid at the moment of the explosion or the beginning of a gun battle. After the battle these fears usually disappeared, but the fear and worries of having no money and not affording school just stay with you. They don't go away, Doc."

To Jack, life in Iraq fighting the insurgents, IEDs, and suicide bombers was relatively more peaceful than fighting for a job in his home state or facing rejecting and discouraging words back home that would ignite his fears and worries!

His statement made me reflect on the words of many of my patients who told me, each in her or his own way, that the long-term emotional toll of fear, anger, depression, and guilt, that results from rejection and/or verbal emotional abuse is far worse than the long-term pain of being physically threatened or abused. The war of words encountered by many soldiers during their deployment from friends, family, or a rejecting and unsupportive environment is actually worse and emotionally more destructive than the war they're encountering in Iraq and Afghanistan. Words spoken from uncaring, uncompassionate tongues hurt more! They can kill you on the inside even as you still appear to be alive on the outside.

That was Jack's first and last visit to the Troop Medical Clinic. He left the next day with a few of his returning unit friends driving back home to their families and loved ones. I will always remember him as a worried warrior who found peace in his heart in the midst of Iraq's battlefields and lost it in the safety of a city mall.

Whatever the reason(s) for our loss of peace—be it exploding IEDs in Afghanistan and Iraq, abuse, losing a job, or financial meltdown, we can find a true, steady, and unchanging source of peace in God's unconditional love. This was demonstrated to the human race not just by words but by a dying action when "...God so loved the world that He gave His one and only Son, that whoever believes in Him shall not perish but have everlasting life" (John 3:16).

Peace, I leave with you; my peace I give to you; not as the world gives do I give to you. Do not let your heart be troubled, nor let it be fearful.

—John 14:27

You will guard him and keep him in perfect and constant peace whose mind is stayed on you.

—Isa. 26:3

CHAPTER 4

COMPASSION

Compassion

Do to others as you would have them do to you.
—Luke 6:31

I'm my brother's keeper

"IT TOOK A co-worker's suicide to teach me about caring for the person who is sitting next to me," said First Class Sgt. Jonathan.

Just minutes before, he was passionately telling me about his love of heights and the intense high he gets from his civilian job cleaning skyscraper windows. It was during one of these dangerous assignments, cleaning the sixteenth floor window panels of a seventy-floor skyscraper, that he witnessed the death of his co-worker.

"We were suspended on the outside of the sixteenth floor, cleaning windows on a clear day. He decided to jump and take his own life."

The death of Jonathan's colleague changed his life forever and launched him into a journey of self-examination and reshuffling his own life priorities.

"On that day, I decided to always pay more attention and to listen and look after those who are around me."

The death of his buddy was indeed a turning point in his life. He was no longer content to just be a platoon's leader, but he wanted to also be a shepherd who watches over his soldiers.

"I've fifteen soldiers in the barracks who are my responsibility. I find myself always watching over them. Who is lonely and depressed? Who is hurting or angry? I want to be there for each one of them, to listen and to care. We really are our brother's keepers."

"Doing that impacts their lives in a big way because you become 'salt and light' to them. You know the Bible teaches us to be salt that brings taste and good flavor to someone's life, and light that lights up someone else's darkness and enlightens our dark world," I said.

He nodded in agreement and shared a story of a marine whose words and actions influenced his life and became "salt and light" to him at a very dark time in his life.

"About fourteen years ago, I was going through a very sad time in my life. I remember sitting down, sad and alone, in the barracks when that marine came in and saw me looking depressed. He sat next to me, looked at me, and in the most caring voice asked me a simple question that made me realize that someone cares about me, 'Are you okay?' I'll never forget his words and what they meant to me. It's amazing how we always remember those people in the past who cared about us when we desperately needed it, but how easily we forget those who chose not to care."

His words reminded me of the many people in my own life, past and present, whose encouraging, caring, comforting words and actions will forever be carved in my memory. Much like that marine, they were the salt and light of my life who will forever remind me of God's love, mercy, and goodness.

It was time for Jonathan, a soldier who boldly decided to be his "brother's keeper," to lead his troops for more afternoon training.

"Thank you, Doc. I never forget a good conversation," he said as he firmly shook my hand.

> Let no debt remain outstanding, except the continuing debt to love one another, for he who loves his fellowman has fulfilled the law.
> —Rom. 13:8

> As a father has compassion for his children so the Lord has compassion on those who fear Him.
> —Ps. 103:13

Those who care

> It is more blessed to give than to receive.
> —Acts 20:35

Many of the stories I've heard showed me the abundance of caring hearts behind the bulletproof body armor.

I can't forget soldier Janice, who came rushing to see me during her lunch break carrying a bag loaded with diapers, nonperishable goods, and cloth.

"Dr. Hanna, would you please take this to your church? I know a poor child will need it more than me or my daughter," she said with a kind, tender voice.

Other stories of kindness that touched my heart include that of two soldiers who had just come from Iraq. One of them shared what he viewed as the most uplifting part of his mission—showing kindness to the Iraqi children.

"The Iraqi children used to wait for hours for my Humvee to drive by the neighborhood," he said. "They knew I would always bring those sweets and other goodies. I will never forget their little bitty hands reaching out for the candy in my hand. Seeing how happy they looked when they ate the sweets and chewed the gum made me feel real good. You know, doctor, helping the Iraqis rebuild their lives made it all worth it, but I worry about them a lot, especially the children, after we leave."

Another soldier, Sgt. Jerry, remembered his noncombat assignment in Rwanda at the height of the genocide that claimed massive numbers of innocent lives. Many years later, he still lamented not been able to use his M16 to protect the innocent ones who were brutally massacred during the ethnic genocide.

"My only regret was being in the middle of it all but yet not taking an active part to stop the killing," he said.

The noncombat nature of his assignment prohibited him from doing that. His only assignment that put him in the middle of the evil genocide was leading a convoy of soldiers to save a Rwandan priest, who was under siege in his church.

"By the time we arrived it was too late. He and the others had already been killed by the mob," he said, sadly.

And then there was Private Tammy, who was going to Afghanistan for her deployment in two weeks. When I saw her for a visit and asked if she was afraid of the mission awaiting her, her only concern was for soldiers in her unit who come from their homes with "worries and difficult issues that make them unable to adjust, and they end up being misunderstood."

"I'm really worried about one of the soldiers in my unit. She tends to keep to herself. Something is bothering her, but she doesn't want to talk about it. I'll be praying for her," she said.

Like the other soldiers who cared for strangers and were ready to sacrifice their own lives for them, Tammy's compassion took her away from her own comfort zone to care for the others in her unit and to seek in prayer help from God above for her brothers and sisters in arms.

All of them seemed to take the focus off their own needs and come to this one realization—it is better to give than to receive. They all found joy in their random acts of kindness, expecting and getting nothing in return. With hearts of compassion such as this, I can't help but feel thankful those powerful M16s and the other destructive weapons at their disposal are in good hands—hands that will use them to free, save, and protect.

COMPASSION

One man gives freely, yet gains even more; another withholds unduly, but comes to poverty. A generous man will prosper; he who refreshes others will himself be refreshed.
—Prov. 11:24-25

I tell you the truth, whatever you did for one of the least of these brothers of mine, you did for me.
—Matt. 25:40

CHAPTER 5

COURAGE

Courage: Photo provided by Camp Atterbury Public Affairs

You are my hiding place; you will protect me from trouble
and surround me with songs of deliverance.
—Ps. 32:7

Beauty in a Black Hawk

JENNIFER, A TWENTY-SEVEN-YEAR-OLD brunette, gracefully entered the exam room in her well-pressed pilot's uniform, and after the physical exam, we began to talk. I was very impressed by her demeanor and confident smile and wanted to know more about her.

"Wow! A Black Hawk helicopter pilot! How did you end up being one? How in the world do you fly this big, scary machine?" I asked, smiling.

She smiled back confidently. "Well, I always wanted to be in infantry but since women can't be in infantry, I chose to be a pilot, the next best thing I can do as a woman in the military."

It was so easy to see the zeal she had for her job as she began to tell me about how much safer, more modernized, and easier to navigate are the Black Hawks she flies compared to the older helicopters flown during the Vietnam War.

As she talked passionately about the challenge of flying that giant, menacing machine, I couldn't help but think about the fact that she would soon be flying her Black Hawk in potential enemy territory as she began her deployment.

"What you're doing takes a lot of courage, Jennifer. Do you get scared?"

"I wanted to do something more challenging than my civilian job in sales. So I joined the National Guard and started training twice a week, flying helicopters. I always believed that I must do my best to be the best that I can be."

"What gives you the courage to fly in enemy territory where you can be shot down?" I asked.

"I rely on my faith in God, doctor, to keep me going. I don't know how I would do it without Him," she said and shared with me her and her husband's new spiritual journey.

"We regularly go to church together. It's good for us."

I once heard a preacher say that faith and fear are on opposite sides of the same coin, much like heads and tails. Fears cease when we have strong faith in a real God Who loves, provides, and protects us as we believe in Him and follow His purposes for us. The absence of faith means the presence of fear, and the presence of faith silences our fear no matter how dark the valley we might be in. That's why I believe that building my faith, one life experience at a time, makes perfect sense.

It was uplifting to see how Jennifer used her faith in God to overcome her fear of flying and risking her life in hostile lands. Beauty and courage in a Black Hawk, flying with wings of faith, is what came to mind as I said good-bye to her and wished her God's protection in the mission ahead.

> For God did not give us a spirit of timidity, but a spirit of power, of love and of self-discipline.
> —2 Tim. 1:7

Bravery: A marine story

> Not by might nor by power, but by my Spirit, says the Lord Almighty.
> —Zech. 4:6

"I don't want stitches, Doc," said Sgt. Randy as he proudly displayed a four-centimeter-long laceration on his right elbow. "I'm only here because of the medic. He insisted I get it checked out. Can you just cover it with a bandage and send me to the barracks with antibiotics?"

He must be kidding, I thought as I measured the depth of the wound.

"Not a good idea, Sgt. It will be infected without stitching it, and you will end up with a big scar," I said, convinced he would have no objections now to closing his gaping wound. But then he surprised me with his proud declaration.

"Doc, I'm a marine. I don't mind at all about the scar."

"You guys are the few, the proud, the first ones sent to battles, right?"

"That's us," he declared.

His response made me wonder about how he viewed his upcoming deployment to Iraq and whether he was afraid.

"Randy, have you thought about the possibility of being killed?" I asked.

"It's true the chance of dying is higher for those of us on the front line. But then we're all going to die one of these days, and it can happen anywhere. It doesn't matter where you are. This happened to a soldier from our unit; he made it through mortar attacks and IEDs but died in a car accident when he was on R&R (rest and recuperation) visiting his family. I'm not afraid of dying."

His courage impressed me and reminded me of another brave young marine, who said to his worried family members before going to Iraq, "Life is short. I would rather do something worthwhile, dying young defending my country, than living a long life doing nothing of value."

Randy left the exam room without the stitches, but to his dismay returned shortly afterwards at the urging of his commander and medic for some old-fashioned skin sutures, as I had recommended.

His story reminded me of the wise words of a veteran army commander who feared greatly for the lives of some of his young, inexperienced soldiers who might not apply wisdom in their pursuit of bravery on the battlefield.

"The ones who want to act too bravely without focusing or thinking end up being injured or killed."

Perhaps Randy and many others can take his words to heart and reflect on this important question: Can someone be too brave for his/her own good? It's an important question, not only for a soldier on his way to war, but also to each one of us facing difficult situations and potentially unsafe relationships in everyday life.

We need more than bravery in our lives. More than anything else we need clarity of thought and wisdom from God above as we navigate through the darkest valleys of our lives.

> The fear of the Lord is the beginning of wisdom, and knowledge of the Holy One is understanding.
> —Prov. 9:10

CHAPTER 6

DEATH AND HEALING THE GRIEF

Death and Healing the Grief

Losing my friend

> Yea, though I walk through the valley of the shadow of death, I will fear no evil; For You are with me; Your rod and Your staff, they comfort me.
>
> —Ps. 23:4 NKJV

IT HAD BEEN almost a year since the death of Sgt. Isaac's best friend, a medic, but the memory of that tragic day still lingered on.

"He wasn't just my roommate and best friend, but he was the only medic in our unit. I was the one in charge of retrieving his body after he was killed by a sniper's shot. For a long time after his death, I fell into depression and lost over twenty pounds. You know how it is—you just stop caring after losing your best friend," he said, remembering the tragedy.

Despite his severe feelings of depression, Isaac continued to patrol the hostile streets of Iraq after his friend's death. "The patrols were as dangerous as they'd always been, but everything around me felt different after his death. Something changed in me. I knew I wasn't the same after his death," he recalled.

While his unit waited for a new medic, a lot of the soldiers, including Isaac, decided to forego treatment for what they considered "minor problems like sprains, aches, and depression."

"I didn't want to bother the medics and docs in the hospital with minor things when they were dealing with gunshot wounds, trying to save lives, and receiving soldiers in body bags," he said, explaining why he and the other unit soldiers had decided to suffer with their "minor" problems.

Isaac's journey of healing began when he decided to reach out to his buddies in the unit and forge close friendships with the Iraqi soldiers whom he trained. The compassionate care he received from them felt genuine and comforted him.

"I will never forget how one of the Iraqi soldiers considered it his duty to keep me alive. Every time our convoy was hit by an IED or there was a mortar attack, he would throw himself on top of my body, covering me from shrapnel, ready to be killed for me," he said. He felt grateful and thankful to a stranger who always seemed ready to die for him.

"I was so appreciative of what he was doing, but I had to tell him to stop risking his life because I felt that was unfair to him. He was putting his life on the line for me."

I could see in his eyes a deep sense of comfort as he shared his story. Less than a year ago, the death of his friend had nearly claimed his mind and soul as depression overwhelmed him. Yet even amidst the mortar attacks and enemy bullets, he found comfort not only in the care and sacrifices of his "band of brothers," but also in an Iraqi soldier, a new friend, who was literally willing to die for him. To these soldiers, there are indeed things worth dying for, and death is not only the end of one realm but it's the beginning of another one.

Isaac's encounter with death reminded me of a story told by one of my patients about a priest who was surrounded by young priests who wanted to comfort him on his death bed. One of them asked him, "How do you feel about dying?"

He answered, "Like a school kid finally off for a long summer vacation." To him, death for a believer in Jesus Christ is best described by the apostle Paul's words, "Absent from the body is being present with the Lord."

I was inspired by how he survived the loss of his friend by surrounding himself with caring people. Even more importantly, his story of caring characters—a soldier killed by snipers as he tended the wounded, soldiers from his unit, and a stranger, all ready to sacrifice their lives for one other—reminded me of the words Jesus said two thousand years ago. He described His reason for coming to earth as the Son of God to die for the sins of the human race with this statement of love: "Greater love has no one than this, that he lay down his life for his friends" (John 15:13).

After all, to die for someone else is all about that—love.

CHAPTER 7

DECEPTION AND TRUE FREEDOM

Deception and True Freedom

The tongue that brings healing is a tree of life, but a deceitful tongue crushes the spirit.
—Prov. 15:4

A financial wolf in sheep's clothing

THE FIRST TIME I saw thirty-nine-year-old, six-foot-tall Staff Sgt. Ronald was for a vague, "I've got something on my privates, Doc," complaint. There were no surprises on his "privates" that he hadn't anticipated.

I confirmed to him what he already suspected, saying, "Ron, this looks like genital herpes," as his eyes quietly focused on the empty exam room walls. He appeared distracted, his eyes wandering between the floor and the walls. I began to tell him about the culture needed to confirm the diagnosis, the treatment, and long-term care for his lifetime disease.

"I know I got it from my girlfriend. She cheated on me once when I started my deployment. That's just the one time I knew about," he said quietly.

After her betrayal, Ron's "much younger" girlfriend convinced him to "take her back" when she knew of his pending deployment and for the last "six-seven years" she had lived permanently in his home, took over his car, and almost all of his paycheck.

"She always says she is looking for a job but never seems to get one. I feel bad for her; she is always so depressed but then never wants to get help. She says she loves me and threatens to commit suicide if I break up with her or if I kick her out of my house."

I could sense his feelings of desperation and entrapment as he began to think about his bleak financial future and the seemingly dead end path he was on. "I'm walking while she drives my car. I have no money left at the end of the month after she uses all of my paycheck," he said, angrily stumbling on his words.

Ron knew he was trapped in a vicious cycle and approaching his future and retirement years alone and nearly emptyhanded. He was desperately in need of a change in the course of his life before it was too late. Perhaps his genital herpes diagnosis was a warning sign, a tip of the iceberg of worse things to come if he didn't quickly reverse the course of his life path.

We talked for few more minutes about the physical, emotional, mental, and spiritual risks to himself in his current relationship. He was painfully aware and deeply affected by all the betrayal and being taken advantage of by a woman whom he adored. He knew what he needed to do, but he just couldn't master the strength and clarity of thinking needed to get away from her. His thinking seemed clouded and confused, and his soul was plagued by a myriad of emotions—probably fear of abandonment, loneliness, guilt, and similar emotions that he had been manipulated into so as to stay in this seemingly parasitic relationship.

Ron needed, like we all do when we face similar life situations, a renewal of his thinking. His story made me think about the all too common reality of manipulation. To be manipulated by someone's deceptive sweet talk, smile, seductions, or her/his shaming and shouting must really hurt, especially from someone you deeply love like what was happening to him.

Some have become skillful with manipulative tactics, which I call the five Ss of manipulation (Sweet talking, Smiling, Seduction, Shaming, and then, when all fails, Shouting!). They influence the thinking and consequently the feelings and behaviors of those whom they manipulate. They use these five Ss as a weapon to control those close to them and to achieve their selfish goals. Their sweet talk of "Oh, baby, I love you or I love you to bits"; big, inviting smiles that can almost melt an iceberg; seduction with words, fast cars, suggestive looks, flowers, timely birthday gifts, presents, and irresistible seductive kisses and embraces; shaming others with zeal while putting on a teary poor-me-I am-a-victim act that is meant to make their listeners/victims feel guilty; and shouting with visible anger, threats, and intimidating words are all deceptive shows and highly crafted acts, ploys, and lies that they skillfully use to control those who are closest to them.

Their goal is to use their bodies, minds, spirits, and every available resource they can get their hands on for their selfish pleasures and goals. The reality is they don't genuinely care about or love the ones they manipulate because they are only concerned with their own interests. They use those whom they deceive as the farm cows are used for their milk production, and then when their milk is depleted and they are too old, they are processed for meat and their bones are sold for other uses. Unfortunately, with tools such as the five Ss of manipulation, a manipulated person is led to believe the lie that he/she is cared for and loved. Sadly, these five Ss are so craftly used that they become like chains or an invisible fence that keeps the manipulated one imprisoned in a dark cell of confusion, fear, guilt, and shame. It is a powerful fence that keeps him/her in captivity until no longer needed, much like a weary cow in a smelly, cold, barn milked daily for a deceiver's usage and pleasure, taking his/her energy, time, peace, and of course, money.

Poor Ron, his life was sucked out of him by another human being. His soul drained, he looked tired and exhausted. It must be tiring and exhausting to not be loved but used, like a weary, ridden horse in a long race, by someone you deeply love and trust. Years of his peace was stolen and worn like a ring on her slippery finger, taken off and on at her pleasure. This must have left him feeling used and abused.

His story reminded me of the words Jesus spoke two thousand years ago about how to recognize a wolf in a sheep's clothing. He once told a large crowd to basically use this litmus test to distinguish the wolves from the sheep.

"By their fruit you will recognize them. Do people pick grapes from thorn-bushes, or figs from thistles?" (Matt. 7:16). "A good tree cannot bear bad fruit, and a bad tree cannot bear good fruit" (Matt. 7:18), which means we all have to look at someone's actions (the fruits) and not her/his words to determine that person's heart and motives.

Someone once told me the words and actions said during an outburst of anger show us the real picture of someone's inner heart's motives and character more than any polished looks or words he or she says. True love doesn't only say words of love but also does actions that only a loving heart can do—showing patience, humility, gentleness, and self-control, among others. Indeed we all have to evaluate the fruits, the words, and behavior of those around us to know the real contents of their hearts. That will help us decide if we are being used and taken for a ride or if the person in question is not putting on a show but is genuine, compassionate, and caring.

Ron, like all of us, had a desperate need to transform his life by the changing and renewal of his mind with thoughts and beliefs that are truthful and positive—thoughts from the very heart of God Who created him that assure him of being loved, worthy, and accepted. For a moment, I wondered about what would happen once his girlfriend got all she wanted from him. Would she see him as an obstacle, lose interest in him, and dump him at a crucial time in his life when he needed her most? Unfortunately, it seemed to be heading that way unless she rethought her behavior, changed her heart, and began to genuinely care for him.

Ultimately, Ron's knowledge of God's truth that he is unquestionably valuable, loved, and forgiven will set him free from being somebody's doormat. Judging by his decision to return for few more visits to tell me about his own faith and God story, I can only conclude that sharing my words with him seemed to offer him hope and encouragement in a difficult situation that could potentially destroy his peace and even his life.

> Trust in the LORD with all your heart, And lean not on your own understanding; In all your ways acknowledge Him, And He shall direct your paths.
> —Prov. 3:5-6 NKJV

> Then you will know the truth, and the truth will set you free.
> —John 8:32

Dear John letter, a story of betrayal

> In my distress I called to the LORD, and he answered me. From the depths of the grave I called for help, and you listened to my cry.
> —Jonah 2:2

Sgt. First Class Daniel looked very cool, calm, and collected as I proceeded with my routine demobilization physical exam.

"So how was your experience in Iraq?" I asked, expecting no big stories. His "I almost died, Doc" statement took me by surprise and triggered my curiosity. For the rest of the visit, he told me about his combat experience in Iraq that had nearly turned tragic.

"I almost didn't make it back alive. I got one of them 'Dear John' phone calls. It used to be 'Dear John' letters back in World War II," he said, managing a brief chuckle. "That's what they used to do to end a relationship. Now all you need to end it is one phone call," he explained.

After ten years of a seemingly happy marriage, Daniel's wife ambushed him with one of those "dear John" phone calls ending their relationship during some of the most violent combat days of his tour of duty in Iraq.

"She left home, moved in with her girlfriend, and filed for divorce. She told me she was in love with her," he said, recalling the call that forever changed the course of his life. He remembered the utter devastation of a phone call that rocked the very foundation of his soul and drove him to a dark, endless pit.

"I broke down and was in a state of shock. I lost all self-control and couldn't take it anymore. All I wanted was to die," he said, remembering the day his heart shattered.

After his wife broke the news to him, Daniel entered into a dark tunnel of depression and began to volunteer for the most dangerous assignments of his unit, hoping for one enemy bullet that would end his life. Miraculously, a Canadian mental health combat crisis team stationed at the same base with his unit began to take notice of his suicidal tendencies.

"They figured out I was too much of a danger to myself to be on any mission and recommended my unit commander take my gun away."

The Canadian team didn't stop there but was able to convince Daniel's commanders to not send him back to the States. He remembered how adamant their team was in insisting that it was best for him to stay in Iraq instead of going back home. They felt strongly that he was in danger of harming himself if he were to return too soon.

"They were right, Doctor. I was going to kill myself if I was returned back home."

Consequently, Daniel was allowed to stay in Iraq and was immediately reassigned to a new job training Iraqi soldiers. His heartfelt appreciation for the lifesaving intervention of that Canadian team was palpable. "They made sure that I felt useful at the camp and as I got busy with helping others, I started to feel better. I felt needed and my depression began to lift. I no longer wanted to end my life. I owe a lot to the Canadians. I owe a lot to the Canadians," he repeated.

As I listened to his captivating story of survival, I couldn't help but see the invisible hand of the divine orchestrating his rescue through the compassionate hearts of Canadian professionals and a caring commander who listened, from what seemed like a sure death.

Looking at his calm face, I would have never guessed he has just been through a living hell in that isolated military camp in Iraq's hot desert.

"I'm feeling well now, Doc. I've already forgiven my ex-wife and she tells me I'm her best friend now," he said calmly.

His story reminded me of a young married female patient who had decided to live a wild life of a single woman, partying all night with her girlfriends during her husband's deployment in Iraq. All my attempts to convince her of the error of moving in with a new man she had just met in a bar, emptying her husband's bank account while he was away, and then filing for divorce as soon as he returned from combat, failed. She betrayed him and did exactly what she wanted to do, destroying her home and family in the process.

Another wife made a choice to cheat on her man a mere month after he deployed to the combat zone and ended up being pregnant. The news of her betrayal nearly devastated him, and after extensive soul-searching and counsel from family and close friends, he decided to forgive her and to adopt the newborn baby girl as his own daughter.

Daniel's story of betrayal and that of others deeply hurt by their wives' heart-shattering adulterous affairs made me wonder and reflect on this most painful subject. Does the person, man or woman, who is contemplating or already in the midst of betrayal, know how devastating and destructive that action is to his/her spouse or significant other?

Perhaps what's needed is a moment of silence, a timeout if you will, where a person walking or about to walk on that dark path could hear the cries of the soul as the betrayed person is engulfed in utter pain and terror—the kind of terror that Daniel and the other soldiers faced as they wrestled with their angry, hurt emotions. Daniel knew, firsthand, that betrayal can kill the very person the betrayer once loved and cherished.

And there are those who are totally repentant for the pain they have caused and the trust they have broken, and feel lucky to be accepted back into the relationship. I wonder if the suffering they caused their spouses to endure will forever be their reminder to never again harm the very person they vowed to love and cherish, until death do them part.

As the visit drew to a close, I asked Daniel about his faith in God, and if the turbulent storm he had experienced made him feel closer to Him. He was quick to tell me his faith in God greatly deepened as he faced the worst crisis of his life. Through the heaviness of his pain, he reached in desperation to God and ultimately came into a new place of peace that he never fully experienced before his "dear John" phone call.

Many months after he left the exam room, his statement, "Doctor, my faith in God helped me forgive her," rang in my ears. After all, it was Daniel's faith in a real, compassionate, and all-powerful God that literally brought him out of the depths of his brokenness and anger to the new heights of peace and forgiveness of the woman who betrayed his trust, stole his peace, and almost pushed him emotionally down to his death.

As I reflect on his story, I am reminded that when life looks desperate and hopelessly dark and gloomy, there exists a beacon of light, just like a flame of a lighthouse, guiding our soul's lost ship amidst its ocean of fear and loneliness, into the safety of shore. This light is God. It was God's unconditional love and goodness that Daniel saw in the eye of the storm, and it was that love that brought him home safely.

> Blessed is the man who trusts in the LORD, whose confidence is in him. He will be like a tree planted by the water that sends out its roots by the stream. It does not fear when heat comes; its leaves are always green. It has no worries in a year of drought and never fails to bear fruit.
> —Jer. 17:7-8

> And forgive us our debts, as we forgive our debtors.
> —from the Lord's Prayer in Matt. 6:12

Two deceptive exes

> The wisdom of the prudent is to give thought to their ways, but the folly of fools is deception.
> —Prov. 14:8

DECEPTION AND TRUE FREEDOM

Private First Class Sherry came early one morning to the Troop Medical Clinic for a medical evaluation and refills for her antidepressant medication before her upcoming deployment to Iraq. She had a big smile on her face as I began to examine her chart.

"How are you doing with the Zoloft?" I asked, hoping to find out more about her.

"I'm feeling much better now, doctor. I needed to be on it when I was going through my second divorce. My bad luck—both of my ex-husbands cheated on me. The second one was even a minister," she said.

"A wolf in sheep's clothing! That's not good," I said as I thought about the web of deception she must have endured from men she once trusted.

"My second husband tried to come back, but after lying to me so many times, I couldn't trust him anymore," she added.

Yet despite her setbacks and all the trials she has endured, Sherry didn't lose her faith in God. For the next few minutes, we talked about God's restoration of her "wounded soul" and a Bible verse that she said describes best her belief and conviction, "For God will restore to you the years that the locust has eaten" (Joel 2:25).

"He is working to restore me, Doctor," she said, her voice full of hope.

Fortunately, Sherry's rocky journey of two failed marriages where her trust was deceptively betrayed didn't destroy her own trust in God. Her story reminded me of a story I heard about a giant South American snake that coils itself in such a way until it looks like a small pool of water when the sunlight shines against its silvery skin. Thirsty deer and other unsuspecting small animals get quickly devoured by the snake when they reach out to drink from what appears to be a pool of fresh water. Sherry, like all of us, can easily be deceived by appearances and devoured by those whom we trust; much like that unsuspecting deer lowering its head to quench its thirst.

As I began to listen to Sherry's journey of healing, her pursuit of God, and the love she has for her three daughters, a thought crossed my mind. Some people ambush our lives as deadly tornadoes and violent winds that wreak havoc in our lives, leaving us feeling hurt, used, and broken in body, mind, and spirit, while others come into our lives like a gentle breeze, a breath of fresh air, and a stream of fresh water that satisfies the thirst of our soul for God's love, peace, and encouragement. It's ultimately our individual decision to either bring to those who cross our life path the heart of God—His forgiveness, love, and acceptance, or bring them destruction, pain, suffering, or death. It's our call—to be a tornado or a gentle breeze to every soul whose own life's journey crosses ours.

Sherry was left to pick up the pieces of her heart's debris after two brutal storms that nearly derailed her life. But despite that, her journey of soul restoration that started with the renewing of her trust in God seemed well under way even as she was about to go to the unknown future awaiting her in the deserts of Iraq.

> Those who hope in the LORD will renew their strength. They will soar on wings like eagles; they will run and not grow weary, they will walk and not be faint.
> —Isa. 40:31

CHAPTER 8

LIFE-CHANGING DECISIONS

Life-Changing Decisions: Photo Provided by Camp Atterbury Public Affairs

> Peace I leave with you, My peace I give to you;
> not as the world gives do I give to you. Let not your
> heart be troubled, neither let it be afraid.
> —John 14:27 NKJV

One dangerous decision

"I AM BACK," said Sgt. Fernando, announcing his return from his four-day pass. I had seen Fernando on few other occasions in the Troop Medical Clinic, and the intriguing conversations we had previously about our immigrants' stories and our new home America were still fresh in my mind.

"You are back! Welcome! I hope you had a great time with the family?" I asked, wondering about his very last visit with his wife and twelve-year-old daughter before deploying to Iraq.

He looked distressed this time. I knew his decision to volunteer to go to Iraq had been a hard pill for his wife to swallow. His four-day pass seemed to bring the seriousness of his decision to the forefront again.

"My wife is afraid that I will be killed in Iraq," he said, sounding tense.

Even though Fernando had an opportunity to be excused from this deployment, given his wife's medical condition and his young daughter's age, he had decided to pack up and leave with his unit.

"My wife's best friend will stay home with her and our daughter," he said. "She will be fine. But I must go to Iraq, Doctor. My wife is no longer able to work. I am the man of the house, the only provider for my family. I have to take care of them," he said, explaining his decision.

His financial obligations that necessitated working two full-time jobs and sixteen-hour days had become quite burdensome to him.

"I want to finish my college degree so I can better our lives. I need the extra money from my deployment to pay for the house mortgage when I start school."

Fernando's decision to go when the war was at its worst with ever-mounting casualties was very difficult for both his daughter and wife to accept.

"How is your daughter dealing with your decision to go?" I asked.

"I love my country. I want Samantha to know that I am no coward who runs away from my duty as a soldier. I want her to know that Dad must do what needs to be done," he explained.

"What about your wife?"

"She's afraid. I told her one can die anywhere when it's his time to go, at war or at home. I knew of these two soldiers who came back home safe from Iraq but were killed in America. One was stabbed to death; the other died from a drive-by shooting."

LIFE-CHANGING DECISIONS

He looked a bit uneasy as he labored to explain his motive to volunteer for deployment despite his family's misgivings. I wondered for a moment if his wife's fears and worries were starting to take a toll on him.

Aware of his interest in spiritual matters and conversations about God in our previous chats, I wondered about how he spiritually viewed his decision. "Fernando, do you have peace about your decision?" I asked.

For the next few minutes he tapped into his spiritual knowledge and we began to talk about the biblical meaning of peace.

"There is a Bible verse that has always helped me whenever I found myself facing a major decision in my life," I said. "Follow after peace" (Psa. 34:14).

"You know, it's important to have peace about our major life decisions," I continued. "One strong verse that's also very helpful is in the Old Testament book of Amos. It says that it's never safe to be out of the will of God. What that means is that you will feel peace and can rest, relax, and feel confident when you're in the will of God. You might have fears and worries about your decision, but you can still feel confident and secure if you find deep peace in your heart with what you believe is the best thing to do. This sense of peace is actually telling you where the safe will of God is for you. Does that make sense?"

"Yes, it does! I do have peace about my decision. I believe it is God's will for me as a husband and father to provide for my family's needs," he said, confidently. His bravery and deep love for God, family, and country were inspiring. To Fernando, the dual honorable mission of fighting for both country and family became a path of no return. He made up his mind.

"You know, Doctor, I'll die when my day comes, at war or here at home. If it's my time, death will find me," he said as he firmly shook my hand.

That was the last time I saw Fernando. He stood by his decision and left with his unit for Iraq a few days later.

> Teach me to do your will, for you are my God; may your good Spirit lead me on level ground.
> —Ps. 143:10

Life-changing choices

> If I take the wings of the morning, and dwell in the uttermost parts of the sea, even there Your hand shall lead me, and Your right hand shall hold me.
> —Ps. 139:9-10 NKJV

Soon after finishing the medical exam, I looked at twenty-year-old Private First Class Chad's boyish face and asked him one of my favorite questions, "So Chad, what made you join the army?"

I wasn't sure what to expect—a post 9-11 sense of duty to defend America, perhaps a golden opportunity to pay for college tuition, or a job that pays the rent. I was particularly interested to see if he understood how his one choice to join the army would forever alter the course of his life. The power of a single decision forever changing the course of our lives was to me a fascinating topic to ask him about.

"I bet joining the army has changed your life. Have you made other decisions that have changed your life in a big way?" I asked.

Luckily, the topic seemed pretty fascinating to him as well.

"You bet. I've made a lot of those life decisions that you're talking about since I was a child, Doc. For example, deciding to get married before deploying to Iraq. Definitely, that wasn't the plan," he said and began to laugh.

It was "one-in-a-million chance" that his girlfriend would get pregnant the day she paid him a visit during his most recent out-of-town AT (annual training). But nevertheless, she did, and he found himself trying to figure out what to do as he suddenly faced a major crossroads in life with life-changing decisions to be made.

"I still can't believe it. She just spent one single night with me, just one night, Doctor. It was the last day of my three-week-long AT. We were 100 percent careful and sure there was no way on earth she was going to get pregnant, but she did."

Chad, already planning to marry his sweetheart after returning from his deployment, found himself "confused, not sure what to do. Should I do the right thing and marry her now or wait till I come back?" It didn't take him long to decide to do the right thing and marry his girlfriend right before reporting to this camp for military preparation for deployment.

"Her pregnancy was so unexpected. I felt it was a sign that I won't come back alive and it was meant for my seed to be passed on by conception before I leave for Iraq," he said, explaining his decision to marry sooner than planned.

Wow! What a disturbing, fatalistic thought to carry with him into combat.

I offered him few calming words, attempting to reassure him of a safe return to his wife and baby, something I knew no one could guarantee him. I could see in his eyes his hope and fear as he pondered the changes in his life.

"My entire unit came to my wedding at the chapel. I had a full military wedding. One day I was a single guy with a decent job, then a moment later a married man who is saving all my money for a down payment for a condo for my wife and our newborn. I know my life will never be the same since the day I decided to get married."

From a young age, Chad had understood how a single life decision can forever impact the rest of his life. He recalled how as a fifth grader he was forced to make such a decision after his parents' divorce.

"I found myself having to choose between either staying with my mom in Nebraska or moving to New York with my dad and stepmom."

At the time, that didn't seem like a big decision to him, but its impact shaped his whole adult life.

"What amazes me is if I hadn't chosen to move to New York with my dad, I wouldn't have joined the army. I wouldn't have met you today at the TMC (Troop Medical Clinic), Doctor," he said, expressing his sense of wonderment.

"One more question for you, Chad. Have you ever seen the hand of God in those major life decisions?" I asked as we both headed to the exam room door.

"Yes, I have. I believe only God can give us the wisdom to make the best decision for our life."

I couldn't have agreed with him more.

Heaven knows how every decision I make today will affect me for the rest of my life and either lead me on the right path or the wrong one. When I am at those crossroads of important life choices, there is one biblical Old Testament verse that always serves as light to my feet and reminds me that God will guide my steps in those confusing, dark alleys of life decisions.

> Trust in the LORD with all your heart and lean not on your own understanding. In all your ways acknowledge him and he will make your paths straight.
> —Prov. 3:5-6

Soon after this visit, Chad left with his unit to start his battlefield assignment. His story made me think, long after he left, about the divine privilege granted to each one of us mortals—the gift of choice. To all of us is granted the power to choose any course of life we want to and change our ways, thoughts, attitudes, or beliefs if we thus desire. The choice is always ours and no one will do it for us unless we decide to let others control our lives. We can choose to pursue the way of God—forgiveness, good life, love, and laughter even as we face the hardships and tears—or the way of evil and darkness—hate, pride, selfishness, and rage. The choice is always ours to get healed from our inner turmoil, shame, low self-esteem, and toxic emotions or stay in hiding, burying our pain deep inside.

Two thousand years ago, Jesus, God in human form, asked a crippled man, who for thirty-eight years had lain on a dirty ground reaching out for handouts from others, a soul-searching question. It was as if Jesus knew the man's deeply hidden reluctance to get well and his fear of abandoning a lifestyle of total dependency on people for his daily needs. Jesus looked compassionately with laser-beam precision at his fearful, full-of-reasons–and-excuses heart and asked a simple question—one He still asks us today when we find ourselves hopelessly chained in an abyss of depression, guilt, and anger and buried in the darkest pits of bitterness, loneliness, and emotional brokenness: "Do you want to be made well?" (John 5: 6).

But before we "get well" we must wholeheartedly "want to be made well." The choice was totally the lame man's as it is ours today to say a simple "yes." As we set aside our excuses and nod our heads in agreement to the same invitation to "Get up! Pick up your mat and walk" (John 5:8), we begin to experience the miraculous healing of the darkness of our souls. We begin to walk again. As we allow God into the story of our lives and choose to listen and obey His voice, we begin to experience, like the crippled man, true healing for our souls, a new beginning, and a renewed, joyful life.

LIFE-CHANGING DECISIONS

God's power and resources are limitless. He can easily and miraculously use natural means to provide for us and heal us—family, ministers, good friends, your church, a new job, a caring counselor, a doctor, or the right medicine. He can also provide all of the above and many more things in supernatural ways beyond our human means or understanding. In essence, God has all the means and desire to heal us, provide for all our needs, and bless every area of our lives. But all these blessings start with our decision to make the right choices that will place us in the center of God's will, goodness, caring, and loving presence—choices that draw us closer to Him rather than moving us further away.

Indeed, to us is given the ultimate right to freely choose to accept or to decline. And like the crippled man who finally chose to be healed, it is ultimate wisdom to say "yes" to the same offer Jesus gave him two thousand years ago to be made well. Of all the life choices we have to make, choosing to courageously accept God's healing hand, to pursue peace with Him, and to live our lives in love, goodness, and peace with others is one crucial life decision we can't afford to miss. Of all life's important decisions, this is *the* most important one that we must not delay or fail to make.

> Jesus answered, "I am the way and the truth and the life. No one comes to the Father except through me."
> —John 14:6

> Search me, O God, and know my heart; test me and know my anxious thoughts. See if there is any offensive way in me, and lead me in the way everlasting.
> —Ps. 139:23-24

CHAPTER 9

DADDY'S LOVE

Daddy's Love

And let us not grow weary while doing good, for in due
season we shall reap if we do not lose heart.
—Gal. 6:9 NKJV

All for my children

THIRTY-EIGHT-YEAR-OLD SGT. LARRY entered the exam room holding tightly to his bag of meds.

"Doctor, I have to go to Iraq. I'm on a lot of medications, and my blood work is a little bit off but I'm fine," he said, looking tense.

Larry's sole purpose for visiting the clinic was to make sure his multiple medical conditions and abnormal labs would not deter him from deploying with his unit. His strong determination to go to the theater of operations triggered my curiosity. I pulled his chart and started looking at his long list of medications and his slightly elevated kidney function test on the most recent blood work.

"So Larry, why do you want to go to Iraq so bad?" I asked.

He answered me with a strong southern drawl. He told me about his "seven days a week, dead-end job" that prevented him for the last seven years from spending time with his three children and wife. He also shared his dream of finishing nursing school, so he could work less and make more money to support his family.

"I want to see them grow to be good kids. All I want is to spend more time with them and my wife. I can't afford to do that now."

It was becoming clear to me that deployment to Iraq was his one and only opportunity to escape the enslaving grip of his financial mess. It was his ticket to financial freedom and to more family time.

"A better job with better hours, so that I can spend more time with my family," he repeated.

"How is the family dealing with your deployment, Larry?" I asked, wondering about his three children and wife.

He paused and then answered with a quiet, reflective voice. "I took each one of them separately to the fun places they love. I went fishing with my ten-year-old and took my eleven-year-old to the movies. Sarah, my thirteen-year-old, loves skating; I took her to the rink. I told them that Daddy has to go away for a while to do his job as a soldier, and that it's important for me to do that, so we can have a better life when I come back. It was hard for them, but they all said they understand my reason for leaving," he said, his eyes beginning to tear.

For a moment, I thought about Larry's story—a soldier with multiple medical diagnoses and a long list of medications, who volunteered for combat in hope of a better life for his family.

I wondered about his source of hope amid all his physical and financial obstacles. "Larry, what keeps you going?"

"God, my Father. He is the reason for my hope. When I see the innocent faces of my little children, I feel so determined to do all I can do for them. What I hope for them is a better life, Doctor," he answered with a strong, unwavering voice.

As he made his way to the exam room door, I could see how well equipped he was—heavy armor, military boots, and Kevlar. But more important, I saw a glimpse of a fine soul, equipped with hope, faith, and a vision that one day his children would have a better life and a future even if it meant giving his life in combat for their sake.

To Larry's great relief, his repeat blood work and blood pressure were normal after starting him on a treatment regimen. I'll never forget his big smile and great sense of joy and appreciation on his last visit when he received the final clearance to go with his unit to combat.

> We are hard pressed on every side, but not crushed; perplexed, but not in despair; persecuted, but not abandoned; struck down, but not destroyed.
> —2 Cor. 4:8-9

> The lions may grow weak and hungry, but those who seek the LORD lack no good thing.
> —Ps. 34:10

CHAPTER 10

DIVORCE AND CHILD CUSTODY WARS

Divorce and Child Custody Wars

Come to me, all you who are weary and burdened,
and I will give you rest.
—Matt. 11:28

Burned out

WHETHER BY SHEER coincidence or a deliberate act of God, stories of divorce and child custody started to pour in one after another in a very short span of time from soldiers of all ranks and files. Sgt. Brian, a thirty-four-year-old attorney who was no longer practicing law, told me one of those unforgettable stories.

"I got burned out and decided to quit my family law practice and started a health products company. I sell vitamins, minerals, male enhancement products, and things like that," he said, whispering his last words as I quickly thought about a potential diagnosis for his chest pain complaint. For the next few minutes, he talked more about himself and the "civilian life" he had left behind as the medics hastily started an IV and shaved off a patch of hair from his chest where they would place the leads of the EKG machine.

He looked visibly shaken as I looked at the monitor and held the printed EKG paper in front of me to read it.

"Is it okay, Doc?"

"It looks pretty good except for your fast heart rate. Your chest pain doesn't seem to be related to your heart; it's musculoskeletal. Do you feel very anxious about your deployment?" I asked.

He looked relieved and smiled. "I believe in God. Thank you for your encouragement," he said as we began to talk about God's divine providence and protection of him on the battlefield.

"For years I worked in divorce, custody, and child support cases. The legal system really stinks when it comes to that. It's not fair to fathers who want to be involved in their children's lives. I felt bad when I couldn't offer fathers hope or a fair deal when they were forced to pay so much child support even when they could barely pay their own bills."

The one-sided system eventually took a heavy toll on him, and he began to feel emotionally drained. "In every case that I represented, dads were denied fair access to their children while they were continuously paying child support beyond their means. I got tired of that and decided to quit. I started my new business just before this deployment."

Brian followed up with me for a couple more visits before he deployed with his unit to combat. He was always grateful for the time we spent talking and sharing about his hopes, dreams, and fear of the unknown that awaited him.

A life crusade for dads' rights

> For the eyes of the Lord are over the righteous, and his ears are open unto their prayers; but the face of the Lord is against them that do evil.
> —1 Peter 3:12 KJV

Shortly after my conversations with Sgt. Brian, I saw thirty-one-year-old Sgt. Sarah, a beautiful brunette lawyer who was preparing to deploy to Afghanistan. After the medical exam and treatment plan, I shared with her Brian's words (of course withholding his name) and asked for a "second opinion."

"Dr. Hanna, all these child support and custody laws make no sense," she said. "These laws were written and put into the books a long time ago by rich white men. Their intention was to make sure that rich men would keep their wealth and power and poor men would stay poor.

"They are designed to take the financial burden of supporting single moms from individual states and handing it over to the fathers. The result of that is what you see now—fathers who live from one paycheck to the next, struggling financially to pay their child support. That of course means they won't be able to get a college degree to better their lives and financial situations. The laws were intentionally designed to keep them poor."

Her passion for the plight of fathers became clearer to me as she began to explain more of the bleak financial picture she found fathers routinely falling into because of these laws.

"A lot of men give up on a college education just to afford their child support payments and end up working two or three jobs, which also means an increase in their child support. So a lot of them end up working jobs that pay under the table. It's a losing battle for many fathers, who end up feeling frustrated and many times giving up on their children. It's a vicious cycle and a no-win situation for them."

Sarah's personal dissatisfaction and frustration with the system continued to mount until she finally decided to radically change her law practice. She scaled down her practice and began charging the bare minimum for the services she rendered to "cash-strapped fathers" who were fighting for more access to their children.

"I've seen firsthand the disastrous effects of these laws. I guess I'm in a crusade to help those who are hurt by them," she said, showing her compassion and zeal for the many alienated fathers.

"Sarah, in your opinion, what's the best thing a father can do to help his children deal with this messy situation?" I asked, tapping into her wealth of knowledge on the subject.

Her answer was quick and reflected her compassion and depth of knowledge about this difficult subject.

"You know, it's like being in the middle of war and being prepared to face roadside bombs and IEDs. They need to be prepared for their post-divorce and custody wars as well. I tell fathers to listen to their children, be positive, and have fun when they're spending time together. They need to be happy and learn to move on with their lives. I tell them to find someone special and be happy. If they can't be happy, they won't be able to show their children any happiness."

Her answer impressed me, and I decided to ask her another loaded question. "What's a parent to do when the ex-spouse starts to speak negatively about him or her in front of the children?"

"No bad-mouthing! It's so important to resist the temptation to say something negative against the other parent. That's only going to hurt the children and will always backfire in the long run on the parent doing the bad-mouthing. The more one talks negatively, the more that builds up the image of the other person in the children's eyes. I've seen that so often!"

"A couple of more questions for you, Sarah, before you go? What if the children are already loaded with negatives against the other parent? What if their minds have been poisoned to hate and disrespect the other parent? What would you tell a parent who has to deal with that?"

"I see that so often," she said. "If the poisoning becomes so overwhelming against a parent or his new family, it's best for the sake of the kids to just temporarily keep away at a watchful distance for a period of time because that will help the children not get overwhelmed or confused. The important thing is to resist the temptation to feed them more negatives against the other parent because the children are already feeling bad and confused. When the children grow up, they will definitely find out about the lies and will be able to tell who was lying and who was telling the truth," she said with a strong, caring voice.

It was time for Sarah to go and get some much-needed rest at the barracks. She picked up her body armor as she made her way to the door, thanked me, and left me with a few more encouraging words.

"Doctor Hanna, I believe adversity helps us grow. It prepares us to serve and help others."

Her words were yet another reminder to me of the Bible verse in the New Testament book of Romans: "And we know that in all things God works for the good of those who love him, who have been called according to his purpose" (Rom. 8:28).

Indeed, parents and children going through the adversity of post-divorce days can certainly grow up one day into much stronger and more compassionate and caring people, who are well equipped to serve and help others. They will be like a beacon of light in the midst of someone else's dark valley of divorce and child custody battles if they persevere, stay the course, and fight the good fight.

I saw Sarah one more time before she left for Afghanistan with her unit but her words of compassion and her crusade for justice and the rights of the child and father will always echo in my mind.

Soldiers in domestic wars

> Do not be overcome by evil, but overcome evil with good.
> —Rom. 12:21

> The LORD is my light and my salvation – whom shall I fear? The LORD is the stronghold of my life – of whom shall I be afraid?
> —Ps. 27:1

Thirty-seven-year-old Sgt. Marvin, a paramedic by trade, was by far one of the skinniest soldiers I've ever met. On his desk, a picture of his three children was proudly displayed. It was during a quiet lunch hour, which he rarely used to eat, that I was finally able to ask him about the picture on his desk. Pretty soon we were engaged in a long talk about his painful divorce and custody battles for his three children.

"For over two years, all I had was about fifty dollars to spend on my boys on the weekends! After child support services deducted almost all of my payroll check, I was only left with six hundred dollars. Doc, to pay for my mortgage, utilities, food, clothes, gas, and car that left me almost nothing to spend on them!"

The pain and passion in his voice was palpable. I listened silently to his intriguing story, which summarized the plight of many other fathers I have talked to who have been through similar ordeals.

"I'm telling you, Doc, there is nothing much you can do for three children with fifty bucks. They wanted to eat out, go to a game, and see a movie. How are you going to do that with fifty dollars? Thank God for my mom. She always made sure my fridge was full of food when the boys were home with me. My soldiers can't believe me when I tell them I just eat one meal a day. I got used to doing that because it was all I could afford those days—no more than one meal a day."

Marvin eventually filed for bankruptcy as his bills mounted and his finances dwindled. His financial situation gradually began to improve after that, and his "empty fridge" days were finally behind him. But he never forgot the "messed up" system that almost destroyed his life.

"The judges and the court are forcing fathers to pay large amounts of money to their ex-wives for child support without any consideration of their financial condition or whether they can afford it or not. They don't care if this money is actually going to the children, or if the ex-wives are making it impossible for the fathers to see their children."

I could see the frustration on his face as he recalled a story of one of his buddies who quit a good paying job two hours away from his home to stay closer to his children's school and spend more time with them. His new job paid him much less, but he was very happy that he was finally able to keep his children with him fifty percent of the time.

"But the judge refused to lower his child support even though the kids were with him half the time," he said. "My buddy wasn't able to pay the same amount of child support with his new job, so he was forced to go back to his old job and spend less time with his kids because of this system that forces fathers to pay more and more child support and throws them in jail if they don't. They could care less that a father who is working his tail off to pay all his child support won't have any time left to spend with his children."

Marvin's own bitter child support/custody story helped solidify his personal views of the biased and unjust laws pertaining to the divorce and child support arena.

"Dr. Hanna, my ex-wife had her unemployed boyfriend and his two kids move in with her and my three boys in the house the judge ordered me to leave and gave to her. The child support check I was sending paid for her boyfriend's housing and his fast food meals while my fourteen-year-old-son was getting Fs in school. He had no time to study because he was babysitting her boyfriend's children. The money that the court ordered me to pay for his afterhours schooling was being spent on her boyfriend and his children."

Despite all the discouraging setbacks, Marvin persevered and was determined to not let the unfairness of the domestic courts defeat him. He continued to see his children and have fun with them even when all he had was fifty bucks and a single meal a day.

I looked at the beautiful picture on his desk with his arms wrapped tightly around their three small bodies.

"I'm glad the court and judges didn't discourage you, Marvin, from fighting for your boys. They look so happy in the picture," I said as my eyes lingered on their big smiles.

"Thanks, Doc, we are very close. You know something? I've seen one of my good friends thrown in jail because he couldn't afford to pay his child support. There's something awfully wrong with having laws that treat a father like a criminal," he said as we started walking towards the door. Marvin with a skinny body, a reminder of his prolonged child custody casualty days, was finally on his way to the mess room for his one meal a day routine that became part of his daily life.

After my long chat with Marvin, I reflected on his words and those of many other soldiers who have also battled the same court system as fathers. The similarities between them were striking. Many of the fathers in the stories were forced to move in with their parents, declare bankruptcy to afford the court-ordered child support, or work under the table to have money for the weekend visits with their children.

One of the soldiers was told by a judge that his wife would still retain custody of their children despite his repeated concern that she was using drugs.

"The judge refused to change the custody orders. My lawyer told me that the court won't care even if I had a picture of her surrounded by drugs." It was only after his ex-wife showed up in court stoned and announced that she was going to rehab for drug addiction that the judge finally decided to give him custody of the children. Another soldier was ordered to go to jail by a judge when the child support services erroneously failed to record his child support payments in their systems.

After hearing so many of these stories, it was inspiring to see how soldiers like Marvin and many others chose to continue to fight for their children despite the minefields of seriously flawed laws that bankrupt fathers and deny their full rights as dads. Theirs, I believe, is the Medal of Honor for loving, caring, and refusing to give up on their children despite the injustices they endure.

What about the women who experience horrible treatment by cheating spouses who drain them, abuse, and then finally abandon them? What about those who find themselves in unfair court-ordered joint custody of their precious children with abusive, alcoholic, and foul-mouthed ex-husbands with endangering lifestyles? Or those single mothers who find themselves alone with children whose dads have vanished or chose to quit their jobs or enroll in college just to escape paying any child support?

As a physician who has handed out multiple tissue papers to many grieving women to dry the tears of abuse and injustice, I will always be in awe of those heroines who choose to turn away from hatred. They resist bitterness as they fight an ultimate battle to see their children grow up feeling loved.

A highly educated middle-aged woman once shared with me how her ex-husband escalated his verbal abuse one notch at a time. He followed that, to further intimidate her, with strategically placing a gun on the living room table and removing it soon after she saw it! Eventually, he pushed her down the steps in a fit of anger, breaking her leg. She, like many others, endured verbal and physical abuse as she held tightly to her children and eventually left after almost losing her life down a long stairway. "You know, the broken leg healed, and now many years after I left him, I don't even remember which leg was broken, but his words, and the verbal abuse took much longer to heal."

In my role as a physician, I have talked to many ladies who have gone through their own tough battles of divorce. To my surprise, those ladies were overtly vocal in their criticism of many women who choose to battle fiercely in the court system, relying on laws that favor them. In their hot pursuit of more and more money, they become calloused to the financial, and at times the emotional destruction that would eventually befall the fathers of their own children.

"Dr. Hanna, many of these women start with being angry, but very soon their anger becomes greed," said my fifty-year-old female patient.

"I just don't understand why a spouse should get half of the marital assets instead of everyone getting only what they came to the marriage with?" asked another female patient.

"He is the father of my children, and I won't take the children out of the state away from him. We have an arrangement where the children spend fifty percent of the time with their father because they need their dad and he is good to them," words said by many of my gracious female patients who have decided to sacrificially put their children's long-term interests above their own emotions, ambitions, and financial gains.

It is because of such noble women who might have also been treated horribly in the court system but who still manage to say with grace, "But men are treated even worse," as one of my female patients put it, that a new dawn of fairness and justice in the court system will one day come. A dawn of a new era where good, hardworking fathers who love their children are no longer driven to financial ruin, their bonding with their children gravely hindered, and their important role as fathers legally diminished to weekend babysitters.

To them and to every woman, who for the sake of peace, love, and the best interests of their children, say a courageous "no" to many a devious lawyer who wants to tempt them to take full advantage of a broken and an unfair system, belongs a well deserved Medal of Honor.

And these words which I command you today shall be in your heart. You shall teach them diligently to your children, and shall talk of them when you sit in your house, when you walk by the way, when you lie down, and when you rise up.
—Deut. 6:6-7

Sons are a heritage from the LORD, children a reward from him.
—Ps. 127:3

CHAPTER 11

FEAR

Fear: Photo provided by Camp Atterbury Public Affairs

Finally, brothers, whatever is true, whatever is noble, whatever is right, whatever is pure, whatever is lovely, whatever is admirable – if anything is excellent or praiseworthy – think about such things.
—Phil. 4:8

A walk of fear and "thought exchange" renewal

"I'M HAVING A *panic* attack," blurted out Private First Class Jason at the front desk medic as soon as he entered the Troop Medical Clinic. "I want to be seen *now, right now!*" he yelled in a loud voice.

As the soldiers gathered curiously around him, his battle buddy rushed forward and tried to calm him down. "I'm sorry, he is pretty scared," he explained as he ushered him quickly to the exam room.

He sat on the edge of the exam table as soon as he entered and, his eyes welling with tears, let out a loud cry. "I need help now, Doctor. I am having a panic attack."

I took a deep breath, pondering the best way to calm him down and what my next move should be as he repeatedly checked the racing pulse of his left carotid artery. "It's fast, Doc…It's so fast."

As he held tightly to his artery, counting his pulse, a list of different treatment options and possibilities raced through my mind: Xanax, Valium, inpatient hospitalization, delayed deployment, or ER referral, among others. I checked his vital signs, did a quick physical exam, which was entirely normal except for his fast heart rate, and reviewed his medical record. Except for his five cups of coffee a day, he was a physically healthy twenty-eight-year-old man suffering from anxiety and a panic attack. I offered him a listening ear after assuring him that his exam was normal and readied myself to hear his story.

"Doc, I don't just want a pill. I want to get to the bottom of my problem," he said as he finally began to calm down.

"That sounds great, Jason. So let's start with the roots then. By the way, five cups of coffee a day with all the caffeine will make your anxieties worse."

"I knew that was coming, Doc. I need to cut that down."

For the next few minutes, I told him about different healthy lifestyle habits that are good for our bodies, minds, and spirits, such as resting, eating a healthy diet, exercising, walking, serving others in need, sharing our feelings, listening to music, and having God in our lives. He listened attentively to my words and began to look much more at ease.

"I was in a Christian school for two years," he said calmly and began to talk about his own spiritual journey. I listened as he shared about how those old school days and his Christian faith once meant a lot to him. With his right hand now firmly by his side, he was no longer counting his pulse but eagerly sharing and listening to words of faith and hope that he once lived by.

"Jason, we are not just physical beings that experience pain, trauma, heat, cold, and sickness in our bodies, but we also have an emotional and spiritual part that can feel loved, peaceful, hopeful, or sad, depressed, and afraid." He seemed totally focused, listening to every word I said.

"Think about it—our souls, minds, and spirits can be beaten up and bruised by many negative, discouraging, no-good thoughts that can lead to ugly out-of-control negative emotions of anxiety, anger, guilt, depression, you name it. You know, your body can get burned if you don't move your finger quickly from a hot stove. You will definitely get heat exhaustion if you march and train too long on a hot, summer day or a serious frostbite if you do the same on a cold winter day.

"But you see, we are all good at keeping our fingers from a hot stove, wearing light clothes, drinking plenty of water, and avoiding direct exposure to the sun on a hot sunny day. When it's cold and freezing outside, we wear heavy clothes and put on our jackets and gloves, right?" I said, poising for a moment to gauge his interest. He looked captivated and nodded for me to continue.

"What I'm trying to say, Jason, is that each of us cares a lot about the wellbeing and safety of our bodies. We avoid and protect ourselves from the burning heat and freezing temperatures that could harm us. But when it comes to guarding our hearts, minds, and spirits from the repeated exposure to negative and messy thoughts, which always generate floods of dark, confusing emotions, we don't do the same. We don't avoid the negative thinking and withdraw quickly from the source of that exposure like we would when we accidentally put our fingers on a hot stove. Do you know what I mean? A lot of us just stay glued and fully focused on many dark, negative thoughts until our hearts and souls burn and begin to fry from them.

"Does that make any sense to you, Jason? I hope this is helping," I said and paused for a moment in wonderment. After witnessing his initial anxious, out-of-control behavior, seeing him so calm and focused on what I was saying was nothing short of a miracle to me.

"I hear what you are saying. It makes sense to keep my mind focused on the positive," he said, and he seemed to no longer focus on his anxiety, fear, and carotid pulse.

It was getting close to time for Jason to go, so for the next few minutes we talked about how our thoughts (T), give birth to emotions (E), which in turn influence our actions (A), or what I coined the TEA effect. We discussed how negative thoughts put doubts into our minds and cause us to question who we are, what our core values are, what our worth is, and whether God loves, forgives, and accepts us. These doubts will produce negative emotions of fear, insecurity, and low self-esteem. On the other hand, positive, loving, caring, and uplifting thoughts renew, refresh, and affirm us. They remind us of God's love and forgiveness and create a shower of healthy emotions that make us feel loved, secure, valued, and freed from guilt and condemnation.

"That's why we desperately need to hear those uplifting words of hope from people who care about us enough to encourage us and keep us focused on the positive no matter how horrific and stormy our past was or our present circumstances are. We need to remind ourselves constantly and surround ourselves with positive people who will remind us of what God thinks of us and make it a habit to practice those good reminders daily," I said.

Indeed, a steady infusion of mind-corrupting killer thoughts from past and present events and experiences weigh us down and load us with fear, confusion, and guilt, much like an invasion of destructive, deadly viruses that must be stopped.

We are all in need of what I call "thought exchange" where our negative and unhealthy thoughts are exchanged with positive and healthy ones much like deoxygenated blood is exchanged in the lungs to the healthy, oxygenated blood that sustains our very lives. But to continuously receive these new thoughts, we must get into the daily practice of being quiet and still in God's presence to receive His Word and His promises of love, goodness, and forgiveness.

Many of us are in desperate need of this habit of thought exchange, as I once told one of my anxious patients who had been tightly grasping negative thinking for years. I suggested she write a list of the top three thoughts that generate feelings of anxiety and fear.

Then, on a separate list, I wrote three thoughts that came from a reliable, pure, and uncontaminated source to be trusted: the word of God in the Bible. The three sentences I wrote emphasized promises that are pleasing and worth thinking about and show God's loving encouragement, caring, and forgiveness. The thought exchange occurred when my patient cut up the paper with the list of negative thoughts, threw it in the garbage, and picked up the list of positive thoughts that was in my hand.

I could see her face brighten as she read it and agreed to deliberately choose to throw any old negative thoughts "in the garbage" as soon as they came and exchange them for positive ones. The idea of being liberated from thoughts that made a yoyo out of her emotional life for many years was worth trying anything for.

We are truly what we think, and if our source(s) of thoughts is contaminated with negatives and we are constantly living with these life-sucking thoughts, or in abusive relationships that are filled with them, we will become like a sick patient hooked to lifesaving breathing, feeding, and IV tubes all connected to contaminated sources of food, fluids, and oxygen. God gives us not only physical life, but also life-sustaining thoughts that will keep us alive and usher us into peace, rest, and a better life.

Like many patients I have taken care of whose only source of survival and life are tubes carrying fluids and oxygen, we are in essence all patients who need life-sustaining thoughts that assure us of being loved, accepted, valued, and forgiven. These thoughts are life to our souls, and it is when our tubes are hooked into the right source— God—that we can receive them and begin to believe them. It is when we trust, accept, and allow them to renew our minds that we begin to put them into practice with passionate acts of kindness, love, and compassion towards ourselves and others, especially those closest to us.

The words Jesus spoke two thousand years ago to a crowd plagued by negative, anxious thoughts about whether they would be able to have a roof over their heads, food to eat, and clothes to wear became alive in the exam room as we both reflected on them. Jesus helped those people to suddenly and cleverly change the focus of their thoughts from negative thinking to hopeful, faith-filled thoughts when He led them to focus instead on the sparrows, whose needs are fully met by God, and the lilies growing on the fields that look beautiful despite their temporary nature.

For few more moments, Jason and I dwelt on God's invitation to switch from negative thinking to hopeful thoughts that assure and remind us of God's love, providence, goodness, forgiveness, and acceptance, a topic fascinating to both of us.

"This can be hard sometimes when we are flooded by negatives, but one thing we can all do is to run away from any sources of contaminated thoughts, drop as fast as we can any rotten, draining, discouraging thoughts and replace them with peaceful, hopeful ones (thought exchange)," I said, summarizing what we seemed to agree on.

As our conversation came to an end, Jason's demeanor was totally different.

"Thank you. Thank you, Doctor. I do appreciate your time. I need to surround myself with positive people. I plan to start going to church and stop my coffee," he said and offered me as a token of his appreciation an invitation to see up close the fighter jets during their precision training, a rare and amazing sight by his description.

"Just ask for me when you come down there, Doctor, and I'll show you around," he said as he made his way to the exam room door.

To the medics' and the front desk soldiers' great surprise, he walked calmly to the front desk and apologized to everyone for his earlier angry attitude and for yelling at them.

I smiled silently as I reflected on God's timely intervention in Jason's life. The medic asked me, "Doc. What did you tell him? What did you give him to calm him down?"

> "Where is your faith?" he asked his disciples. In fear and amazement they asked one another, "Who is this? He commands even the winds and the water, and they obey him."
>
> —Luke 8:25

Emotions, Emotions, Emotions

> But the fruit of the Spirit is love, joy, peace, longsuffering, kindness, goodness, faithfulness, gentleness, self-control. Against such there is no law.
> —Gal. 5:22-23

Like the rising, raging water of a flooded river that sinks, destroys, levels, and kills every living and nonliving in its path, so are our emotions. Like that raging river, they can rise within us higher, higher, and higher and then flood. Who can silence, soothe, and calm the raging emotions within us as they gradually swell and surge? Who can soothe our hearts as waves of overflowing, intense feelings of rejection and loneliness, emptiness and despair, fear, guilt, and restless anger take over our lives and shut us off from reason and good sense? Who can calm our waters when we can no longer be calmed or comforted by even the soothing, gentle breeze of God's voice whispering His love to ears that can no longer hear and eyes in a valley of darkness that can no longer see His light? Who can calm Jason's rising tide of fear, and who can calm down our own destructive emotions before they flood us and those nearest and dearest to us, stealing away every semblance of peace?

What and who can calm our waters and rescue us from drowning in a torrent of killer thoughts and emotions? Do we have self-control as our dam that won't be breached by the deadly rainfall and flood? Can it retain the rising levels of our impounded emotions? Have you, like Jason, let your emotions rise up to flood levels? Have you been able to exercise your self-control like a dam that allows you to release them with a steady and healthy, manageable flow without destroying others and yourself with destructive words and actions?

Emotions are real and are essential to our human experience. There is no sin or shame in crying or in the pain, fear, and anger we all feel as we are subjected to life's sad tragedies, injustices, and rejection and to a world that often shames, uses, abuses, and confuses us. Jesus felt them. He felt anger at the injustices prideful people inflicted on the poor and the believers and at times he felt hurt, unappreciated, and lonely. He shed tears and cried when His friend died and felt the joy of healing and sharing a meal with others. He danced as he celebrated with friends at someone's wedding. But just like He fully experienced emotions and controlled them before they welled up to flood level by spending time in stillness and prayer, resting, and sharing his thoughts and feelings with God, the Father, and others, we must learn to do the same!

Before the rising tide of fear, anger, and other out-of-control emotions grips the helm of our lives, like what happened to Jason, and erode our foundation, destroying us and others in the process, we need to quickly spring to action. Before we cross boundaries that must never be crossed and hurt ourselves, loved ones who trust us, and others who are lost in darkness and desperately in need of light, we must admit our feelings. We must put them to rest with prayer, healthy activities such as sleeping and eating well, resting, exercising, and talking with trusted friends, family members, a pastor, or a professional counselor or physician who can start you on medicine if necessary.

The road of self-control is easier to take when the level of emotions has not risen to the raging point. There is nothing that will raise the level of our destructive emotions, especially anger, more than looking back at our painful past. For example, when we focus on a past experience when we might have been shamed by one or more ruthless people or we suffered traumatic physical, emotional, and mental abuse through rejection, moral failure, or abandonment stirs destructive feelings. The same can be said about dwelling on fearful, humiliating, and choking memories of being overwhelmingly controlled—body, mind, and spirit—by a power-hungry, controlling person.

Your life and relationships can be destroyed by intruding memories—bruising memories of past wrongs and violations forced on you or done by you. Dwelling on memories that bring destructive feelings of deep shame, anger, fear, and pain to your heart and mind will steal your peace, destroy your life, and kill any meaningful relationships in it.

Whatever wrong has been done to you or is now being done to you by unloving, selfish, prideful, controlling person(s) or by the dark powers of evil in this world, you will still need to make major life decisions. You can make a crucial choice to forgive, let go of any inner pride and selfishness, and not let the evil done to you flow through you like a violent river that will assuredly destroy you, the loved ones around you, and potentially future generations.

You can choose today to stop the evil done to you from flowing like raging, destructive waters over the balance of your earthly life and onto others through you. Shamed and hurt people shame and hurt others; controlled people control others; and raging and angry people explode unexpectedly like land mines if stepped on, defiling others and drawing them into a cycle of rage and anger. This becomes a never ending cycle where whoever is now hurt, controlled, shamed, and enraged will be equipped to do exactly the same to others. This is a deadly cycle that, if not stopped, will affect everyone around you and become one sad family legacy to leave behind.

The evil that touched your life can flow through you and touch others around you even into the next generations unless you decide that the cycle stops here and break it with the *power of love*. Our self-erected strong fort walls of pride, self centeredness, and selfishness can keep the poisonous weeds of anger, shame, fear, and past wounds growing wildly in the confines of our hearts, choking us and those closest to us in this endless deadly cycle. But we can end this cycle when we choose to walk in love and humility and begin to deliberately dismantle our fortified walls of pride and selfishness. It's only when we raise the white flag of surrender to God's love and Spirit and begin to build new walls of love—God's love—that we can demolish these thick walls and heal and remove the deadly weeds in our hearts, ending this destructive lifetime cycle.

If we don't choose to accept and walk in God's love, these deadly weeds will continue to bring out the worst in us, which will in turn become a never ending cycle that will harm and bring out the worst in those who love us and whom we care about—family, children, our children's children, friends, neighbors, society, and country.

It is only when our hearts are converted, changed and renewed with the healing touch of God's divine love that we begin to be genuinely humble, forgiving, and loving and look forward to the amazing future that God has planned for us instead of backwards into the memories and feelings of a painful past. It is then that we become like a gentle, meandering river where living water of light, love, peace, and goodness flows in us and through us to touch our families and children, spilling over into a dark, thirsty world desperate for light.

None of us will ever experience a normal life with its joy, peace, tears, and other healthy emotions if we continue to look backwards into our painful past memories while driving on the highway of life. We will certainly crash if we continue to look at the past while trying to live a good and peaceful life.

Ultimately, there is no tear, feeling, or human experience, no matter how painful and unpleasant, that will ever go to waste. From the seeds of our pain and suffering, we will one day see, if we don't give up, lavish trees growing in the soil of our hearts with the fruit of patience, character, love, hope, and new beginnings (to name a few) growing abundantly on their branches.

God will use our pasts of abandonment, rejection, failure, shame, abuse, or control to transform us into stronger and more joyful, loving, and peaceful men and women. We will arrive at our peaceful shore of rest if we persevere and do not give up. We will surely get there if we continue to hope in God's divine plan and purpose for our lives—an eternity in heaven and a better life where no matter what dark and violent storm we are in, we can still feel contentment and God's inner peace.

Jesus tells us about this amazing peace in the New Testament book of John. "Peace I leave you; my peace I give you. I do not give to you as the world gives. Do not let your hearts be troubled and do not be afraid" (John 14:27).

This peace is exactly how one of my Christian patients, a beautiful thirty-seven-year-old woman with a loving husband and four children, including a baby, felt even as she received her terminal cancer diagnosis and as the cancer ravaged through her abdomen, subjecting her to one major colon removal surgery after another. She always looked peaceful as she continued to believe that God, Who loved her and sent His Son Jesus Christ to die for her sins, was always in control of her earthly and eternal life.

With an eight-by-ten-inch color picture of herself, her husband, and their children adorning the empty hospital room wall facing her, she never stopped saying kind words, praying, and smiling every time I saw her, even as feeding lines and IV tubes struggled to nourish her withering body. God used even her human experience of terminal suffering to bring her closer to Him and to bless me and the many others who knew her by opening our eyes to see that all of our human problems grew shamefully pale in light of what she was going through; yet she was comforted by God and was content, praying and smiling with every bit of energy she could muster.

Jesus says, as found in the New Testament of the Bible, that He came to earth so that we can have a better life and live it more abundantly. The teachings of the Bible remind us to forget what was behind and run the race of life looking forward to the amazing future of blessings, peace, and contentment, both here on earth, despite the storms we face, and in heaven after we depart our earthly bodies. This is one life-saving, emotional-fever-reducing medicine that no doctor can prescribe and a self-control mechanism to quell our emotions before they rise and flood us. The Bible contains wisdom of the ages for each of us to choose to live by.

> Get rid of all bitterness, rage and anger, brawling and slander, along with every form of malice.
> —Eph. 4:31

> I will sprinkle clean water on you, and you will be clean; I will cleanse you from all your impurities and from all your idols. I will give you a new heart and put a new spirit in you; I will remove from you your heart of stone and give you a heart of flesh. And I will put my Spirit in you and move you to follow my decrees and be careful to keep my laws.
> —Ezek. 36:25-27 NKJV

I want to go home

> Are not two sparrows sold for a copper coin? And not one of them falls to the ground apart from your Father's will. But the very hairs of your head are all numbered.
> —Matt. 10:29-30 NKJV

"I want to go home. I just want to go home," repeated thirty-one-year-old Private Justin in desperation. Judging by his disappointed look, disgruntled attitude, and multiple sick call visits (six times in less than a month) to the Troop Medical Clinic, it was clear to me that he was overwhelmed by his pending tour of duty in Afghanistan. His multiple medical visits with multiple X-rays, MRIs, and extensive evaluations by specialists found no medical reason to cancel his deployment. Yet, Justin continued to complain of various ailments that didn't make any sense medically. Finally, the army medical board reached the obvious conclusion and decided he was fit to deploy. It was during this visit that I was to inform him of the board's final decision.

I sat on the chair across from him and began to read the binding report that he was deemed fit for combat after a thorough review of his medical condition and that he would be departing with his unit to combat. As I was going over the final decision with him, I could see in his eyes the fear and desperation that filled his heart.

"I just want to go home...just want to go home" was all he could manage to say as his eyes began to tear. He seemed to be gripped by a deep fear of the future that lay ahead. He had run out of all possible appeals and knew the only way out of this camp was going forward to the battlefields awaiting him.

As he sat down on the exam table in total desperation, I wondered what to say that might be of help to him in his predicament. My dad's favorite saying, "The one whose hand is in the fire is not like the one whose hand is in the water" came to mind. There he was—a soldier whose heart was overwhelmed with the prospect of shooting to kill for the first time and the fear of being killed. I was definitely not in his shoes, and my hand was not with his in the fire. I was in no place to judge him.

I wondered if some of the stories I heard from many of the demobilizing soldiers would be of comfort to him.

"Justin, I know this news is not what you were hoping for. Are you willing to hear some stories from soldiers who came back from the front?" I asked as I thought of ways to keep him from falling deeper into despair and depression.

He suddenly became quiet and signaled his interest in what I had to say. For the next few minutes, I shared with him the stories of many who believed their tour of duty had boosted their confidence and inner strength. I told him about those who were very thankful for the opportunity of traveling to remote parts of the world where they experienced for the first time foreign cultures and a chance to make a difference in another human being's life.

"Many shared with me the pain of losing a friend in combat and the fear of going through deadly battles where they fired their weapons as bullets and shrapnel pierced their bodies," I said. "But still, they were all willing to go back, eager to make a difference in the lives of Iraqis and Afghanis, especially those of the innocent little children."

His interest in what I was saying was complete, and so I continued. "Many told me they're looking forward to going back to join the humanitarian efforts to feed the children, protect the innocents, and rebuild what was destroyed, especially democracies in Iraq and Afghanistan."

He continued to listen silently to what I had to say. I wondered if my words offered him the comfort and encouragement he badly needed. At that moment, I decided to change the direction of our conversation and began to talk to him about our human destiny and our individual God-designed life purpose that may very well include the road he found himself travelling now.

"Justin, have you thought that in the greater scheme of things, going there might actually be part of God's purpose for your life? You've tried everything in the book to avoid going to combat but every single attempt has failed, and here you are here today! Could this actually mean that mobilizing is an integral part of your life purpose destined for you by God? Is it possible that what you will do, perform, help, or say over there will be exactly what someone else desperately needs and that you're the one purposed by God to do that?"

Judging by his strong interest in the topics of God, destiny, and life purpose, his engaging questions, and drastic change in demeanor by the end of the visit—from tears of despair to quietness and reflection—I wondered if he was beginning to look at his deployment through a lens colored with God's higher life purpose and plan for him.

Soon after he left, I reflected on his story and the change of heart that can come when we view what seems so overwhelming and scary to us from God's point of view. To God, we are not born by accident, and each of our individual lives is according to a plan and a purpose.

After repeated unsuccessful attempts to go home, Justin found himself instead going to join his "band of brothers" in the theater of operations, not just in body but hopefully in spirit as well. His only way out was marching, even as fear gripped him, with boldness and a sense of purpose through the unknown that awaited him far away.

> For you did not receive a spirit that makes you a slave again to fear, but you received the Spirit of sonship. And by him we cry, "Abba, Father."
>
> —Rom. 8:15

CHAPTER 12

FOCUSING FOR SURVIVAL

Focusing for Survival: Photo provided by Camp Atterbury Public Affairs

Therefore since we are surrounded by such a great cloud of witnesses, let us throw off everything that hinders and the sin that so easily entangles, and let us run with perseverance the race marked out for us.
—Heb. 12:1

Distractions that kill

"I'M GLAD TO be home," blurted thirty–two-year-old Sgt. First Class Jonathan as he entered the exam room. His personality was very upbeat and friendly. With multiple deployments under his belt, he looked very confident and exceptionally easygoing.

"I started when I was nineteen," he said.

He was a natural comedian with a fascinating gift for storytelling. His ability to talk about the harsh realities of war with an ingenuous mixture of humor, sadness, and compassion captivated me.

"I care about my soldiers like my own family, Doc," he said.

Soon after ordering a steroid cream for his skin rash, I asked him about his best advice to the younger, less-experienced soldiers on their first deployment.

"I learned a lot from the older soldiers. I'm teaching my soldiers the best thing that I was ever taught—to stay focused on the battlefield, pay attention, and have common sense," he said. Then, in a serious tone of voice, he proceeded to tell me about, "the surest way to get killed in Iraq."

"The first thing is we need more troops in Iraq to get the job done. We advance from one building to another, house to house, and fight hard to clear the streets from insurgents, only to see them return soon after we leave. We need more soldiers to get the job done and prevent them from coming back."

What he said made a lot of sense to me and to the fighting troops and their commanders on the ground. I nodded in agreement as I continued to listen to his cheerful voice.

"A lot of enemy hits are preventable if our soldiers follow exactly what they've been trained to do—listen carefully, watch for changes like sudden silence, a street that is suddenly deserted, a stranger in town, or when children stop playing and run to their homes. They must pay particular attention when people in the neighborhood signal to soldiers not to enter a house from this or that door or give them a sign to wait and not keep moving," he said.

I knew I was listening to a soldier who must've learned the hard way from his many years of multiple deployments to Iraq, beginning with the first Gulf War.

FOCUSING FOR SURVIVAL

"One must focus and pay attention to all these subtle changes. You know, Doctor, you would find some of the soldiers with little experience rushing to use a radio to call their commanders instead of waiting. They end up revealing their position and setting up IEDs and enemy fire."

"Something else," he added and began to explain how each soldier must learn how to fire his M16 at the enemy when he is lying on the ground. "It's different."

Every time I shared Sergeant Jonathan's words, they seemed quite helpful to many young soldiers on their first deployment. His words were a reminder of the high price one can pay for being distracted and unfocused. It's indeed one thing to be distracted and miss an appointment, a highway exit, or your mother's birthday, but quite another to be unfocused and distracted and losing your physical, emotional, and spiritual life in the process. His words made me think about the more serious consequences of living an unfocused life: wandering away from God-given opportunities, losing peace and security, and missing all the danger and slow down warnings in life.

The race of life is one of constant battles, much like that of a soldier in combat. To run our life races well, we need to stay focused on our higher, God-given call and purpose and look forward to our life in the future, not backward into a long-dead past.

> So we fix our eyes not on what is seen, but on what is unseen. For what is seen is temporary, but what is unseen is eternal.
> —2 Cor. 4:18

Focusing on what's good

> Do you not know that in a race all the runners run, but only one gets the prize? Run in such a way as to get the prize.
> —1 Cor. 9: 24

"You've been to seven deployments! How in the world did you do it?" I asked old Sgt. First Class Andrew, who had just returned from his last tour of duty. Andrew, now a weapon trainer at the base, was quick to share his secret of surviving multiple war assignments while keeping his big smile still intact.

"It's about staying focused on the right things, Doctor. Right after each combat mission where our unit was hit with mortar attacks, IEDs, or enemy bullets and suffered some casualties, I came back to the barracks and immediately started to exercise, play basketball, or read my Bible. That was my only way to change my thoughts and focus from what I'd just experienced in combat to new things and activities that help me feel good."

His words made perfect sense to me. By changing the focus of his thinking as soon as he could from the bloody and gruesome battles he had just experienced to the good, healthy distractions of basketball, exercising, and Bible reading, he was able to keep his thoughts positive and uplifting. That in turn generated in him positive and peaceful emotions even in the midst of his dangerous assignments and surroundings.

His words reminded me of a similar tactic that Jesus used two thousand years ago. He once told a large crowd of people, who were plagued with many fears and worries about daily life, such as where their next meal would come from or whether they could afford clothes or a roof over their heads, to stop worrying about these things. Instead, He invited them to change their thinking to focus on the simple, well-fed little sparrows and the spectacularly beautiful lilies of the valley—all provided for and well taken care of by a loving God, Who will also take care of all of our needs.

"So don't be afraid; you are worth more than many sparrows," Jesus said.

—Matt. 10:31

"Not dwelling on what I just saw—blood, dead bodies, and other disturbing images of combat—helped a lot. One of our unit soldiers wanted to be by himself and would always go back to his tent and stay alone after each one of our convoy escorts and missions. He didn't want to join us, talk, or occupy himself with activities that were available to him. He didn't do well after he came back home; he shot himself," he said, reinforcing his point.

Many months after my brief encounter with Andrew, I found myself using his example to help many patients whose fears, worries,

FOCUSING FOR SURVIVAL

anxieties, and toxic, negative thoughts have paralyzed them. I often tell my patients that dwelling and focusing on the past and on the experiences that generate such deadly, destructive thoughts is as damaging to our hearts, minds, and spirits as the damage caused when our fingers are left to dwell on a red hot stove. The main difference is that we're all smart enough to pull our fingers quickly from the hot stove before they burn, but we're slow to withdraw and foolish enough to keep our minds and thoughts focused on negative and toxic words and thoughts that come from our past and present.

Many of us entertain and hold tightly (instead of just briefly glancing at them and moving on) such thoughts; nursing and rocking them to sleep like precious little babies, even as they steadily burn and fry our minds, thoughts, and emotions. Unfortunately, some refuse a helping hand and sound wisdom but choose instead to dwell in a polluted pool of dark thoughts. They harden their hearts to God's help that often comes with timely advice of a caring person, a counselor's compassionate words, or a desperately needed medicine, even as they slowly drown in more confusion.

But living a life where dark thoughts lead us astray into unhealthy paths of emotional turmoil where we hang on tightly to old wounds and bitterness is not what God, our Creator, meant for our lives when we were born. We were created as men and women to have a good life with a divine purpose. Yet until we choose to totally surrender the control of our lives to God, we will continue to be controlled by our pride, anger, selfishness, shame, and guilt.

The good news is that we can all have a new beginning, free from anyone or anything controlling our thoughts, emotions, or life paths. We can be controlled by nothing and no one except by God. It's in surrendering to God's control of our lives that we find lasting inner peace and true freedom. This spiritual path is like the first day we were born except it's being born again from above by the Spirit of God Who comes to dwell in us, as Jesus told a Jewish leader, Nicodemus, over two thousand years ago (John 3:3-8).

The Bible explains that we find this freedom and ensuing peace when we willingly remove ourselves from our throne and relinquish control of our lives to God, believing and confessing that Jesus Christ is our Savior and Lord. Then comes a lifelong spiritual journey through the wilderness of life where we learn to surrender different areas of our lives to God's direction, purpose, and control. A journey where we learn with God's help to be light and salt to a dark world and to let God's Holy Spirit produce in us what the Bible calls the fruit of the Spirit: love, joy, peace, patience, kindness, goodness, faithfulness, gentleness, and self-control. After that comes God's promise of a joyful eternal life. "He will wipe every tear from their eyes. There will be no more death or mourning or crying or pain, for the old order of things has passed away" (Rev. 21:4).

Before he left, Andrew and I agreed on the wisdom of these powerful words found in the New Testament: "Finally brothers, whatever is right, whatever is pure, whatever is lovely, whatever is admirable – if anything is excellent or praise worthy – think about such things" (Phil. 4:8).

We both know that with God's divine love and help, it's never too late to rid ourselves of our old toxic thoughts and replace them with new, healthy, peaceful ones that will keep us in God's good and perfect plan for our lives. The choice is ultimately ours whether to dwell with the new or the old and hence to determine the path we end up taking.

> So teach us to number our days, That we may gain a heart of wisdom.
> —Ps. 90:12 NKJV

CHAPTER 13

GOD, SPIRITUALITY, AND NEW BEGINNINGS

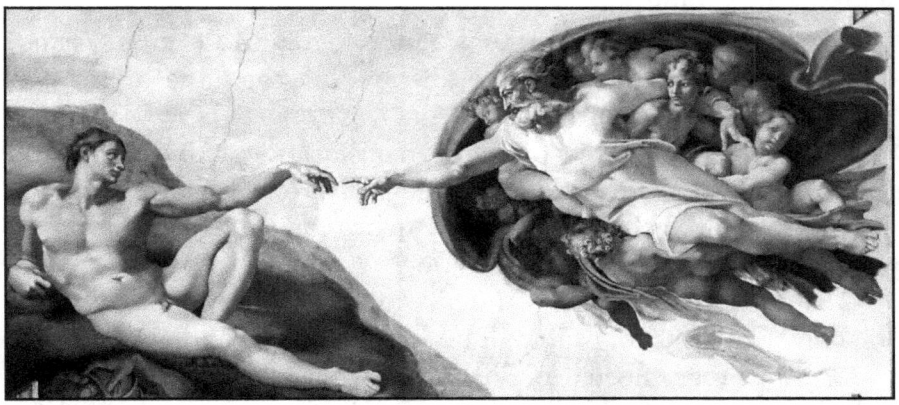

God, Spirituality, and New Beginnings

> What a man desires is unfailing love…
> —Prov. 19:22

A long search for love – when God becomes real

"ALL I NEED is to break this migraine attack. If I can just sleep, I'll be fine," said twenty-one-year-old Private First Class Samantha as she walked slowly towards the exam room table. Her frequent visits to the Troop Medical Clinic with migraine complaints prompted me to look closer for any underlying depression or anxiety that she might be reluctant to talk about.

Soon I could tell that she was starting to feel comfortable as she began to open up and talk to me about what was bothering her. She talked about her absent father, whom she had not seen since her early childhood until recently when he suddenly decided to call her, and her lifetime struggle to feel secure and loved.

"I struggled all my life, looking for some kind of assurance that my parents love me, especially my dad. I haven't seen him since he left home when I was only five. We've just started talking," she said.

Fortunately for Samantha, her relationship with her mom was stable and had remained strong throughout the years.

"She is watching my ten-month-old baby till I come back," she said. "I can't trust anybody else. I have no idea what I would do without her…I love her."

Samantha's yearning for her daddy's love never ceased. Yet her disappointment with his failure to show her the fatherly love she desperately yearned for remained.

"He conveniently went out of town on vacation with his girlfriend the day I had my deployment farewell party. He wasn't even there to tell me good-bye before coming here to be mobilized. That hurt me," she said, barely hiding her frustration.

"Samantha, in what ways did missing your dad's love shape your life choices?" I asked, probing into her hidden emotions.

"I think that affected me in so many ways, especially the way I dealt with my life problems. For the longest time, I looked for love in relationships…with the wrong type of men. Living with my ex-boyfriend was the dumbest mistake of my life."

For the next few minutes, she talked about her past shame, wounds, fears, and hope. I could tell the sense of relief in her voice; perhaps sharing these emotions and talking about the challenges of the strained relationship with her dad was therapeutic to her.

Samantha grew up missing her father's love, and her natural desire to be loved by a father figure would not be satisfied. Eventually, what was normal—the need to be loved—became an out-of-control intense craving for love that led her to dependent relationships with the wrong men who took advantage of her, including a boyfriend who had almost derailed her life.

Her thirst to be loved was not quenched by any of her physical and love relationships with men. Instead, her soul's thirst worsened, affecting her emotions and probably inflicting her with frequent crippling migraines.

Sadly, many daughters, like Samantha, never experience a mother's or father's love before they leave to college or to homes of their own.

Unfortunately, many, but not all, parents and single parents are too busy and no longer care. Some fathers and mothers have become too wrapped up in themselves and their own selfish goals to notice their children's desperate need for genuine love, guidance, acceptance, and encouragement.

I believe that is like sending a son or a daughter into a dark, dangerous, predator-filled world equipped only with low self-esteem and lacking confidence. It's the equivalent of sending a soldier to war without any food, body armor, or a loaded M16.

Her story reminded me of a story in the Bible that I've often mentioned to my patients about a woman Jesus saw near the village well drawing water. He approached and asked her for water but then surprised her by telling her that "the water that I give you if you drink it you will never be thirsty." Jesus knew that she was a woman desperate for love, who lived with a man without marriage, and that she had been in and out of relationships with other men all her life. Like Samantha, she was also desperate for love and tried to quench this inner thirst with relationships that could not satisfy her.

Jesus' words to the woman at the well were a bold statement that He alone could satisfy her inner thirst with his unconditional love and presence in her life. He says these same words today to Samantha and to humanity. We all, like that woman at the well, are thirsty for love, security, acceptance, value, and forgiveness, and He alone has the water that will satisfy our souls.

Samantha was very appreciative, and before she left with her migraine medicine we talked about a Bible verse on love and its healing power. She left with a big smile, a thank you, and a hug. She continued to do very well, finished her training, and deployed to Afghanistan with her unit.

> For I am convinced that neither death nor life, neither angels nor demons, neither the present nor the future, nor any powers, neither height nor depth, nor anything else in all creation, will be able to separate us from the love of God that is in Christ Jesus our Lord.
> —Rom. 8:38-39

Change from the inside out: new beginnings

> O Lord, you are our Father. We are the clay, you are the potter; we are all the work of your hand.
> —Isa. 64:8 NKJV

Soon after I diagnosed Sergeant Jeremy with bronchitis and prescribed an antibiotic, we had a brief chat about how deployment has affected his life.

"I'm thankful to be here," he said.

To Jeremy, this deployment had proved to be a new beginning. It provided him with "finally a chance to leave my girlfriend, who nearly ruined me and my children with her drug habit.

"I pray a lot here and I thank God every day for giving me this chance to put my life back on track," he said. "I'm going to leave my kids for the next eighteen months, Doc, and it had better be for something good like getting to know God, working to put my life together, and saving money for their college educations."

"Are you afraid of going to Iraq?" I asked.

"I volunteered to go there. I found out the hardest thing about changing my life around is the fear of making the change, but I knew that I desperately needed a fresh start and needed to be at this deployment camp."

His desire and passion to start anew seemed to ignite in the loud, vigorous daytime training and in the quietness of the dark camp nights. It was his deep desire for change that had motivated him to volunteer for this deployment, and his zeal and passion for a new beginning will keep him marching steadily towards his goal.

"Doc, all these changes are good for me. Even my blood pressure is better," he said, cheerfully on his way out of the exam room.

After he left, I reflected on his inspirational story. Often in life we get ourselves involved with the wrong people—an abusive relationship, a foolish financial deal, or situations that make us feel stuck—and we hopelessly try to regain our lost sense of peace.

And much like Jeremy, we often yearn for a new beginning and for God to rescue us from our humanly impossible dilemmas and put our lives back on track. Just like he ventured and volunteered in hope of a new page in his life, we too need to walk boldly towards what is good and new. As we steadily walk away from threatening, destructive relationships and bad memories of the past, we will assuredly arrive one day in the total freedom that God has for us in our own personal life camp.

But can change really happen? The answer is yes for those who sincerely want it and are no longer comfortable with the old. A patient once told me, "My ex-husband has changed so much. He cares a lot about the children now, and we are becoming friends. But I just don't understand why he didn't want to change when we were still married."

Yes, change is most definitely possible, but unlike Jeremy, we often choose not to walk on its rugged road, or we resist it until it is too late. The walk of change is not for the timid, prideful, and fearful.

Nothing will fire you up to walk away from the old and venture boldly into a new beginning like remembering the smelly, stinky odor and the bitter, rotten taste of a painfully sinful past with its abuses, hurts, and wrong choices. It is in taking a long, deep look at such warlike destructiveness and shame that we wake up, stand up, and walk away, saying in our hearts, "No more."

> The Spirit of the Lord is on me, because he has anointed me to preach good news to the poor. He has sent me to proclaim freedom for the prisoners and recovery of sight for the blind, to release the oppressed, to proclaim the year of the Lord's favor.
> —Luke 4:18-19

Finding God in a military camp

> And so we know and rely on the love God has for us. God is love. Whoever lives in love lives in God, and God in him.
> —1 John 4:16

Private Emily zoomed into the exam room looking angry and frustrated.

"Doc, good luck. You've got an angry patient in the room," whispered the medic in my ear. "She was screaming at everybody at the front desk."

"Are you a shrink?" Emily asked defiantly as soon as I entered.

"Not really. I'm a family physician. So what brings you to this humble dwelling?" I asked, wondering about her next move.

"Good! I'm sick and tired of therapists and shrinks. I don't want to have any more therapy."

But soon she began to calm down and tell me about her life story. She talked about her ex-boyfriend, whom she had broken up with after a ten-year relationship, who was actively stalking her, and her frustration with her new manic-depressive boyfriend who wanted to call it quits.

"My ex is threatening him. He says he can't take it anymore and wants to break up with me."

Adding to Emily's frustration was her relationship with her mother.

"It's been over five years since my brother was killed, but Mom is still crying every day and blames herself for his death. It wasn't her fault, you know, but she is always questioning why it happened, 'Why did I move to this neighborhood? What could I have done to prevent it?'"

Eventually, her mom's constant tears and lamentations began to take a toll on Emily, and she started to feel overwhelmed.

"I feel she is becoming too dependent on me. I tell her 'I love you' all the time, Doctor, but she says she can't believe it. She goes to church…says she is religious, and I keep telling her about God but she still can't get rid of her guilt," she said, in disappointment.

I wasn't sure why Emily decided to tell me about her boyfriends, her brother, and her mother's ordeal, but talking about them seemed to make her much more at ease. I quietly listened as she talked for few more minutes about them and her feelings. But suddenly she stopped and looked at me with a tender and peaceful smile and said in a calm voice, "I'm just so happy…to be away from it all. I feel that I can start a new page in my life…to have a new relationship with God, the Creator of the universe, and find rest…away from everything."

Was that the same Emily who was just yelling at the medics and was overly worried that I was a shrink? I marveled.

Her face looked peaceful as she thanked me for listening to her. She left the exam room and stopped by the front desk to apologize to the medics, whom she had previously blasted with an angry voice on her way in!

After our encounter, I reflected on her story and the obvious change in her demeanor. It would be easy to take some credit for her sweet change, but Emily could have felt better with anyone who showed her respect, caring, love, and compassion by the simple act of *listening*.

To someone who is in emotional turmoil, listening is a potent medicine that reaches a wounded heart with one clear message: "You're not alone, you're not crazy, you're loved, you're worthy, and yes, you can begin to hope again because everything will be okay very soon."

Would you please take the time to thank someone who listened to you when you most needed it and be quick to listen to someone hurting who needs your listening ears today?

> This is love: not that we loved God, but that he loved us and sent his Son as an atoning sacrifice for our sins.
> —John 4:10

Finding faith in a military camp

> Now faith is being sure of what we hope for and certain of what we do not see.
> —Hebrews 11:1

"How are you doing, Carol?" I asked the twenty-three-year-old corporal from the upper Midwest as I glanced briefly at the Prozac dose listed on her chart.

"I feel much better now, Doctor. God helped me deal with so many problems in my life that nearly tore me apart," she answered.

"Do you want to talk about it?"

"I don't know where to start, Doctor. It seems like everything was happening at the same time—I caught my husband in bed with my best friend, he had lied until I caught them together. Then I went through divorce. I got deployed around the same time and then left my daughters with my mother to come here. I think that's plenty," she said, pausing briefly to catch her breath.

"My goodness and you're still alive! I can't imagine what you've just been through! How did you survive that?"

For the next few minutes, Carol talked about her faith in God and how her relationship with Him had sustained her in those dark, scary, and lonely days of her life.

"My faith in God saved me," she said confidently.

After her visit, I briefly reflected on her confessed faith in God that has sustained her during her darkest and loneliest hours. It's that faith that quelled her fears when she found herself in the pitch dark days of betrayal, divorce, and separation from her children.

God knows that fear, a natural tendency bestowed upon us to help us navigate safely away from the physical, emotional, and spiritual dangers of life towards right and safe relationships and places, can also be a force that will paralyze our souls and keep us hiding in the bunkers of life.

This is why we find in the Bible the command "Fear not" mentioned 365 times—the number of days in a year! As a reminder that God is always in control of our lives and whatever happens even during our worst moments, He tells us to "fear not." And even if death is our lot in one of our life's worst storms or when our numbered days come to an end, God remains in control and with us at that last moment and forever in eternity.

Our life situations and the different storms that hit our lives can indeed be menacing and scary, but God wants us to focus on Him and not on the storm; on His massive power, forgiveness, mercy, and grace and not on the comparatively weaker power or potential damage of the storm attacking us.

Our fears will indeed begin to vanish as we move our eyes from the adversity cornering us from all directions and begin to focus on God and have a stronger faith in His power and goodness towards us. This is when faith kicks away our fears, and we start to see that as faith takes over our hearts and minds, our fears begin to fade away.

This is the fear-busting faith that Carol talked about and that gives us inner peace and assurance that it will all be well with our souls even in the midst of the raging battles of life. And it's that same faith that Carol will soon need to sustain her on the war front with her unit's soldiers as they face the deadliest moments of their lives.

> And without faith it is impossible to please God, because anyone who comes to him must believe that he exists and that he rewards those who earnestly seek him.
> —Heb. 11:6

> God is our refuge and strength, an ever present help in trouble.
> —Ps. 46:1

God's love shining through a cat's eye

> Not only so, but we rejoice in our sufferings, because we know that suffering produces perseverance; perseverance, character; and character, hope. And hope does not disappoint.
> —Rom. 5:3- 5

With her small frame and tender smile, Captain Judy quietly entered the exam room. She walked cautiously, avoiding any sudden movements that would irritate her sprained neck. She could barely move it after the morning's combat training. She looked very friendly and younger than her stated age of fifty-two. I admit that it would have been fairly hard for me to conclude on my own that this gentle soul was a brave soldier on her way to war. Somehow, I needed to see her confidently walk to the exam table wearing with pride the ACU (Army Combat Uniform) and its associated heavy battle gear.

After discussing the treatment plan for her neck sprain, Judy began to open her heart. "Doctor, it was so hard to be a female in the military back in the late seventies. I started in the air force and then the navy," she offered. Then with a grin she continued, "Back then, higher-ranked males would say sexually suggestive things to the female soldiers without any fear of repercussions." She added with a chuckle, "I still recall how some of the pilots and flight officers used to ask me if I wanted to join the 'one mile high club.' It took me a long time to know that they were talking about a 'club' where one engages in sex at high altitudes! Doctor, I could almost write a book about all that happened. Thankfully, things have now changed."

But suddenly, the topic changed as she started to passionately talk about her love for animals and their loyalty. I wasn't sure why she suddenly wanted to talk about this topic, but somehow I felt there was a story dear to her heart that she was about to share. I could see the tears starting as she looked at me.

"You know, a society can be judged by how well it treats its animals," she said. "My cat always shows me unconditional love. She is always loyal to me, Doctor." She paused as if to gather emotional strength and began to tell me about a man who was once her husband. "My husband left me after six years of marriage. I loved him... helped him, supported and took good care of him till he finished his residency. But he could never make up his mind whether to stay with me or leave. He finally chose to leave me and filed for divorce. He knew how much I loved him. He left me to marry someone else, and now that I'm getting ready to deploy to Afghanistan, he's starting to call me again. He is not happy, Doctor...he is not happy."

Then she suddenly burst into tears. "I am sorry...I am sorry. It really hurts. It's too late for me now to have a baby. He never wanted to have a baby with me. I had a hysterectomy because of bleeding. I can't have babies anymore."

Her tearful words touched my heart as I felt a surge of compassion towards her. I saw her as God's sweet, kind, and gentle creation and a most loving human being, who was once deeply wounded. What she had thought was a lifetime love relationship ended up being a hurtful and failed marriage to a man who literally stole the best years of her life, ultimately denying her the joy of being a mother. And now, on her way to combat, he suddenly shows up in her life again to complain about his misery and unhappiness with his new wife!

As I saw Judy's tears, I could feel my anger rising towards the injustice that this tender soul has suffered as she saw her dream of love and motherhood unfairly interrupted. But then suddenly, I was comforted by her gentle, brave heart. With her eyes beaming with hope, Judy shared with me how she had found God's comfort in her darkest hours. It finally became clear to me why she had passionately shared about the unconditional love and loyalty of her cat. The tender and quiet tempo of her peaceful voice echoed with hope as she began to tell me about her precious pet.

"You know, Doctor, God touched my heart in the most painful times of my life. I still remember the day my ex-husband hurt me so deeply with very painful words before leaving and slamming the door hard behind him. I was so hurt and just sat on the couch, crying. I felt so sad. Then suddenly, I felt a warm body next to mine; it was my cat that saw me in tears and came crawling next to me!"

Judy's voice began to choke as she remembered what happened next. "At the saddest day of my life, my cat must have felt my sadness. She stood next to me and just stared right at my eyes… so intensely at my tearful eyes. It was as if a kind human eye was looking at me with so much love and compassion. It was like she knew that I was hurt and was telling me. 'I love you. It will be okay' with her eyes."

She paused as she reflected on her next sentence. "Doctor, that was the moment I knew God was telling me through my cat's eyes… that I'll be all right," she said, drying away her tears.

As Judy prepared to leave, I thought about her words. To think that God uses any part of His creation—cats included—to speak love and comfort to a broken heart like Judy's brought me a step closer to knowing the loving heart of God and speaking His main language—love.

Judy left for more afternoon training, but she left me with these powerful words that described her faith, fighter's spirit, and resilience. "I am much stronger because of what happened to me. What does not kill you only makes you stronger."

> However, as it is written: "No eye has seen, no ear has heard, no mind has conceived what God has prepared for those who love him."
>
> —1 Cor. 2:9

"I Dreamt of Jesus, Doc"

> Whether you turn to the right or to the left, your ears will hear a voice behind you, saying, "This is the way; walk in it."
> —Isa. 30:21

At the end of Manuel's physical exam, his last before leaving for Iraq, I asked if his faith in God had helped him deal with the sudden news of his deployment with his unit all the way from Puerto Rico. For the next few minutes, we talked about God, life, death, war, and a dream that worried him.

"Before my deployment, I started to pray a lot to God and ask Him to show me His will for my life. A few days ago I dreamt of Jesus. In the dream, I saw Jesus standing in a real nice garden with flowers and green grass. In the dream I wanted to move closer to Him, but I had to walk across a dangerous field to go to Him. Suddenly, I saw a man running towards Jesus to kill Him. I ran quickly to stop the man, pulled my military knife, and killed him before he could hurt Jesus," he said, concluding the story of a dream that left him puzzled.

His sister had offered him her own interpretation of the dream. "She told me, 'Manuel this is a sign that you shouldn't go to war because Jesus doesn't want you to kill people,'" he said, recalling her words. He looked pretty concerned about his sister's interpretation and seemed interested in my own opinion.

Judging by the confused look on his face, I ventured with my two cents' worth interpretation of his dream.

"Hey, Manuel, in the dream you seem to care enough about Jesus to want to risk your life for Him. Could it be possible that your dream is Jesus' way of reminding you that He will be with you on the battlefield where you will be fighting to protect what's important to Him?" I asked, offering my own thoughts on his intriguing dream.

He listened attentively to every word I said and seemed to find comfort in knowing that Jesus would be with him in combat.

"I've been praying a lot since I found out about my deployment," he said, expressing his relief.

Somehow his sister's interpretation of his dream didn't resonate well with him. I could tell that the simple notion that Jesus isn't condemning him for going to war, but is right there by his side watching over him, brought him a deep sense of calm. As we talked more about his faith and courage that led him to risk his life for Jesus in the dream, Manuel wondered if the dream was a sign that a higher purpose would be served after all by his combat deployment: a divine purpose and a noble cause that he was now willing to give his life for, just like in the dream.

I've often marveled at the way God uses dreams, as the Bible mentions, to communicate with those who pray to Him and earnestly seek Him like Manuel began to do after he heard of his deployment. Witnessing firsthand the positive influence of the dream on him, and how much it fueled his courage and zeal as a soldier with a mission, strengthened my own faith in God's reality, His love to us, and His guidance.

But just as the gentle, quiet sound of the leaves moved by an unseen soft breeze is drowned out in a loud, roaring storm, so is God's whispering voice to our hearts silenced by the loudness of our world and the fierce storms of our lives. It's in those difficult moments of life's crossroads, such as the one Manuel was facing, when we reach to the depth of our heart and release our cries to God that we're finally able to tune out all the voices and noises in and around us. Then we're finally able to hear the still voice of God in a song, a smile, a kind and caring word, someone's compassionate acts of service, and yes…in a dream.

> So do not fear, for I am with you; do not be dismayed, for I am your God. I will strengthen you and help you; I will uphold you with my righteous right hand.
> —Isa. 41:10

> For he will command his angels concerning you to guard you in all your ways.
> —Ps. 91:11

Ingrown toenail, guilt, and God

> I, even I, am he who blots out your transgressions, for my own sake, and remembers your sins no more.
> —Isaiah 43:25

Twenty-four-year-old Private Rick limped slowly into the exam room, his right foot barely touching the floor, and loudly announced the reason for his visit.

"I need my toenail removed. It hurts to march, Doc," he said, pointing at his infected right great toe.

I looked at the nail and pushed gently on its sides.

"I can remove it, but I think you should try antibiotics and warm soaks first. What do you think?" I asked. I started to review his chart as he sat in the exam room, contemplating his next step.

"So you're all the way from New Jersey and on your way to Afghanistan?" I asked. "Tell me, how are you handling all these changes in your life, Rick?" My question drew his attention, and for the next few minutes he totally forgot about his infected toe and began to passionately talk about the major life changes and challenges he had gone through in the last year and about his rocky journey of faith.

"Just a year ago, I was walking the streets of our neighborhood, breaking the law and getting myself into all kinds of trouble. I was pretty violent and scared a lot of people," he said, recalling that violent chapter of his young life.

His rough life on the streets had landed him a place in front of a merciful judge, who challenged him and gave him a second chance.

"The judge gave me only two options—to clean up my act, change my life around, and start a new page, or go to jail. At that time, I just had a baby with my girlfriend. I knew I could no longer continue my old ways."

To his credit, he chose the former. He enlisted in the army and brought his military enlistment papers to the judge, pleading with him for mercy.

"I took my signed papers to court and asked him to give me a second chance. I told him I'd already cleaned up my act and gave him my word I wouldn't break the law any more. He believed me and decided to let me enlist in the army instead of sending me to jail!"

Soon after the birth of his daughter, Rick married his girlfriend and embarked on his military career. To him, those sweeping life decisions were a breath of fresh air, but they also ushered him into a new and confusing spiritual journey. He shared with me how the old buried sense of guilt that usually hovered over him anytime he thought of God during his menacing street life days came back to haunt him.

"When I was walking the city streets, breaking the law, thinking of God made me feel guilty. I intentionally kept God out of my mind and tried not to think about Him," he said. He paused as if struggling with his own understanding of God and the new spiritual crossroads he now faced.

"Now that I'm going to combat, I'm starting to feel afraid again of being close to God. I feel the same guilt I felt before because when I go to Afghanistan I will be using my gun to shoot people. That's why I try not to think of Him, Doctor," he said.

Rick's words made me wonder about the depth of his spiritual battle and the inner tug of war he must be experiencing in his soul. On one hand, he seemed to yearn for God in his life as he faced the unknown of war, but on the other hand his old fears of a God Whom he perceived to be angry and unloving haunted him and kept him away from Him. To Rick, facing life and death moments without God were troubling, but so were the guilty thoughts of having God close to him when he pulled the trigger of his M16 to kill the enemy.

I briefly changed the subject to his infected toe and pressed gently on it to drain any remaining pus. "I'll try warm soaks and antibiotics first before you remove the nail," he said, barely showing any sign of pain, and quickly resumed his briefly interrupted reflection on God, war, and guilt.

Sensing his uneasiness about his own view of God, I offered him a few encouraging words in hopes of easing his burden before his pending departure. I told him of a few Bible verses that I had heard from a well-known, reputable pastor, Charles Stanley, about war and God's help to those who fight for justice and freedom.

"Rick, I really believe God will be with you in the battles that you will face."

With his facial features more at ease and his voice relaxed, he said before leaving with his toe bandaged, "Thank you, Doctor. It helps me to hear that. Can you please give me the website of the pastor? I want to read more on that."

A few days later, he returned for a follow-up visit. His ingrown toe nail was healing well, and so was his attitude and view of God.

"I looked at few Christian books, Doctor, and checked the website you told me about. I've also been talking a lot with my brother about God...about being a sinner who needs Jesus Christ in my life for my sins to be forgiven."

His changed attitude towards God and his zeal to dig deep in the well of spirituality took me by surprise.

"I already went to Chapel and that was good. You know, my wife is a Buddhist. I've no idea what she will be thinking when I tell her about all of this," he said with a chuckle.

Rick, like many of his fellow soldiers heading for combat, found himself in a spiritual quest for God and meaning to his life. As life's transient nature and the inevitability of death suddenly became real to him, the reality of God and His love, forgiveness, and acceptance became just as real.

He left the exam room for the last time not only with his toe feeling much better, but even more importantly, his soul no longer experienced guilt or fear of the very same God Whose presence he would need in the heat of his upcoming battles.

> When you pass through the waters, I will be with you; and when you pass through the rivers, they will not sweep over you. When you walk through the fire, you will not be burned; the flames will not set you ablaze.
> —Isa. 43:2

Losing God after the storm

> You will seek me and find me when you seek me with all your heart.
> —Jer. 29:13

Staff Sgt. Ken, a stern looking soldier in his mid forties, had just returned with his unit from his long tour of duty in Iraq and seemed eager to get his final physical exam out of the way so he could go home.

"My better half has a couple of projects waiting for me at home. I'm planning to take a short vacation before I go back to my highway patrol police duties," he said. His face looked somehow sad as he forced a faint smile. I wondered if something was bothering him or if he had experienced something traumatic during his tour of duty.

"So Ken, do you have a church or a support group back home?" I asked, wondering about his support network.

After a brief moment of silence, he sighed. "My wife goes to church. She has faith, you know, but I have a problem with God."

His words fueled my curiosity. "Something must've happened. Do you feel comfortable talking about it?" I asked.

He began to tell me in his low-pitched voice about how he and his wife were both involved in the church that she still attends, and how all of that suddenly changed with a single bullet he fired as a trooper.

"I was on patrol when I got dispatched to a bank robbery scene. When I arrived, I saw a young man, the robber, running out of the bank with a gun in his hand. He saw me and pointed his gun at me. That was when I shot him. He was killed on the spot." He paused and after a brief silence added, "I didn't know he was only a twelve-year-old child with a BB gun."

With tears welling in his eyes, Ken described his shock when he saw how young the bank robber was and the painted BB gun lying next to his dead body. After a full police investigation of the shooting, his name was completely cleared, but the *memory* of that tragic day had not cleared from his heart and mind.

"You were doing your duty, Ken. There was no way for you to know," I said, scrambling to find the right words to comfort him.

"It's not easy to live with yourself after killing a twelve-year-old with a BB gun," he said. "That was when I stopped going to church."

His melancholy voice reflected the torrent of guilt that must've swept over him on that dark day of his life. *Why did he decide to share his story with me? Was he hoping for a word of comfort to take away the heavy burden of that day?* I wondered.

Following that tragic day, Ken's wife, family, and church gathered around him and reminded him of God's love and forgiveness. Their support helped him during his darkest hours but his alienation from God and a deep inner sense of guilt remained.

"It's just not easy to live with killing a twelve-year-old," he repeated.

For a brief moment, I reflected on his soul's anguish and pain. It was clear to me that Ken didn't lack any social support. He seemed to have plenty of head knowledge about God's love and forgiveness even as he struggled with believing it and forgiving himself. So for a brief moment, I probably repeated what many others must've already told him about how he did his job to the best of his ability and about forgetting what is already behind and looking ahead. I told him about God's grace and love, purpose, and plan for his life, and about putting our hope, despite life's setbacks, in the great future that God has destined for us here on earth and for eternity.

Somewhere in the course of our talk, I began to notice a gradual shift in his demeanor as his facial expression appeared to be more at ease. Somehow talking and reflecting on God, Who still loves and accepts him despite what happened and Who wants to pick him up and lead him like a good shepherd into new green pastures in his life, seemed to greatly refresh him. Hope, like a spring of fresh, living water, seemed to gently flow into the dry soil of his guilt-ridden heart. Perhaps that was my own hope for him, but he did seem much more relaxed and at peace as our visit came to a close.

It was time for him to go. He thanked me with one long, strong handshake that every one of my carpal bones felt. That was his way of showing appreciation, I believe, to a total stranger who listened to the inner cries of his heart.

For many months after our encounter, I reflected on Ken's story. For Ken and each one of us, talking about God's love, acceptance, and forgiveness is just that—talk. But it's when God's love touches us, such as when a caring person puts his or her arm of compassion on our shoulder and talks to us through words of love and comfort, that God's healing love becomes real. Perhaps, on that early morning in the Troop Medical Clinic, God used me, as He has used many others in Ken's life, to bring His reality, love, acceptance, and forgiveness to him, not just as another "talk" but as a reliable truth he can believe in. Ultimately, it's that belief that will liberate his soul from the darkness of that very sad day in his life.

> Peace I leave with you; my peace I give you. I do not give to you as the world gives. Do not let your hearts be troubled and do not be afraid.
> —John 14:27

The Milky Way on Interstate 46

> Lift your eyes and look to the heavens: Who created all these? He who brings out the starry host one by one, and calls them each by name.
> —Isa. 40:26

Watching the splendor of the Milky Way, with its billions of stars adorning the night skies over eastern Indiana as I drove on Interstate 46 to the campgrounds, was one of the most awe-inspiring moments of my life. I remember how the majestic view of the Milky Way stars began to gradually dim and fade away as the pollution of the city lights stole the heavenly show above. For it was only in the stillness of a dark night that the greatness of the Milky Way became visible and in total focus.

Every time I experienced the disappearing of the majestic beauty of the star-laden skies by the pollution of the streetlights, I pondered how our human mind and heart can similarly be polluted and darkened by life's past, present, and future setbacks and negatives—sickness, relationships going sour, abuse, toxic in-laws, put downs, disrespect, heartbreaks, and financial disasters. I thought about how repeated exposure to such toxic life pollutions slowly and subtly removes us from the inspiring, uplifting, bright majestic sight of God's reality and love and ushers us into the darkness of emotional negativities and confusion. As we lose touch with God's majestic love, peace, and power, wrong beliefs about Him, life, and ourselves fill our skies and we gradually slip into a pit of darkness with its guilt and fear, emptiness, and depression. It's truly never about God turning off the light of His unconditional love, but it's always about us being so blinded by the toxic negatives that we start to lose sight of Him and His outstretched hands of love and mercy.

Who and what is keeping you and me from seeing the reality, goodness, love, and power of God—our soul's Milky Way? No matter what or who obscures this life-changing, amazing sight, I will always remember the awesomeness and magnificence of the Milky Way on Interstate 46 and the loss I felt as it gradually faded away in the pollution of the city lights.

> Oh, the depth of the riches of the wisdom and knowledge of God! How unsearchable his judgments, and his paths beyond tracing out! Who has known the mind of the Lord? Or who has been his counselor? Who has ever given to God, that God would repay him? For from him and through him and to him are all things. To him be the glory forever! Amen.
> —Rom. 11:36

> For in him all things were created: things in heaven and on earth, visible and invisible, whether thrones or powers or rulers or authorities; all things were created through him and for him.
> —Col. 1:16

Miracles on the battlefield

> You are the God who performs miracles; you display your power among the peoples.
> —Ps. 77:14

"I've seen a couple of miracles in Iraq. Only God could've saved the lives of many in my unit, Doc," said Sgt. Jerome, who had just returned from his tour of duty in Iraq. Two of those miracle stories from the battlefield were obviously near and dear to his heart. He wasted no time talking to me about them soon after his medical exam.

"It started as a routine mission but suddenly our platoon came under heavy enemy fire. One of the soldiers got hit and quickly started falling down. We thought a bullet or shrapnel went though his right thigh as he screamed in pain, holding his leg, saying, 'It burns...It burns.'"

Jerome recalled how he and his buddies expected the worst as the platoon medic began to tear through his BDU (Battle Dress Uniform) looking for a bleeding femoral artery that could easily send him to his death. But to Jerome and the medic's surprise there was no bleeding, no bullet hole, nothing but a burn mark on his skin!

"All we found was a bullet hole in his right pocket. We found the bullet inside the pocket, surrounded by the four sides of a cross that he kept in his pocket. The cross wrapped around the bullet, stopping it from advancing!" he said, reliving the moment of wonderment that he and his platoon soldiers experienced. "The cross saved his life. He would've bled to death during the enemy fire. That was a miracle!" he said.

I could see in his eyes how genuine his excitement was as he continued with another miracle story from the battlefields of Iraq.

"One of our soldiers was hit by enemy fire. The bullet pierced through his IBA (Interceptor Body Armor), and when he fell down, we all thought that he was dead. But, miraculously, the bullet was stopped by a Bible that he kept in his chest pocket. The Bible pages saved his life, Doctor."

Apparently, the bullet had advanced through the Bible's pages and then stopped before piercing his heart or going through his main arteries. Interestingly, as Jerome recalled, the soldier didn't believe in God and was "resistant to Him, despite carrying that Bible in his pocket."

Shortly after the incident, both Jerome and the soldier who had miraculously escaped death began to attend church regularly and read the Bible.

Soon after he left, it dawned on me that equally striking as the physical miracle Jerome and his buddy experienced was the even bigger miracle of changed hearts, from spiritual indifference to a closer, personal, and deeper walk with God.

> This is the confidence we have in approaching God: that if we ask anything according to his will, he hears us. And if we know that he hears us – whatever we ask – we know that we have what we asked of him.
> —1 John 5:14-15

> He performs wonders that cannot be fathomed, miracles that cannot be counted.
> —Job 5:9

Starting all over again - no more drugs

If we confess our sins, he is faithful and just and will forgive us our sins and purify us from all unrighteousness.
—1 John 1:9

With a vast assortment of colorful, scary-looking tattoos covering most of his upper body and a friendly, big smile, Sgt. Sam was definitely a soldier of many contrasts. His rough, external appearance stood in sharp contrast to his kind smile, soft-spoken voice, and gentle demeanor.

"Man, you must really like tattoos! So what does this one mean to you?" I asked, looking at a big colorful one adorning his left arm.

"It means nothing now, Doc. They are all from my old days when I was drinking and doing drugs. I had a messed up life until I found God."

For the next few minutes, he talked passionately about his personal God story and how his life was changed when he became a Christian. His newfound faith in Jesus Christ steered him away from the old destructive road of drugs and addictions onto a new path and a new passion for helping young men and women break free from their own addictions.

Sam's personal crusade to help young, confused kids break free from the strong, evil jaws of drugs had taken him to community centers, high school classrooms, and multiple other outreaches. He spoke about the evil of drugs and addiction, encouraging his listeners to start a new page and not give up.

"Alcohol and drugs almost killed me, Doc. I want to help these kids before it's too late for them," he explained.

"Sam, what you're doing is great. So what helped you make this big change?"

"God. I couldn't have done it without Him. He changed me into a new man. My wife stood by me when I was at my worst. She helped me cut my old drug and alcohol addiction. I owe her a lot," he said.

Long after this visit, the impact of Sam's story stayed with me. There he was, a caring soldier on his way to war who didn't consider it shameful to share his past failures and pain with perfect strangers. He was changing his world, one lost soul at a time. His was a higher mission, beyond the one he was about to embark on in the deadly battlefields of Afghanistan—a mission to free young souls imprisoned by deadly addictions and lead them to the freedom that he himself had finally come to enjoy.

As I reflected on Sam's story, I found a similarity between the freedom he found when he closed his old chapter of addiction and that of closing an old, unused bank account. By signing your name on a paper that the bank manager brings you to close the account, you are declared forever free from it, no longer associated with it, and can once and for all forget all about it.

In a similar way, God in His mercy and goodness is like that bank manager who brings you the closure of the bank account papers to sign. He allows us to forever sign off on our past and frees us from it—our sins, shame, failures, and messes—like an old, closed bank account.

To me, Sam's decision to close the old, dark, drug-filled page of his life and open by faith a new page—believing in Jesus Christ—summarized the story of the Bible. Jesus, the Son of God (God in the flesh), full of love, came to earth to die for the human race so that all those who ask for forgiveness for their sins and believe in Him and His resurrection from the dead will forever be free from their old accounts of sin—once and for all.

> For the eyes of the LORD range throughout the earth to strengthen those whose hearts are fully committed to him.
> —2 Chron. 16:9

CHAPTER 14

HEALING CHILDHOOD WOUNDS

Healing Childhood Wounds.

He heals the brokenhearted and binds up their wounds.
—Ps. 147:3

Picking up the pieces

"WHAT WAS YOUR childhood like, Diana?" I asked the thirty-two-year-old beautiful blonde army officer sitting across the table from me. After hearing about my plan to write a book to help the soldiers, she gladly agreed to my great delight to talk to me about her rough childhood. I had heard a glimpse of it during our occasional morning chit chats at the Troop Medical Clinic before the start of our busy days, and now I couldn't wait to hear the whole story. With her big, welcoming smile, she quickly answered.

"Dad was abusive and mean to me. I remember how he poked fun at me and made me feel so little with his words. I was like his scapegoat. It was hard for me to feel joy or believe that I would achieve victory in my life. I felt my spirit was crushed," she said, her eyes welling with tears.

Her words took me totally by surprise. I had a slight idea from our previous conversations that she occasionally battled with worry and anxiety, but I never imagined that Diana, with her lively, positive, and uplifting personality, once lived in such a toxic environment. Her dad's alcoholism eventually earned him the title of the "town's drunk," and his anger escalated and became uncontrollable even over small things.

"There were times when he became angry if I just turned on a room light," she said. "He would just go out of the room and slam the door so hard. I remember how bad I felt when I saw the paint falling from the sides of the door as it was being slammed."

Her words made me pause and think about the unsettling image of a frightened child whose world of security and innocence crumbled and shredded as those broken paint pieces fell down the door sides as he raged.

But things only got worse for Diana and her mother, who chose to stay in the relationship "because of her religious beliefs and a roof over our heads," she explained.

To escape the turbulence at home, Diana began to spend as many school nights as possible in hotel rooms, at her uncle's, and at her best friend's home in pursuit of peace and rest for her young heart. Yet despite her predicament and the devastating effect on her, she made a vow to survive and to one day excel in her life.

I worked, worked, and worked. I knew I needed to buy a car to be able to get out of the home, and so I studied hard to finish high school. Thank God for Mom. She helped me build my faith in God. We both found strength from each other and our church," she said.

But the pain and hurt that she had experienced began to gradually take a toll on her, and she found herself sinking into a dark, deep abyss of anxiety and depression.

"I became anorexic and had to be hospitalized when my weight dropped to sixty-seven pounds," she remembered. Miraculously, when she was eleven years old and all seemed so dark and gloomy, a Christian counselor stepped suddenly into her life and helped pull her out of her slippery pit of anorexia and despair. Sadly, her father's unpredictable outbursts and shoving and yelling didn't stop until he was disabled by multiple sclerosis six months before the disease claimed his life. He spent the remaining days of his life in a nursing home, totally dependent on Diana and her mom for his basic needs.

"Mom and I visited him daily. We brushed his teeth and attended to his other needs. As his disease got worse, he wanted to know about how I was doing and seemed to care about me. He told me 'I love you' just before he died," she said, and her eyes began to tear.

Diana remembered how she had struggled with her own feelings as she saw him crippled by MS and lying helplessly on that nursing home bed. "I knew I had to forgive him. I did. He cared about me deep inside, but he just wasn't able to handle being diagnosed with MS. He was a good musician and a great athlete, who loved riding his motorcycle and playing basketball before he got sick. As his disease progressed and he was no longer able to do the things he loved to do, he became very bitter and lashed out at me and Mom," she softly whispered as she leaned forward and began to share her own journey of healing.

"I lived a lot of years in my childhood home. It's been over ten years since I left, but I still don't feel comfortable in new surroundings and occasionally I feel sad and anxious. But you know, every day feels better than the one before it. I thank God for my husband; he helped me deal with many of my issues, especially during the first year of our marriage. We've grown closer to each other as we both grew closer to God," she said with a sweet smile.

As she finished her last sentence, a thought crossed my mind. There she was, a woman of noble character, a healer, and a well-trained high-ranking officer in the army, who had survived a childhood of pain, tears, and fear. Her emotional rollercoaster had taken her down into a dark pit that almost claimed her life. But despite her past living-hell days, the soldier who sat across the table from me was not a defeated, bitter woman, but a victorious, positive one whose childhood dream to one day survive and excel in life was finally becoming a reality.

Then as if she had read my mind, she smiled and interrupted my silent reflections with her soft voice. "Dr. Hanna, I don't know how my life would be today if I had lived an easy, sheltered life growing up. All I know is I've come to appreciate even those painful conflicts and adversities of my childhood home because they helped me become the person I am today."

Diana's story was inspiring like many others and reminded me one more time of the New Testament Bible verse found in Romans 8:28, "And we know that in all things God works for the good of those who love him, who have been called according to his purpose."

She knew it well, and for few minutes she shared with me how her Christian faith had strengthened because of what she had gone through and her firm belief that God indeed worked out all those tragic days to shape, refine, and build her character. As an officer in the army, offering direct care to many soldiers on their way to combat, she had indeed touched many lives with her refined character and compassionate hands. She chose to be better and not bitter because she decided to see her life experiences—both the good and the bad ones—with an eye of faith in God's promises.

When I finished the writing of this story, an important thought flashed through my mind. As a young, innocent child, Diana had no way of knowing the difference between wrong and right, between a truth and a lie, or justice and injustice. It was during those most vulnerable childhood years that negative words and deeds hit the shore of her innocent mind like raging waves, carving negative, and disabling thoughts that brought her emotions to a crisis state. She was simply too young to know any better. She didn't have the knowledge of God's truth—His love, forgiveness, and acceptance.

She also didn't know how much He saw her as valuable and worthy, to stop the endless flow of damaging words and actions.

But now as an adult, Diana knew the lifesaving spiritual truths she once lacked. This knowledge liberated her from the bondage of the past and brought her into a dawn of a new beginning in her life.

> He tends his flock like a shepherd: He gathers the lambs in his arms and carries them close to his heart; he gently leads those that have young.
> —Isa. 40:11

> The LORD is a refuge for the oppressed, a stronghold in times of trouble.
> —Ps. 9:9

CHAPTER 15

HUMOR IN WARTIME

Humor in Wartime.

A happy heart makes the face cheerful,
but heartache crushes the spirit.
—Prov. 15:13

A soldier and her rat

SGT. SHARON'S EKG looked perfectly normal. Her brief episode of chest pain the night before had given her quite a scare and an early morning trip to the Troop Medical Clinic for an evaluation.

"So, Doc, what do you think is wrong with me?" she asked.

"Your EKG looks great, Sharon. Tell me what happened. Were you exerting yourself when you felt the chest pain?" I asked.

She looked somehow embarrassed. "Well, yesterday I was at my brother's home to spend the night. When I entered the guest bedroom and turned on the light, I saw this big, fat rat sitting on top of the pillow and looking directly at me. I screamed so loudly, Doctor, and started feeling this sharp pain in my chest."

I wasn't sure if I should sympathize with her or start laughing. Somehow, the image of that big, fat rat resting comfortably on her bed, only to be unexpectedly startled by a bright lightbulb was too funny for me to pass up. *Her heart is fine, and a good hearty laugh never hurts*, I thought.

I managed to muster a very serious look, put down my eyeglasses, and asked her with a straight face, "Sharon, do you think you woke up the rat when you turned on the light? Do you think you might have disturbed this poor rat's deep sleep?"

After a brief moment of silence, apparently processing the silly words I'd just uttered, she burst out laughing at the goofiness of what she had just heard.

"I woke up what? That fat, rotten rat almost gave me a heart attack!" she said, laughing hysterically, telling every soldier she met in the hallway about her doctor's silly joke. She continued to laugh every time she saw me, repeating what she coined as the "poor rat story" to many of the deploying soldiers heading for combat.

> Blessed are you who hunger now, for you will be satisfied. Blessed are you who weep now, for you will laugh.
> —Luke 6:21

Ben and Lenny's comedy team

> A cheerful heart is good medicine, but a crushed spirit dries up the bones.
> —Prov. 17:22

To me, army medics Ben and Lenny from the upper Midwest were natural-born comedians. They were known by all the Troop Medical Clinic personnel for their spontaneous comical skits and off-the-wall humorous remarks. Sick soldiers waiting to be seen often heard Sgt. Lenny firing his trademark phrase, "You know, I don't care what people say about you, I still think you're the best." Not to be outmatched, Sgt. Ben was often seen doing his own lunchtime show, gathering the medics during the break and teaching them an improvisation of what he fondly called, "the nipple dance," a dance performed by a male Panjabi-Indian singer who lightly hits his chest while swaying to the music. His "that's crazy talk, Doc" became a signature lighthearted phrase that he routinely used in response to any physician's request or medical order.

Sgt. Ben kindly invited me during a lunch break to join him and his faithful followers for a free "nipple dance" lesson. After a short time watching him moving his hands skillfully from his chest to his sides and swaying his body as he displayed his own rendition of the Panjabi singer's moves, I stopped him briefly for one question.

"Ben, you're really doing a great job cheering up the soldiers. So what's motivating you to do that?"

His answer cheered me up and convicted me that bringing appropriate humor, smiles, and laughter, whether it's in an exam room to a destitute patient or a lighthearted "nipple dance" in a lunchroom to soldiers in arms, is all about caring and using God's gift of humor to help heal someone's soul.

"You know, Doctor, every one of us here is away from home and family. These soldiers can't just pick up and go home. They all need to be cheered up and have a good laugh."

I couldn't have agreed with him more.

> There is a time for everything, and a season for every activity under heaven…a time to weep and a time to laugh, a time to mourn and a time to dance.
>
> —Eccl. 3:1, 4

A tick abuse story

> All the days of the oppressed are wretched, but the cheerful heart has a continual feast.
>
> —Prov. 15:15

"My shoulder is killing me, Doc," complained twenty-year-old Private Dustin. As I began the exam, I could see the thick layer of dry mud on his shoes and uniform. "Sorry, Doctor, I just came from field artillery training," he said, pointing at his sore shoulder.

I quickly began my routine evaluation and checked the range of motion of his shoulder, stopping momentarily to inspect a big, black female tick deeply embedded in his upper arm. Dustin had no idea the tick was even there, getting bigger as it feasted freely in his bulging deltoid muscle.

"They are everywhere in the field. I burned a few of them today, but my buddies must've missed this one. We always check each other after we leave the field," he explained, pulling his lighter to show me his favorite method of terminating his ticks.

I briefly glanced at the flame of his lighter and quickly began the process of meticulously pulling the tick from its warm surroundings. After carefully dislodging it in one intact piece, I placed it on a metal tray, thinking of perhaps a "nicer" way to eliminate it. I began to squeeze it with a set of surgical tweezers as it ran energetically around the tray, escaping from my grip. After a few more failed attempts to stop it, I decided to change my strategy. I reached out to the two percent lidocaine tube and squeezed enough of the numbing medicine to cover it and then quickly transported it into a clear plastic bag before it recovered.

"I just burn them, Doc," said Dustin after watching enough of my failed destruction attempts. "I just burn these darn things," he said, flicking his lighter on, ready to inflict the final blow to his tick.

"So Dustin, do you think what we are doing is considered tick abuse?" I asked as we both began to laugh, wondering how to kill the energetic tick. He continued to laugh as I handed him his instructions on how to monitor the healing of his old tick site.

"My lighter works better, Doc...and no, I don't really think it is tick abuse."

He left the exam room with a follow-up plan to be checked for Lyme disease exposure. He had a big smile on his face as he left to join his unit, leaving his big tick behind, totally numbed up in a plastic bag and on its way to microscopic analysis.

> He will yet fill your mouth with laughter and your lips with shouts of joy.
> —Job 8:21

CHAPTER 16

LEADERSHIP

Leadership: Photo provided by Camp Atterbury Public Affairs

The man of integrity walks securely, but he who takes crooked paths will be found out.
—Prov. 10:9

Good leaders, bad leaders

LISTENING TO MANY soldiers' conversations about good versus bad leadership has helped me to evaluate my own leadership skills, weaknesses, and strengths. Sooner or later all of us find ourselves in some form of leadership position where someone views us as role models. Every one of us, but soldiers in particular, detest and can't tolerate oppressive, controlling, and uncaring leaders while they have great admiration and respect for the good ones who consider the physical and emotional safety of their followers as a very high priority.

James, an E7 (a high-ranking soldier), shared with me how he became very unhappy when he overheard "an E7 ordering a lower-ranking E2 and E3 to get out of their chairs as they waited to be seen by the medical staff in order to make copies for him."

"He gave them a big pile of papers to copy for him! They were enjoying watching TV and waiting for their name to be called. Then he started bragging to me that he gets to watch TV while they are copying his papers. It's just plain wrong to use people like that. A higher rank doesn't make him better than them. It doesn't make an E2 or 3 soldier less of a person," he said passionately.

Wise words to live by! I thought.

A few days later, I was a third party in an intriguing conversation between two female soldiers, both E4s—Tammy, a twenty-eight-year-old active duty soldier, and Cindy, who had just turned twenty-six and was on her way to her first deployment in Iraq. Both of them joined the army after 9/11 when a wave of intense unity and patriotism engulfed the nation. Soon after witnessing their big hugs and listening to a few of their loud, excited shouts of, "Oh, my God! Oh, my God, I can't believe you are here," I asked them to tell me about some of their trials and tribulations with leaders.

"An E6 officer who wants to pull rank on me because I'm an E4 makes me feel so mad," Cindy said.

"Oh, I hate that! The leaders who do that are just hungry for power and that is what attracts some of them to the military. They find power in their military rank—something they can't find anywhere else," Tammy responded.

"You are right," answered Cindy. "Some of these higher ranked soldiers think I am stupid because of my E4 rank. They can't understand that I have a B.S. degree. I have done more things in this world than many of them could ever imagine doing. At least I have learned what not to do and what not to be when I get my promotions."

"I just try not to be bitter when I see them doing that," Tammy said.

After listening to them with a few occasional interruptions, I offered them my ten cents' worth of an idea. "I guess whatever you guys are experiencing can make you better or bitter. If you learn how to deal with bad leaders, you will learn how to be good leaders yourselves, right?"

They both agreed, and for the next few minutes I told them stories I had I heard at the base about great leadership, including "Sgt. Adam."

"Sgt. Adam," I said, "is one of your own commanders. He believes that as a leader he must build his soldiers from the inside out."

They listened attentively as I told them more about his caring, serving, and strong leadership style. I could tell that what I said was encouraging to them. Bringing to their attention examples of strong and caring leaders such as Adam and many others seemed to take their focus off the few bad apples that had thus far plagued their short military careers. We thanked one another for the lively conversation and rushed to face the obstacles of the day that had just started.

Evangelist Billy Graham once wrote in his book *The Journey*, "When a soldier submits to the authority of his commanding officer, he obeys what that officer tells him to do. If a patient submits to a doctor's treatment, he or she does what the doctor says to do. If a player submits to the direction of his coach, he does what the coach instructs him to do. And when we submit ourselves to the King of Kings and the Lord of Lords, we obey what He tells us to do, because we know His way is right."

Indeed, at the hand of a caring and strong leader who is committed to doing the right thing and can be trusted, obeying authority becomes the tool that will bring out the best in every soldier. Submitting to such authority and obeying it is much easier and brings greater results than submitting to leadership that one views as oppressive and not right.

Yet no matter who has authority over us on earth, a good or a bad leader, we can all feel safe and secure as we trust, obey, and submit to God's ultimate authority over us. Authority is indeed a powerful thing; it can either lead us wisely to safety or blindly to destruction.

When pride comes, then comes disgrace, but with humility comes wisdom.

—Prov. 11:2

Leadership from the inside out

The path of the righteous is level; O upright One, you make the way of the righteous smooth.

—Isa. 26:7

As first in command of his big unit, thirty-year-old Sgt. Adam decided not to delay his FOB (forward operations base) training despite his severe cold symptoms. He came to see me when he could no longer ignore his symptoms, especially his hoarse voice that was now quite noticeable.

"I know I needed to see you earlier, Doc, but I wasn't going to miss going to the FOB with my unit," he said.

His gentle demeanor, friendly smile, and passion for his troops intrigued me. I felt he was a perfect candidate to teach me a thing or two about the most important qualities of a strong military leader who can be well liked and trusted by his soldiers on the battlefields of Iraq and Afghanistan.

"I'm glad you finally decided to take care of your cold. Please take this antibiotic and rest today and tomorrow in the barracks," I said at the conclusion of my exam. "Hey, Adam, I've seen in the past leaders who seem hard and uncaring when they exercise their authority. You're a leader of a big unit. What's your opinion about the best way to lead?" I asked.

His response impressed me and led us into an intriguing conversation that became the heart of this story. "I lead them from the inside out, sir. Each one of my soldiers has a different set of life experiences—some good and helpful, others bad and hurtful. It's only when I know each one of my soldier's stories that I can build them up and help to lead them to their fullest potential. I can lead them best when I show them that I care. I do believe it's my calling to build them up, be their mentor, and even a father or mother figure to them, Doc," he said, clearing his hoarse voice.

His words sounded very genuine and made a lot of sense to me. I began to ask more questions, hoping to tap into his refreshing insights on leadership.

"What are the things you do to help build them up?"

"First of all, I always remind myself that some of them might be hurting emotionally and need help to deal with that before they can reach their fullest potential. What I do is reach out to the one who is hurt, listen to what's bothering him or her, and try to help. Some of the soldiers need more attention and help than others, but I use what I call a 'hands-on approach' with all of them."

"What's the hands-on approach?" I asked.

"That's how it works, Doc. I show them respect and tell them my objective is to build them up to be leaders who will help me, in turn, do my job as their commander. I then promote them when I'm convinced they are ready to lead. They will, in turn, help me train the new soldiers in our unit to become future leaders. That's what I call a hands-on approach—building them from the inside out."

"Does it work?" I asked.

"It does. One of my soldiers is a pristine beauty queen who won many beauty pageants. She was sent to me by her old unit commander who couldn't handle her because she had a problem obeying authority. She started defying my leadership as soon as she joined the unit. I knew I needed to reach out to find what was bothering her on the inside before I could help her reach her fullest potential," he said. But soon enough she realized that he genuinely cared and began to open up to him about her own painful story of childhood rape and other traumas that had affected her attitudes and behaviors.

"She was one of eight children and grew up into a lot of money. Her father died when she was very young, and she missed out on his authority and discipline. To her, the army was the best way to promote herself as a beauty queen."

As her unit commander, Adam took it upon himself to offer her not only discipline and guidance but also care and compassion.

"She lacked having a father in her life and told me that she feels like I'm that father figure. That was fine with me as long as it helped her to trust me and talk about what was bothering her. I made it a point to remind her that I believe in her and that she must do her part."

"Do other soldiers get upset when they see you pay that much attention to her?" I asked.

"One of the female soldiers did. She was jealous, but then I quickly reminded her that she too had had bad life circumstances before she joined the army and had needed just as much time, attention, and understanding. I told her what they both had in common: a very painful life experience and a need to be encouraged to be a leader."

As the relationship got worse between the two soldiers Adam found himself working very hard to bring peace between them before the unit's deployment to Iraq. He found himself using the best of his leadership skills to help mend their broken relationship and eventually his effort paid off.

"The soldier who got upset at the 'beauty queen' admitted she was jealous and decided to apologize. I wanted them to trust each other before going to combat. They would need each other there," he said. But rebuilding the trust proved to be a challenge as he recalled. "It was very hard for them to trust each other after what had been said. So I told them both that each would have to show respect to the other even if she doesn't like her, and that each could definitely find something in the other to be thankful for because that would help them build respect for each other."

Adam's passion for unity and trust between each member of his unit was refreshing. His next words described his leader's heart best. "I told them that when they are in a convoy, sitting tightly next to each other in a Humvee, each will feel thankful for the other, and a strong bond will begin to form between them. I kept on telling them to be sure to remember my words—a strong relationship and trust will develop when they are sitting for a long time in a Humvee under heavy enemy fire not sure where the next IED will be."

What a great leader, I thought. His words made a lot of sense to me. Learning to find something to be thankful for in someone I might not like makes it possible for me to respect that person and gradually trust him or her if that person has proven worthy of that trust. Great words of wisdom to both soldiers and civilians squeezed in important work relationships where there is no other option but to get along with those we might not like.

"What a way to lead, Adam. Where did you learn to do that?" I asked.

He smiled and answered as he cleared his hoarse voice. "Doc, you just never know who God brings your way to help you make an important change in your life. That happened to me when I was twenty-three years old. I was young and haughty and didn't care much about respecting others. I was hired at that time as a supervisor in a manufacturing plant with a good number of employees, including an elderly man who had been there for many years, reporting directly to me. After this man heard me enough times yelling at my employees and ordering them around, he took me to the side away from everyone, looked me straight in the eyes, and told me, 'Listen to me, boy! Don't you ever treat your employees this way! These are the people you will need one day. You must show them respect.'"

After a brief pause and reflection he added, "You know something, Doc, I never forgot his words. They have changed me forever and made me finally see that everyone must be treated with respect. God brought him to my life on that day to teach me to respect others even when I don't agree with them or don't like them."

His words made me think about the good that can come from caring, humble leaders whose desire is to serve, help, and lead justly and the harm that comes from arrogant leaders whose intoxication with power makes them disrespect, control, mislead, and break the spirit of their followers. The former ones help others grow and excel as they feel encouraged and rewarded, but the latter ones discourage and hurt the very people who look up to them and they eventually end up being disliked and disrespected.

His hands-on approach to leadership made me think about the other end of the spectrum—those who choose a hands-off approach when it comes to taking care of those entrusted to their authority. Their leadership is viewed as taking advantage and using others because they are interested in what their followers will produce for them, and not in each individual person. Such leaders don't take their followers' needs as their own and won't fight for their people. But it's only when I know that this person in authority cares for me that I begin to do what is expected of me with passion and take his cause and make it my own.

Our universe exists and is faithfully maintained by a hands-on God Who loves us and cares for the weakest and least among us. Our world couldn't exist if we had a hands-off God; our homes wouldn't survive hands-off husbands, wives, fathers, or mothers, and our society and nation would slowly die with hands-off teachers, doctors, CEOs, lawmakers, judges, pastors, military leaders, soldiers, families, friends, babysitters, and presidents. Good things happen when we care, especially when those entrusted with the gift of leadership, position, and authority care, and very bad things happen when those in power no longer care.

One of my military affiliated patients said it best. "Many of those who enjoy the power and use it to put down others come out of the military expecting everyone around them in the civilian world to obey them and do it their way. They end up being shocked, angry, and frustrated when the world doesn't listen to them, and they no longer have the power or position to control everyone around them. I know one of them who nearly committed suicide when he could not make life go his way."

Shortly after this visit, Adam led his troops to Iraq. I have never forgotten his story about how God brought an elderly employee to his life to help him change. I came to realize long after his visit that God had in turn brought him to my exam room to help me and others reading this story, to serve, care, and lead others with love and respect.

> The LORD is my shepherd, I shall not be in want.
> —Ps. 23:1

> As a shepherd looks after his scattered flock when he is with them, so will I look after my sheep. I will rescue them from all the places where they were scattered on a day of clouds and darkness.
> —Ezek. 34:12

My troops come first

> So give your servant a discerning heart to govern your people and to distinguish between right and wrong.
> —1 Kings 3:9

LEADERSHIP

Sgt. Major Dean, a forty-five-year-old commander of the largest platoon in his home state, had the big task of preparing his troops for war zone deployment and the heavy burden of leading them in combat. I could tell by his badly sprained arms and back muscles that the rigorous training had taken a toll on him.

"This old body is aching all over, Doctor," he said.

After prescribing the routine 800 mg dose of Ibuprofen for his aches, I asked about his most important priority as the highest-ranking leader of a regiment as big as his.

He smiled and said without much hesitation, "That's my job—to help my soldiers, who depend on me. They are my responsibility and I care about each one of them."

"Thanks, Sgt. Major, for your service to the country. Your troops are lucky to have you," I said as I handed him the "No marching or strenuous training for three days" slip. He thanked me and folded the instruction sheet neatly and put it in his pocket.

"I need to get well...my soldiers need me. We're all here preparing very hard to defend our country. I want to show them by example that they must see the doctor if they are not feeling well. They need to feel well before mobilizing. I'll do what you tell me, Doctor," he said.

After Dean left, I thought about his strong convictions as a leader. I have often heard of Jesus referred to as the ultimate example of leadership. He led others by serving them, such as when He washed the dirty, dusty feet of His disciples teaching them to lead others by serving them.

Dean had not said a word about his faith or spiritual beliefs, but his selfless caring, serving, and compassion for his soldiers inspired me and reminded me of Jesus' teaching and God's higher ways.

> A generous man will prosper; he who refreshes others will himself be refreshed.
> —Prov. 11:25

No pregnancy allowed on my watch

> May the God of peace...equip you with everything good for doing his will.
> —Heb. 13:20-21

"Not on my watch, Doctor," said twenty-two-year-old Private Jill, laughing as she explained her assignment of "making sure the female soldiers in my unit don't get pregnant."

Her "job description" was one I had never heard of before, and I started to ask her about it. With great passion, she began to tell me about her assigned duties and how her job had helped her fine tune her leadership skills.

I admit, it was initially hard for me to see how any leadership skills could possibly develop from the unique role of being the watchdog of her unit soldiers' sexual behavior. But as I listened to her, I quickly changed my mind as she began to passionately tell me about the benefits and challenges she had to overcome in the course of her unique assignment.

"I feel it's important for the male and female soldiers here to be friends. It wouldn't be good for any of them to be sexually involved," she said in a serious tone of voice.

"So Jill, what's the hardest thing about your job?"

"At times it feels scary, and I get anxious. But I keep reminding myself that what I'm doing is very important for the soldiers… making sure no one gets pregnant. I try to stay focused on doing my job well, Doctor."

She then added with a sense of pride before leaving, "All my soldiers work together as friends, and my job is to keep it that way. A woman who is thinking of getting herself pregnant better find another military camp to do that. I won't let that happen here under my watch."

After she left the exam room, I paused to reflect on the significance of her story. I've often heard the stories of high-ranking military commanders with vast responsibilities facing the challenges of preparing and leading their troops to combat. Jill's responsibilities were quite different from theirs, but to her they were just as important. Her story will always remind me of the great wisdom of performing any job or any life assignment that I'm faced with, no matter how small or trivial it might appear to be, to the best of my ability.

To me, the life lesson learned is that real satisfaction should be in a job well done and not in the great significance and prestige that come from performing a specific job. Ultimately, it is to God that I stand accountable for doing my job, and it is to God I will one day answer if my job was well done.

He guides the humble in what is right and teaches them his ways.
—Ps. 25:8

CHAPTER 17

MAMA'S LOVE

Mama's Love

Love never fails.
—1 Cor. 3:18

Fighting for Mom

IT WAS ABOUT mid morning when twenty-four-year old Julio came charging into the exam room with an obvious limp, his appearance tense and very frustrated. Apparently, he had run into a metal locker in his barracks as he walked in total darkness to the bathroom, injuring his left great toe.

"I got so mad, Doc. I know it was dumb, but I screamed at the locker and kicked it hard with the same foot," he said, pointing at his swollen, black-and-blue toe.

I examined his bruised toe carefully amidst his "Oh, s---! No, be careful!" and ordered an x-ray.

"I doubt it's broken, but I want to make sure before sending you back to marching. So hey, what happened to the poor locker. Did you break it?" I asked, displaying a serious look and hoping to infuse some goodhearted silliness into the situation.

After a short pause he began to laugh loudly. "What? The locker? That b---- is doing well, sir," he said and continued to laugh.

Noticing how that joke had put him at ease, I began to ask him about his background and the family he had left behind.

"You're all the way from New York? Did you spend your childhood there?" I asked.

"What childhood? I've never had one, Doc. I became a man at age nine. I mowed grass, ran errands for the neighbors, and did some construction for extra money," he said, shaking his head.

Julio's parents had separated when he was only two years old, and his mom took him and his younger sister with her out of the mainland US to the city of her birth.

"Mom caught Dad cheating on her and decided to go back to her family. I'll never forget how hard she worked but still couldn't make ends meet—we were so poor!" he said, remembering the depth of their poverty after the divorce.

Desperate to find new love in her life, his mother settled for dating abusive men who mistreated her and endangered her life. He recalled how exceptionally brutal the last man that she dated was.

"He was almost seven feet tall and very violent. She was totally helpless and couldn't get out of the relationship."

For a brief moment, I was able to see Julio's genuine love for his mom as he recalled one of the darkest nights in his life where his mom was almost killed and he nearly ended up in jail. "He started beating her repeatedly with his big fist. I was sure he was going to kill her, and I had to stop him. I ran to the bedroom, brought a gun, pointed it directly at him, and shouted at the top my voice, 'You stay away from her or I swear I'll shoot you…I'll shoot you.' I was only fourteen at the time. I really meant it. I was ready to pull the trigger."

But the giant man refused to move an inch and continued to beat his mom uncontrollably. That was when things began to get worse, and Julio became emotionally out of control and no longer himself.

"I aimed the gun at his chest and cocked it. I was ready to shoot him and he knew it."

At that exact moment, his mom ran quickly and stood between her boyfriend and the gun and started crying at the top of her lungs, "Drop the gun! Drop it! Drop it!"

Immediately after that near-tragic incident his mom decided to send him to the States to live with his father before his out-of-control anger landed him forever behind bars.

"That was the first time I had seen my dad since my mom took me and my sister out of the country. He felt so bad for not keeping in touch with us all those years and blamed it on Mom. He told us she refused to let him talk to us."

After a brief pause and a moment of reflection, he said what is probably deep in the heart of every child whose parent has given up on her or him too easily in the face of negative brainwashing or unfair custody and visitation rules.

"I didn't know whom to believe. I told him, 'Dad, you're supposed to be a man. We were just children, Dad…just kids. Why didn't you try harder for me…for my sister?'"

Despite their dad's failure to fight for them and do his best to stay in touch with them, Julio and his sister were quick to forgive him and start a new page in their relationship with him.

"I'm finally getting to be close to him. My dad and I started a business together. I want him to be close to my family, especially my son. He's still not there yet, but I'm not giving up."

Julio, who had almost committed a murder to save his mother from an abusive boyfriend, never forgot about her after he joined his dad in America. He recalled how hopelessly unable she was to leave the man and his final appeal to her to come and join him and his family in America.

"It was only after I told her that I'd be traveling with my brother-in-law to bring her back to the United States that she decided to leave her boyfriend and come to America," he said.

His deep love for his mother and the great joy in his heart over her safety was palpable. "She is here, finally here close to me. She has at last found love in her life—a good man who loves her and respects her. I made sure of that, Doc, the first day I met him. I told him, 'We'll be on good terms as long as you don't lay a hand on her.'"

It was time to review his x-ray result. Luckily, he didn't have a fracture, and I was able to carefully "buddy tape" his great toe to the toe next to it without much difficulty. It was time for him to go back to the barracks for foot elevation, icing, and rest. As I handed him the final instructions, I reflected briefly on his story of childhood survival, near tragedies, and triumph over adversity. There was yet one more question to ask him before we parted ways.

"Julio, what lessons have you learned from your life experiences? I'm sure someone out there will learn from your story."

"You know, Doctor, we're finally close to being a family again. Mom and Dad are both happy now with new loves in their lives. Mom was deeply hurt, but she was willing to forgive Dad and start anew because of my sister and me. I appreciate her so much for doing that. We all had to go through so much forgiveness. To answer your question, Doc, I believe there is a purpose in everything. Maybe God meant for me to go through this, so I can be a better father…and a stronger man."

Not only that but his previous words, "We were just kids, Dad," were indeed powerful appeals. To every father who is about to give up on his children because of the inherent injustices of the child custody rules, Julio's words serve to challenge him to never give up on his children.

As he stepped out of the exam room with his heavy military gear and an obvious limp, he left me with an inspirational life melody, loaded with beautiful tunes of victory over adversity and the healing power of love and forgiveness.

Hatred stirs up dissension but love covers over all wrongs.
—Prov. 10:12

> I thank God every time I remember you.
>
> —Phil. 1:15

A mother-son bond of love

> Love is patient, love is kind. It does not envy, it does not boast, it is not proud.
>
> —1 Cor. 13:4

"Don't misunderstand me, Doc. I know I must take care of my wife and children first, but Mom has always been there whenever I needed her," said Sergeant Frank in response to my question about how he misses his family. His love and appreciation for his mom was evident, and I couldn't wait to hear his whole story.

"She must be a great lady," I remarked. It was easy for me to see how appreciative he was of her as he began to talk passionately about her endless life struggles, including enduring his father's abuse and cheating. He could barely hold back his tears as he told me about how she silently endured hurt and betrayal for many years and about her love for him and his brother that drove her to immigrate to America from her familiar overseas home surroundings to work as a nanny to help them.

"She was able to survive her separation from my father. He never treated her right in all the years they were married. And even when she knew he was seeing other women, she still chose to treat him with respect. My mom is a very good person, Doc. She is so good, that's why so many people take advantage of her," he said, his eyes welling with tears.

Frank's parents' separation when he was fifteen years old was a very pivotal moment in his life. The memory of that day left a lifelong impact on him and almost two decades later the memory still lingered on.

"I'll never forget that day. I remember the pain I felt and the promise I made to myself when I left home with Mom for the last time. I vowed that if I ever had a family in the future, I would never let my children suffer the same pain I felt on that day. I will never do anything to break up my family."

His parents' permanent separation was followed by a very turbulent period in his life. He began to smoke heavily and do other reckless things to escape the inner pain he felt. He continued on that destructive path until he was "finally able to see that Mom had made the right decision."

"Mom worked so hard to save every penny for our needs that her face started to look tired and wrinkled. My father spent all the money he earned from his private business as soon as he received it. He never thought about his many business expenses that had to be paid at the end of every month. He spent the money on his women and began to call Mom 'grandma' in front of his friends, as she began to look older than her age," he said.

Eventually Frank's dad lost his business, became diabetic, and gradually lost his women and friends.

"Twenty years after she left him, he came to America and wanted to get back with her. He wanted her back after he had lost everything, including his health. But you know, I wasn't going to let him take advantage of her again. I made it very clear to him that he must respect her wishes and never pressure her into a relationship with him. She has finally found peace in her life, Doc, and I wasn't going to let him hurt her again."

Frank's turbulent childhood shaped him into a man who wouldn't follow in his father's footsteps of ruining his own home. His experience has also made him a better parent to his children. He told me about how much he loves his children and about his desire to discipline them well and serve as a good role model in his home.

"My children will learn kindness and respect because they see my wife and me being kind and respectful to each other. Our children will learn to be unkind and disrespectful if that's the way we treat each other. Children learn from what they see, and in my home they will learn to be kind and to respect others."

It was time to go. He stepped down from the exam table, put his body armor on, and with Kevlar in hand, made his way to the exam room door.

"One more thing, Doc," he said as he opened the door. "I learned a lot growing up. I needed discipline from my parents—all children need it. I want to teach my children what the Bible teaches, 'The beginning of wisdom and understanding is the fear of God.' God is like a parent who disciplines us too."

Frank's story brought to life one of Jesus' last sentences before his "It is finished" cry on the cross. The New Testament book of John describes a precious mother-son encounter when Jesus was hanging on the wooden cross about to take his last breath. "When Jesus saw his mother there and the disciple whom he loved standing nearby, he said to his mother, 'Dear woman, here is your son,' and to the disciple, 'Here is your mother.' From that time on this disciple took her into his home" (John 19:26-27).

Just as fathers, including stepfathers, are vitally important to their children, the role of mothers, including stepmothers, is magnificently and equally as vital. The significance of a loving mother-son, mother-daughter relationship transcends into the realm of the divine and comes from the very heart of God. It's a holy assignment like no other.

Frank's love for his children and wife was planted tenderly by his loving mother, much like St. Augustine's mother, Monica, planted the seed of Christian faith in her son and continued to pray for his soul until he left his immoral life to become a spiritual giant, a theological father of reformation and a bishop in the fourth century church. And such is the influence and legacy of a caring, godly mother who loves her children.

A few days after this visit, Frank left with his unit for the combat zone. But his gratitude, inspiring love, and devotion to his mother, and the life lessons he learned from his own childhood storms, I will never forget.

> Her children arise and call her blessed.
> —Prov. 31:28

CHAPTER 18

MARRIAGE AND WAR

Marriage and War

> He who finds a wife finds what is good and receives favor from the LORD.
> —Prov. 18:22

Always in love

WITH A BIG smile revealing her perfect teeth, Corporal Jessica looked more like a model from the pages of *Vogue* than a soldier in arms. After addressing her urgent medical need, I asked, "Are you worried about going to war?"

"I'm more worried about getting wrinkles. You know all the heat and my smoking will wrinkle my skin by the time I come back," she said.

"You must be kidding. You seem more worried about wrinkles than bullets," I said as we both started laughing.

"You are right, Doctor, you are right."

"So Jessica, how is your husband handling your deployment?" I asked, noticing her wedding ring.

"My husband is also deployed. We were friends for six years before we got married. We're both very committed to each other," she said.

"So how do you keep your relationship well?" I asked as I thought about the challenges that deployed couples face.

She answered without much hesitation, "You know, Doctor, I see married couples who say that they love each other but end up fooling around. My husband and I respect and care for each other. I think it's important to be friends with your spouse. We're friends."

"How are you guys keeping in touch?" I asked.

"I write him one letter every day, put it in an envelope that I design myself, place a nice stamp on it, and then take it to the post office to send it. There is just something very special about receiving a letter in your hand from someone who cares about you and spent time to write it and send it."

Her words captured my imagination and reminded me of the great joy a single letter from family and friends used to bring me. In our fast-paced life, the soul-enriching, almost forgotten art of letter writing and waiting for a letter, activities that involved patience and anticipation, has been almost totally replaced by the instant gratification of technological advances—e-mailing, instant messaging, and texting. The amazing tools and the wonder of instant communication, things we're all dependent on today, have forever added a fast food mentality to our lives and snuffed out of many of us the patience and joy of letter writing and the anticipatory, growing experience of waiting. Exercising patience while waiting for anything or for anyone from whom we might need urgent care, such as waiting for a doctor, has become a rarity.

"What about him, how is he keeping in touch with you?" I asked, cutting short my thought process.

"He calls me a lot and e-mails me about his day," she said and then stopped. I could tell something was bothering her. "You know, Dr. Hanna, he tells me about some of his unit buddies who yell and fight with their spouses on the phone…it's so sad. I just want to do for him what I want him to do for me."

Her words impressed me. She used Jesus Christ's words, also known as the Golden Rule, "Do unto others what you want them to do to you."

"You know, Jessica, it's great what you're doing. The way you care about your husband shows me that you don't just talk about the Golden Rule but you actually practice it. Many people claim to be Christians but they don't care to follow Jesus' words," I said as I reflected momentarily on her choice of the F word on couple of occasions during the conversation (followed by the apologetic "Sorry, Doctor, please excuse me").

"I don't go to church, Doctor, but I care about people. I just wish spouses at home could understand the stress their spouses face during deployment away from home, be more understanding, and listen to them."

It was time for Jessica to go. "You've taught me a lot, you know," I said as I opened the door for her.

"It's good to learn from one another," she said with a beautiful smile as she left to join her unit.

> If I give all I possess to the poor and surrender my body to the flames, but have not love, I gain nothing.
> —1 Cor. 13:3

Betrayal and regrets

> For this reason a man will leave his father and mother and be united to his wife, and the two will become one flesh.
> —Eph. 5:31

"My wife has no ambition, Doc, no motivation. I tell her that all the time," said Sgt. Curtis moments after the exam. His marriage was on the rocks and on its last breath with all attempts at marital reconciliation by the military base's social worker leading nowhere.

"She's got issues. I won't be going back to her," he said.

Their relationship had been heading south for a while with endless fighting between them at a base in Europe, which finally led to a final warning by his commanding officer to "fix it or she leaves." She had left the military housing and returned to the States after that ultimatum. Soon after her departure, Curtis surrounded himself with beautiful European girls like Anita who captured his attention with her "big breasts" the first time he body searched her at the main gate of the base.

Not long after that body search, Anita and other attractive women swept him off his married feet and distracted him with late night partying and money spent on him when he ran out of cash. But most of all, he was swept further and further away from his wife and his original beliefs.

"My wife is not like those women. She is not motivated like them. I've been telling her for years to go to school, so she can get a decent job but she wouldn't do it until just recently. I plan to move on," he said, comparing his wife to the other women.

It was at that moment that Curtis suddenly stopped talking and began to pay attention to the sacred music playing on my CD. He seemed totally absorbed by the inspirational, calming piece coming from the corner of the room.

"I used to sing it in the choir," he said and became silent. After a short pause he said, "I used to attend church, Doc. My preacher used to talk to me about God…to stay away from drugs. I'd like to go back," he said as his excitement about Anita and the women in his life gave way to a moment of reflection on long-forgotten sacred memories.

A week after this visit, Curtis returned for a follow-up visit. He seemed troubled by something and wanted to talk.

"Two years ago, before I married my wife, Renee, I was having second thoughts about getting married to her. I broke up our relationship and started to date a beautiful European woman, Monique," he said.

It wasn't long after their first date that they fell in love, and Monique told him that she was, "the happiest woman in the world" the day he proposed to her. But soon after he placed the golden engagement ring on her finger, he changed his mind and decided to secretly marry Renee instead. "We had had a baby together, and I felt it was the right thing to do. But I continued to see Monique. She was thinking all along that we were going to get married," he said, his voice dropping to a whisper.

But it didn't take long before Curtis' double life and unfaithfulness to both women was exposed.

"They ran unexpectedly into each other at the PX (the army's equivalent of a department store) and got into a big fight. My wife showed Monique the wedding ring on her finger and screamed loudly at her to "stay away from my husband," he recalled.

Curtis remembered his girlfriend's utter shock as she gazed with total disbelief at the wedding ring a few inches away from her face.

"She cried so hard before she dashed out of the PX. That was the last time I saw her," he said. With his voice increasingly quieter, he began to tell me the tragic chain of events that followed.

"It was late at night when I got a call from Monique's best friend, crying and blaming me for what happened to her. After she ran out of the PX in tears, she drove her car fast and crashed it. She was found dead," he said as silence swept the exam room.

His words took me off guard as his story took a sudden dark twist. I could tell that the part he played in Monique's untimely death weighed very heavily on him. Why did he decide to share this guilt-ridden, sad episode of his life with me? Could this be the first time he had shared this story with anyone? Had this seemingly unresolved inner guilt contributed to his troubled and unstable marriage and to his reckless extramarital affairs? I wondered.

To me, the deep remorse I heard in his voice reflected the depth of the guilt he felt for betraying the trust of an innocent woman, leading to her brokenness and death—guilt heavier than the bulky body armor he proudly wore and a burden too heavy for him to bear alone.

Sensing the depth of his inner struggle, I prayed silently for wisdom to find the right words. "Curtis, I remember how touched you were the last time you were here by the song that was playing on the CD. You told me that it reminded you of the church choir that you once sang in and a time in your life when you felt close to God."

He nodded his head in agreement as his eyes began to tear. I sat on my chair pondering what to tell him—words that would judge and condemn him for his part in destroying an innocent soul who loved him, or words of compassion that would help heal his own soul's brokenness. The latter won out, and I began to comfort him.

For the next few moments, I talked to him about topics he once believed in and that many years ago meant a lot to him—a language of love, forgiveness, and redemption that he once spoke and understood. I reminded him of what he already knew—our natural human tendency to sin and God's immediate willingness to blot out and forgive our sins and shortfalls when we accept Jesus Christ and His death on the cross, confess our sins, repent (turn away from our old, sinful ways), and ask for His forgiveness.

I talked about Jesus, God's love and forgiveness, and forgiving himself and starting a new page in life, free from the dark prison cell of guilt and condemnation with Curtis, a former choir singer, as he sat quietly and listened.

"Does that make sense to you?" I asked.

"It really does. Thank you, Doctor," he said, fighting back the tears.

I saw Curtis one more time before he left with his unit for combat. He was much more at peace, regularly seeing the chaplain, and receiving excellent personal counseling from the army behavioral health team at the base. He left me with these hopeful words, "Thank you, Dr. Hanna. The social worker talked yesterday on the phone with my wife for a long time. Maybe it will work out between us when I come back."

As he walked out of the exam room for the last time, I thought about how heavy a load guilt is. Perhaps crossing safely through the river of guilt's raging waters would help him calm his inner anguish, focus, and win the battles awaiting him in the hot deserts of Iraq and the cold, deadly mountains of Afghanistan.

> For God, who said, "Let light shine out of darkness," made his light shine in our hearts.
> —2 Cor. 4:6

> Do you not know that your bodies are temples of the Holy Spirit, who is in you, whom you have received from God? You are not your own; you were bought at a price. Therefore honor God with your bodies.
> —1Cor. 6:19-20

I love my wife

> Love is patient, love is kind. It does not envy, it does not boast, it is not proud.
> —1 Cor. 13:4

After examining Sgt. Bill's back and prescribing Ibuprofen for his pain, I noticed his shiny wedding ring and asked him, "Was it hard to say good-bye to your wife?"

"Yes, that was very hard," he said. "I have known her for twenty years, Doc, fourteen of them as my wife."

Talking about his wife brought a big smile to his face. He was eager to tell me more about the love of his life, and about one of the happiest days of their lives.

"I took her to an exotic getaway vacation. I thought that would be a great place to get pregnant and sure enough she did! I bought four EPT pregnancy tests and repeated the urine test four times before I could believe it," he said.

Before this pregnancy and after many miscarriages she had began to despair and point a finger at him. "She started to blame me! Do you believe that, Doc? I told her she got pregnant so I can't be the problem," he said, recalling his wife's many previous unsuccessful attempts to have a baby before their memorable getaway vacation.

Her long-awaited pregnancy proved to be very complicated as she battled with joint pain, multiple ailments, and a dreaded lupus diagnosis that required strong blood thinners following the birth of their beautiful daughter, Kim. Then suddenly, nine months after the delivery, the unexpected happened. He vividly remembered that moment.

"I left for work early in the morning, but then I came back home unexpectedly to pick up something I forgot. As soon as I entered, I heard my nine-month-old baby crying hysterically, and I knew something was terribly wrong. My wife knew exactly how to calm Kim down and would not let her cry that long. When I saw her, she was lying on the floor with foam coming from her mouth. She was unconscious. It was a miracle that I came back home to find her before something bad happened to her."

He frantically called 911, and for the next twenty-one days stayed by her ICU bedside, pleading, "God, she isn't ready to die; my daughter and I are not ready for her to die," as she battled for her life. Suffering from a brain hemorrhage, she was in a coma for three weeks. After she had received "nineteen bags of IV and many blood transfusions," his only hope was a miracle from heaven.

Adding to Bill's fear and confusion was the air of suspicion that surrounded him as the physicians and medical staff tried to piece out the reason for her collapse and brain bleed.

"Some thought her bleeding was caused by trauma. I felt like I was a suspect," he said, his voice reflecting that sad moment in his life. Fortunately, that suspicion didn't last long as her team of physicians found out about her history of lupus and her list of medications, including blood thinners.

I could sense the love he felt for his wife from his voice as he finished the rest of his story. Love and commitment had kept him fully focused on the journey of her recovery and healing.

"She is finally able to walk on her own, and her arm is regaining its full strength. It's a miracle that she is alive and we have a child together. You know, we talk every day on the phone after training. It took her some time, but she can talk very well now. I feel very good that her best friend will be with her during my deployment, so I don't have to worry," he said, reflecting on the love of his life he was temporarily leaving behind.

For many months after he left for the theater of operations, I reflected on his loyalty and deep love for his wife. His story will always remind me that love is a decision and not a fleeting feeling or an emotion that waxes and wanes, rises and falls. Lying in a coma on an ICU monitored bed with IV fluids sustaining her very life couldn't have been romantically arousing or attractive. But out of his heart flowed a decision to love his wife and not give up on her as she lay down in that lonely hospital bed at her weakest and her worst. The promise he made to his beautiful bride "to love and to cherish...for better or for worse" on a joyful wedding day a few years before, he kept later even as a ventilator tube taped to her mouth would not let her utter a single word of love back to him.

> It always protects, always trusts, always hopes, always perseveres.
> —1 Cor. 13:7

It's hard just being friends

> Where has your lover gone, most beautiful of women?
> —Song of Songs 6:1

"Are you okay?" I asked Private First Class Pam, an attractive twenty-five-year-old from the Midwest, as I saw tears rolling down her gentle face. One moment she was smiling and talking enthusiastically about how her training was progressing, and the next she was in tears.

"It's not easy when the only private time I can spend with my husband, Dan, is during training when everyone is around," she said.

Pam and her husband, newlyweds, were soldiers in the same unit and both had been ordered to deploy at the same time. The effects of the rigorous training and regulations that limited their private time together was starting to take a toll on her, and all she could do about it at the moment was to let her tears flow in a closed room where no one but her doctor could see. As a bride whose wedding had been only a few days before she reported with her bridegroom to the camp, all she could do was train vigorously even as she silently cried.

"It's wearing me down, Doctor. It's hard to see him every day and act like friends instead of holding each other and spending our honeymoon together somewhere romantic," she said, wiping away her tears.

For a moment I reflected on her dilemma and her sweet love and desire for her husband. There she was, a strikingly beautiful bride, deeply yearning for her groom in the midst of intense war preparations that couldn't be altered. Like a love bird separated from her loving mate, she silently cried, hoping for even a moment with her lover.

"I can tell how much you love him," I said. "You guys must have a great romantic love story!"

"We complete each other, like two separate pieces of a puzzle. The first time we met was at our AT (annual training). There were a lot of guys who wanted to date me, but there was something special about him that separated him from the rest. He wasn't the tallest or the best looking, but he made me laugh. I thought about him a lot after AT and was so happy when he called me after we went back to our different states," she said as tears gave way to a beautiful smile.

Pam gladly agreed to go out with him when he asked her, and their love relationship blossomed and grew, leading to their holy matrimony just before reporting to duty here.

"We decided to get married sooner than we originally planned when we received our orders. But our wedding was still great! Even the local newspaper wrote about us on the front page—we were our town's heroes," she said, reminiscing about the joyful moments of the greatest day of her life.

I could sense her calmness and see how relaxed her face looked as she walked down memory lane with her mind no longer fixed on the pain of not spending private quality time with her husband, but on the joyful memory of a beautiful wedding day. Sharing her feelings and love story seemed to soothe her heart. Somehow, it took her mind away from the daily grind of combat training, artillery firing, and rigorous marching on rugged uncharted terrain with her wet and muddy uniform, to the day when a beautiful bride walked gracefully on a clean, colorful carpet in her white dress to her groom's anxious arms.

"It felt good talking to you. Thank you so much for listening," she said with a wide smile and gave me a big hug.

I'm not sure how I helped her, but she was obviously feeling much better by the time she left. Perhaps all it took was listening to her not only share the pain of her temporary separation from her man here at

MARRIAGE AND WAR

the camp, but also the joy she had experienced as she permanently united with her beloved in a small church few days ago.

A few days before she mobilized to the theater of operations, Pam returned to say good-bye to me, with her husband by her side. She wanted me to meet him, and thankfully there were no more tears but many smiles and laughter this time around.

> I belong to my lover and his desire is for me.
> —Song of Songs 7:10

> But as for me and my household, we will serve the LORD.
> —Josh. 24:15

No loyalty

> There is a way that seems right to a man, but in the end it leads to death.
> —Prov. 14:12

"So what do you think, Doctor…is it STD? I'll be leaving 'on pass' tonight to see my girlfriend in North Carolina," said twenty-three-year-old Private Romeo, explaining the reason for his "personal issue" medical visit.

After a thorough medical exam, I delivered to him the good news, "Looks like an inflamed hair follicle. No herpes, Romeo."

Elated by the news, he smiled. "Thank you, Doc. This is good news. You know, I have two girlfriends I'm seeing back home. They both say they love me and are already fighting with each other. I want to make sure I don't catch anything."

It sounded to me like a web of triangular mess with one of his ladies headed for a heartbreak and the other one struggling with trusting him.

But then he suddenly added an additional crucial character to his already entangled story. "I was able to finally convince my wife that we should start dating other people just for the sex, you know. We're so far away from each other, she's in Central America and I'm here. We're still married, Doctor, but I can't stay too long without having sex."

"Did she agree to that?" I asked, trying to make sense of what I'd just heard.

"At first she hated the idea, but then I convinced her that she can also do the same while I'm away from her," he said nonchalantly.

What a mess! I thought. Romeo's cast of women lovers has now expanded to include his lawfully wedded wife. Beyond the obvious—acquiring STDs or getting one or all of them pregnant, there was the looming emotional pain of rejection and feeling used awaiting them by the end of his sexual crusade.

"But, Romeo, what if your wife ends up falling in love with one of the guys you've been encouraging her to sleep with? The reason I'm saying that is because sex isn't just a physical fusion of two bodies. It's also an emotional fusion of feelings, especially for a woman. So what if one of these men ends up winning her heart, and she finds herself in love with him? What if you end up losing her? Have you thought about this possibility?" I asked.

There was suddenly silence in the room. I wasn't sure if what I just said had made him mad or if he had decided to ignore me.

But then he nodded his head in agreement and said, "You're right, Doctor, what you say makes sense. I love her. I don't want to lose her to someone else."

At that moment it occurred to me that Romeo might've never experienced in his childhood home the importance of being sexually loyal and faithful to one's own spouse. Perhaps he never saw in his life experience marriage as a God-established institution meant to be a safe relationship where a man and a woman can have peace and feel loved, appreciated, accepted, respected, and secure as they face life's endless challenges together. With time on my hands until my next patient, I thought a mini talk about this important topic might prove to be of benefit to him.

"Romeo, you know those vows you exchanged with your wife on your wedding day, to love and be loyal and faithful to one another. These were promises you both made on that day before God and people to be only romantically in love with each other and to not sleep with anybody else. As a married man you show loyalty, love, and respect to your woman when you don't break your promises to her. And the same applies to her. God wants us to love our spouses and to be loyal to them, and of course they are supposed to do the same. It's the right thing to do, don't you think?" I asked, wondering about his response.

To my surprise he seemed deeply touched by the words I'd just uttered. I'll never forget the look in his eyes when I finished with this statement. "Romeo, you got to fight for your woman; you *do not* want to lose her!"

He nodded his head and with fire in his eyes, like a tiger ready to defend and fight for his lifetime mate till the very end, said with power in his voice, "Thank you! Thank you, Doctor! I'm going to bring her to America. I will bring her here."

> If I speak in the tongues of men and of angels, but have not love, I am only a resounding gong or a clanging cymbal. If I have the gift of prophecy and can fathom all mysteries and all knowledge, and I have a faith that can move mountains, but have not love, I am nothing.
> —1 Cor. 13:1-2

My wife's inner beauty

> A wife of noble character who can find? She is worth far more than rubies.
> —Prov. 31:10

I had seen Sgt. Kyle, a thirty-two-year-old from the Southwest, a few times before this sick call and was always impressed with his gentle demeanor and politeness. As I finished his physical exam, I noticed for the first time the big, bright wedding ring adorning his ring finger.

"Nice ring! So tell me how your wife is dealing with the deployment, Kyle?" I asked as I rested the stethoscope around my neck.

He smiled and began to eagerly tell me about the woman of his dreams. "I've been married, Doc, for ten years to the most wonderful woman. We have children and she is a great mom. I love her," he said and began to tell me his love story.

"The first time I saw her was at my parents' home. She came to visit them, and I happened to be there at the time. I remember I didn't think she was as attractive as the women I was dating at the time, and I hardly paid attention to her," he remembered.

But it was a simple act of kindness that she did at his mom and dad's home on that day that caught his dad's attention and eventually caught Kyle's as well.

He recalled how concerned she was that there were no cold drinks in the house and how she chose to go to the store to buy him a cold soda when he complained about being thirsty. Kyle remembered that he wasn't particularly nice to her the first time they met and wasn't kind when he asked for his drink. To his astonishment, she totally bypassed his rudeness to her and chose to buy him the cold soda anyway. Her choice to not hold his impoliteness against him, willingness to serve others, and her random act of kindness took him and his dad by surprise.

"My dad was so impressed when she came back with the soda. He pulled me to the side and told me, "Son, you mark my words: one day you will marry this girl. A woman who goes out of her way to do something like that for you cares about you and it means she is a good woman. Remember what I'm telling you—you will marry this girl," Kyle laughed as he remembered his dad's words.

Kyle's initial laughter at his dad's "crazy words" that eventually turned out to be prophetic didn't last long as he began to quietly notice her behavior, becoming increasingly impressed by her character and how much she cared about him.

"I fell in love with her," he said.

Their love grew and survived an onslaught of vicious attacks of jealousy from some of the women he had once dated, who tried to break their relationship apart with accusations and digging into his woman's past.

But their relationship weathered the attacks when he decided not to listen to their negatives or focus on her past, choosing instead to start a new life with her, looking ahead towards the future.

"I told them, 'I too have a past but I'm a new person today, just like she is.' They stopped once I told them that I love her for the person she is today and her past is already gone," he said in a quiet, confident voice. Before leaving the exam room he painted with his words another picture of the beautiful woman he would soon leave behind to embark on his risky military mission.

"Dr. Hanna, Dad was right. Here I am ten years later with four children and a lovely wife! And I'm still in love with her."

Soon after he left, I reflected on what I thought was a fascinating part of his love story. In a world where our human worth and value are measured by outer appearances: looks, skin color, and power from our position or possessions, Kyle decided to look at his woman's inner beauty—her heart. It was refreshing to see how her inner beauty of kindness, love, compassion, and caring was worth more to him than the outer appearance and beauty of the women he once dated.

In our media-crazed world where a man or woman's outer self is valued, trumpeted, and praised at the expense of her or his inner beauty of character, it's no wonder so many of us look so darn good on the outside, but are dark, spoiled, and stinking rotten on the inside. Society's message that our outer looks and attractiveness and not the content of our character and morals are the measure of our value and success has been accepted, believed, and incorporated into our inner psyches.

This message has helped to transform many young women's thinking into a flawed mind-set that drives them to live their lives as trophies who must look sensual and thin with a perfect shape, looks, and complexion in order to be won by men. Young men, on the other hand, find themselves groomed by society's mind-set of competing for women like trophies to be adorned, enjoyed, and won with a flashy display of physical appearance, power, position, and possessions. It's not much different from the animal world with the important difference that we were not created to behave like or be animals.

As a physician who routinely treats women and men battling rock-bottom low self-esteem, raging anger, worthlessness, depression, and anxiety (often manifesting themselves as anorexia, bulimia, personality disorders, and a host of other emotional ills), I'm sadly aware of the trauma many have suffered as a result of childhood abuse, domestic violence, abandonment, rejection, destructive control, and rape. But I'm wondering how much of my patients' emotional suffering can also be traced to society's crippling mind-set that conforms men and women to standards no one can measure up to and leaves them feeling rejected and like captives of a never-ending cycle of anger, bitterness, hurting, and being hurt as they move from one bad relationship to another. And by the end of this rat race, everyone ends up drained. It must be very exhausting trying to live as a beautiful trophy and just as tiring to maintain and to take care of one.

Indeed, our culture's loud "praise trumpets" about our outer appearance, possessions, and position will tempt us to be puffed up, prideful, and selfish. They will lead us to lose sight of what really matters—building godly inner character of love, kindness, humility, respect, patience, and self-control, among other solid moral traits.

Like Kyle's dad, who had pointed his son to the real inner beauty of his future wife who nobly chose to forgive Kyle's rudeness in asking for a drink, I hope one day I will also teach my sons to look beyond the outer beauty of a woman, directly into the character of her heart. And I hope to teach my daughters to be no man's trophy but to be women of true character, who will bless their husbands and whose children will one day call them blessed.

Kyle returned for one more visit to say good-bye before he left with his unit for his combat assignment. His radiant smile and passion for his beautiful wife told one love story I will always remember.

> Charm is deceptive, and beauty is fleeting; but a woman who fears the LORD is to be praised.
> —Prov. 31:30

> Love is patient, love is kind…it is not easily angered, it keeps no record of wrongs.
> —1 Cor. 13:4-5

CHAPTER 19

MUSIC AND HEALING

Music and Healing

Sing to the LORD a new song; sing to the LORD,
all the earth.
—Ps. 96:1

My daughter's song

SGT. FIRST CLASS Abel entered the exam room limping from a severely sprained ankle that he had suffered during his intensive training. As soon as he sat on the exam table, he seemed mesmerized by a song playing on my CD that brought him sweet memories from his home in Massachusetts.

"This is my daughter's favorite song. She is seventeen years old. She has church choir practice now. She might be singing it!" he said, forgetting for the moment his swollen ankle. I could tell how the music had softly touched a tender chord in his heart. He missed her and missed his home.

"Johnny, my twenty-year-old son, still lives at home with us. He was still asleep downstairs when I called them earlier this morning," he reminisced.

"You've got a beautiful family, Abel," I said.

"I have four children and a great wife. We lived together for nineteen years and had four children before we decided to get married four years ago. Getting married was the best thing I've ever done for our children. When I first met her, I wasn't into God like she was but I finally listened to her about getting married, Doctor. That was the best thing I did; I'm now a good role model for my family."

I could tell by his peaceful, joyful smile the depth of his love for his family.

The music was still playing when he left the exam room. I will never comprehend how, on that cold, early morning day, a simple song from my CD had transformed the exam room into a tranquil place of rest and respite where his most cherished memories were vividly experienced.

I have heard many stories of patients and soldiers who felt God's voice of love and comfort in dreams or through someone's compassion and tender love, the warmth of a pet's touch, the beauty of creation, the sound of falling rain, the majestic sight of snow carpeting the landscape, the captivating changing colors of the fall leaves, and the awesomeness of sunrises and sunsets. Now I'm able to see how God's encouraging voice of love can also be found in music, even a simple song played on my old CD player.

Sing to the LORD, praise his name; proclaim his salvation day after day.

—Ps. 96:2

Is any one of you in trouble? He should pray. Is anyone happy? Let him sing songs of praise.

—James 5:13

Symphony memories

Praise the LORD. Praise God in his sanctuary; praise him in his mighty heavens.

—Ps. 150:1

As I entered the exam room, I could see Sgt. Damon's eyes locked on the small CD player on my table. I greeted him warmly as I walked in and began to inspect the surgical tray brought in by the medic for the incision and drainage of his large skin abscess.

As Giovanni's soothing classical piano music played, he seemed totally oblivious to the menacing, size-eleven blade about to incise through his inflamed skin.

"My grandparents played in the Boston Symphony Orchestra. That's where they met, fell in love, and got married sixty years ago. This classical piece brings back lots of good memories," he said, pointing at my CD player, "lots of memories."

For the next fifteen minutes, Damon took me with him on a journey down memory lane as I silently listened and drained his abscess.

He talked fondly about his grandpa and grandma's marriage and romance six decades ago as they enchanted the renowned Boston Symphony Orchestra's crowds with their musical gifts. "They played so well. Grandma tried her best to teach me how to play the violin. I wish I had continued like my brother did."

Damon continued to chitchat and reminisce about his life, his new bride, and his young children from a previous relationship. He told me how he terribly missed them as Giovanni's music played while I gently drained and cautiously packed his deep wound with sterile gauze. He was so fascinated by the soothing, gentle sound of the music that filled the exam room that he barely noticed that the surgical procedure was over.

I will never forget the day when a lovely, heavenly melody played by a master musician comforted Damon's heart and evoked pleasing childhood memories in his anxious soul—memories that he deeply cherished and that would hopefully uplift his spirit in the midst of the fierce and deadly battles awaiting him.

> Praise him for his acts of power; praise him for his surpassing greatness. Praise him with the sounding of the trumpet, praise him with the harp and lyre.
> —Ps. 150:2-3

Touched by music

> Praise him with tambourine and dancing, praise him with the strings and flute, praise him with the clash of cymbals, praise him with resounding cymbals.
> —Ps. 150:4-5

Twenty-eight-year-old Private Rebecca looked quite somber as she coughed repeatedly before sitting on the exam table.

"Good morning! I promise to be right back," I said as I rushed to finish the medical care of another soldier. I returned a couple of minutes later only to see her sobbing eyes soaked in tears.

"Are you okay?" I asked.

"I'm fine, Doctor. Thank you."

"I hope you're not crying because I left you?" I asked, hoping to cheer her up.

"No, no, Doc. I just wasn't expecting to hear the worship song playing on your CD. I've grown up listening to it where I used to go to church. It brings many good memories," she said, wiping her tears.

"As the music continued to play, Rebecca looked much more at ease and soon after I finished the medical exam she wanted to share with me what sounded like a major spiritual roadblock in her life.

"I did something bad in the past, something I know I shouldn't have done. I haven't been able to talk about it to anybody. It feels like it is coming to haunt me now," she said in a whisper.

I realized she wasn't yet ready to talk about it. She seemed to have chosen to emotionally isolate herself. Hoping for the right words to comfort her and jumpstart her journey of healing, I said, "Becky, this song brought a lot of tears to your eyes. I don't know what you did, but whatever it is, I believe you will find complete forgiveness from God when you ask Him to forgive you. But you will also need to forgive yourself," I said, mindful of her spiritual roots.

The words I uttered suddenly became like a key that unlocked the bolted door of her deeply bottled emotions. Her eyes welled again with tears as she talked about how much she needed God's forgiveness and how much she missed having a closer relationship with Him. She shared how the Bible verse, "And we know that in all things God works for the good of those who love him, who have been called according to his purpose" (Rom. 8:28), meant so much to her and how it had served as an anchor in her life.

For the next few minutes, Rebecca and I talked about parts of the Bible that reminded her of God's love and forgiveness: The parable (story) of the prodigal (lost) son in Luke 15:11-32, who sinned against his father but was fully forgiven and restored, and the story of a woman who was endlessly searching for love and peace in her life with a series of failed relationships with men and ended up meeting Jesus at a well where she was drawing water. Rebecca knew the story of the woman, also known as the Samaritan woman found in the New Testament book of John 4:4-30, and how Jesus offered her a different kind of water and the same water to all of us today—a spiritual one that will bring our human souls real peace and satisfaction.

"Everyone who drinks this water will be thirsty again, but whoever drinks the water I give him will never thirst," Jesus told the woman.

I could tell by Rebecca's peaceful smile and her gentle request of "Can we pray?" that a ray of bright light had pierced through the thick cloud of guilt that surrounded her.

"Doctor, I feel this is a new beginning in my life. I feel God brought me to sick call to remind me of Him. I feel now that the soldiers of my unit will benefit from me. I want to be used for something good… to help others," she said, her voice filled with emotion.

Rebecca returned to see me for a follow-up visit and treatment of a minor facial irritation that she had suffered during riot control training. Gone were all her anxieties and tears.

"Doctor Hanna, I was sprayed during riot training. But guess what? I took a step of faith today and told my captain after I was sprayed with the chemicals about my faith in Jesus Christ. I feel so good, Doctor! I'm starting to send thank you notes and encouragement cards to soldiers I don't even know. Do you believe that?" she joyfully shouted.

It was hard for me to believe this was the same Rebecca who had cried as she heard a song on my CD a week ago. She was happy and buoyant, the old Rebecca on steroids!

"Glad to see you doing so well. So tell me what helped you feel better," I asked in amazement.

"Psalm 37, the third and fourth verses. I am now able to see how great it is to have my one-year-old, my three-year-old, and my five-year-old in my life. Do you believe that? My husband called me and told me 'Good morning, beautiful'! I asked him, 'Are you freaking drunk?' It was so great, just great, to hear him say that."

"I am so glad, Becky, that you are doing so much better."

"Thank you, Doctor. You know the first day I saw you, I wasn't even planning to come to be seen at sick call. That was a miracle. The song I heard reminded me of my old relationship with God," she said.

Before she left to join her unit, she said these last words to me: "Doctor, the problem is still there, but I am no longer focusing on it and that's why I feel so well. Things will never be perfect until we get the freaking out of here and go one day to heaven."

I couldn't agree with her more. Her statement, "Things will never be perfect until we get the freaking out of here and go one day to heaven" was so simple but yet so profound. To paraphrase, Rebecca had decided to keep the focus of her heart and mind not on her past hurts, present obstacles, falls, and failures, but on God's love, mercy, goodness, and His solemn promise of eternity until the assigned day when her life journey comes to an end.

Rebecca returned for one last time to say good-bye to me before she mobilized with her unit. She was still charged, excited, and passionate about her ministry of encouraging other soldiers the way she had felt encouraged.

Many months after she left, I remembered her jubilant voice as she talked about how two verses in Psalm 37 had touched her heart and changed her life. At times in my life when challenges seem many, I find myself always encouraged and renewed when I open my Bible and read, "Trust in the LORD and do good; dwell in the land and enjoy safe pasture. Delight yourself in the LORD and he will give you the desires of your heart" (Ps. 37: 3-4).

> Let everything that has breath praise the LORD. Praise the LORD. Praise the LORD.
> —Ps. 150:6

God, Master Composer and Conductor of life

> Speaking to one another in psalms, and hymns and spiritual songs, singing and making melody in your heart to the Lord.
> —Eph. 5:19 NKJV

As I sat many a night amid the crowds in the comfort of the historic Ohio Theater watching Japanese maestro Junichi Hirokami, one of the world's best and most warmhearted conductors, leading the powerful and exceptionally talented Columbus Symphony Orchestra with his baton, I often found myself deeply immersed in my thoughts.

As his baton swayed and moved, the captivating music played by each one of the professional musicians on stage pleasantly followed. Regardless of what was on the program—the great Yo-Yo Ma playing his mesmerizing cello, or the wonderfully, unforgettable live recording of Tchaikovsky's Symphony No. 5, with the slightest movement of Maestro Hirokami's hands, strings, woodwinds, brass, and percussion instruments brought the greatest of symphonies vividly to life.

As I enjoyed the awesomeness of the music played, I often thought about God—music Lover, and Master Conductor of the grandest orchestra of all, the orchestra of life. God conducts the symphonies of our lives so superbly if we just let Him. He lifts His baton up to allow the sounds of a long, beautiful, and marvelous piece of music, or a brief, stormy, and somber one to flow. With majesty and perfect precision, He speeds up the movement ushering new tempos into our lives. Then at the right moment lowers His hands all the way down to end one divine musical piece, only to lift them up again to bring a fresh, warm, and fantastic new tune into our lives. He is the Master Conductor, gentle and divine, Who conducts our lives with love, grace, and mercy, creating masterpieces of our lives in ways that no human conductor could ever parallel.

Help us, God, so that we don't let ourselves or others write and conduct our lives' symphonies with anger, abuse, disrespect, manipulation, selfishness, lust, and pride. May we let You conduct our lives with Your directing right hand unto a life of love, peace, and joy. For in God's miraculous notes, love, security, acceptance value, and forgiveness flow to our lives, unlike the injustice, guilt, and condemnation of this controlling, dark world. It's my prayer that I don't let the course of my life be conducted by anyone or anything else but by the One Who composed my life story from beginning to end, and knows best how to make my life into His masterpiece, a symphony of faith, hope, and love.

As you reflect on these words, think about what and whose life symphony you are playing? Who is conducting your life?

The more I reflect on God's grandeur as He meticulously conducts the whole universe with its billions of stars, galaxies, celestial bodies, and planets, the more I marvel at the notion that He still has such deep interest in composing and conducting the stories of each of our individual lives.

To accomplish His grand plan, God has composed for us the ultimate composition, the Bible. He uses people, just like a conductor uses instruments, to deliver its notes—His Word of redemption, love, peace, and freedom to all of His creation.

He teaches and uses us, His creations, as instruments that bring to others the joy of living a free, peaceful, spirit-filled life, instead of a stuff-filled life. His living Spirit wants to lead us to the amazing joy of true freedom found in His love and truth. With His conducting Spirit, He directs us away from an existence-controlled, paralyzed, and hindered by a life of pleasing others and years of time and energy wasted on polishing and fighting for perishable stuff into a new beginning.

We begin to play God's note well when we learn not to find our value in things and in people's approval and when we are no longer prisoners of our possessions or other obsessions.

We play God's conducted divine notes of peace and freedom when we choose to stay focused in heart and mind on God, even when we face evil, hurting words, injustice, and rejection, and when we repay good for evil. And we surely become His best musicians who play His finest of freedom melodies when we learn and encourage ourselves and others to let no human being or material thing steal our liberty and freedom, for without freedom life can't be truly lived. We play it well when we live our lives free from control, abuse, fear, guilt, and condemnation—free to dream, to be Christians even where persecution abounds, to fly like eagles higher and higher, to worship, serve, hope, laugh, and live.

It's when we're tuned to God's life symphony that we can begin to understand why Patrick Henry once said, "Give me liberty or give me death," why many slaves to human greed and injustice chose and continue to choose death over life in their pursuit of freedom from captivity, and what is the main thing George Washington's America has in common with Christianity—God and the pursuit of God's given liberty and justice for all.

Just like America's brave soldiers who choose to fight for the freedom of many from control and injustice, one generation after another, Christianity is also about fighting for freedom from the spiritual and emotional darkness of hopelessness, guilt, fear, and condemnation.

Jesus Christ said on His very first announcement about the objective of His earthly mission, "I came to set the captives free."

There is one more powerful God-conducted musical piece, an important and favorite He never misses: love. God's love, which the Bible best describes in the New Testament verse, "For God so loved the world that he gave His one and only Son, that whoever believes in him shall not perish but have eternal life" (John 3:16) is like the most potent cholesterol-busting drug that heals and gets rid of the thickest cholesterol deposits and plaques that are so stubbornly nestled on the walls of one's coronary arteries. It heals our past hurts, wounds, and shame and when it controls us it becomes that potent medicine that subdues and gets rid of our inner fear and anger and our controlling, selfish, and prideful attitudes and replaces these negatives with love, kindness, peace, and hope. Love transforms an unthankful, prideful heart full of anger, fear, and discontent into one of contentment, joy, and thankfulness.

God's love, demonstrated as the Bible describes by Jesus Christ's life, death, and resurrection for mankind's eternal salvation and a better earthly life, is indeed His most important and striking note. Without that perfect love, all forms of fear and negative emotions prevail; without it we can't change our lives; and without it the symphonies of our lives become those of our own composition, devoid of the healing, loving, and miraculous touch of God. Beyond all things He is the Master Composer and the Greatest Conductor of my life story, and yours.

> And now these three things remain: faith, hope and love. But the greatest of these is love.
> —1 Cor. 13:13

> Lord, make me an instrument of your peace.
> Where there is hatred, let me sow love,
> Where there is injury, pardon,
> Where there is doubt, faith,
> Where there is despair, hope,
> Where there is darkness, light,
>
> Where there is sadness, joy.
> O Divine Master, grant that I may not so much
> seek to be consoled as to console,

not so much to be understood as to understand,
not so much to be loved, as to love;
for it is in giving that we receive,
it is in pardoning that we are pardoned,
it is in dying that we awake to eternal life.

"Make Me an Instrument of Your Peace" by St. Francis of Assisi

CHAPTER 20

PATRIOTISM

Patriotism

He will wipe every tear from their eyes. There will be no
more death or mourning or crying or pain, for the
old order of things has passed away.
—Rev. 21:4

A swimmer's tribute

"THANKS FOR SEEING me, Doctor," said Staff. Sgt. Marco as he coughed his way to the exam room table. He looked much younger than forty-seven, the age on his medical chart.

"You won't need any antibiotics, Marco, just some decongestants and rest," I said as I set the stethoscope on my shoulders.

"You came all the way from Puerto Rico! So how long have you been in the army?" I asked.

"I've been with my unit from Puerto Rico for twenty-seven years, sir! I was originally born in New York. I moved to Puerto Rico with my parents when I was a child and have lived there since then," he explained.

"It's your career! How did you manage to stay that long?" I asked.

"This is my fifth deployment, Doc. It has to come from here, you can't do it if it doesn't come from the heart," he said, pointing at his own heart. "You must do it because you love democracy, you love your country of course, and it's good that you're getting paid but you've got to love what you're doing."

His words made perfect sense, and I nodded in agreement. He then began to share with me what I will always view as one of the most patriotic expressions I've heard—a tribute by a soldier to the memory of his fallen comrades.

"Doctor Hanna, we have lost many soldiers from Puerto Rico in the war. I can swim very well and for the past two years I've joined many professional swimmers in a national race from one side of the bay to the other. I swim wearing my DCU (desert combat uniform) with the names of each of the fallen soldiers written on the back of my uniform. I'm swimming in their memory, for their widows...for their children," he said, fighting the tears.

His words, "I'm doing it in their memory, for their widows...for their children," resonated in my heart long after he had left the exam room. Marco left with his unit shortly after this visit to start his deployment during one of the fiercest phases of the war in Iraq.

> He will swallow up death forever. The Sovereign LORD will wipe away the tears from all faces.
>
> —Isa. 25:8

Not "Born in the USA"

> Blessed is the nation whose God is the LORD.
> —Ps. 33:12

"I wasn't born in America. I came here with my brother at the age of twelve," said Sgt. Jacob soon after I finished his medical exam. Jacob actually had the choice to stay at home if he wanted to because of his wife's disability. He explained to me the reason for his decision to volunteer for this deployment.

"We came to America for a better life, to work hard and achieve our dreams. America is my home now, and I'm proud to be a soldier and serve my country."

"Why did you choose to volunteer, Jacob, if you could've stayed here at home?" I asked.

"My daughter is proud of her dad, the soldier who fights for America. My wife will be fine…she will be fine. I made sure of that. I just didn't want to be a coward in front of my daughter and tell her that I won't go to Iraq. I'm ready to go, sir."

Jacob's words took me down memory lane. I remembered that fall night when I arrived for the first time in New York's JFK airport, a teenager with nothing but a dream of going to college and becoming a doctor one day in America. I had often pondered this question throughout my early years in the US, *Will I ever take arms and defend my new home, America, if I am called to do that?*

As he walked out of the exam room dressed in his full military gear, I could see the American flag proudly displayed on his uniform. The memory of my own naturalization as a new American citizen flashed in front of me—the American flag I firmly held in my left hand and the words I proudly recited as I raised my right hand, "I pledge allegiance to the Flag of the United States of America, and to the Republic for which it stands: one nation under God, indivisible, with Liberty and Justice for all."

That was the moment I knew that America was not only my new home but also that I was ready to fight for her, much like what Jacob was getting ready to do.

"Jacob, America is my new home too. I know exactly how you feel," I said as I firmly shook his hand.

Jacob returned a few more times before departing for combat with his unit. He shared with me during the visits more stories—of his childhood memories in the old country and his love of family, God, and America, his new home.

> Unless the LORD builds the house, its builders labor in vain. Unless the LORD watches over the city, the watchmen stand guard in vain. In vain you rise early and stay up late, toiling for food to eat - for he grants sleep to those he loves.
> —Ps. 127:1-2

CHAPTER 21

PTSD, LIGHT AT THE END OF THE TUNNEL

PTSD: Photo provided by Camp Atterbury Public Affairs

Say to those with fearful hearts, "be strong do not fear; your God will come...He will come to save you."
—Isa. 35:4

Violent dreams

STAFF SGT. CHRIS'S life has never been the same since his last deployment to Iraq. The memory of his combat days has filled his restless nights upon his return with vivid nightmares one after another.

"Every night it was the same dream: mortar attacks, IEDs and explosives detonating. I was always physically fighting with the enemy in my dreams—wrestling, kicking, and hitting back—just like it was in combat.

"My poor girlfriend! She got kicked, hit, and choked as she slept next to me. She would wake me up before she got hurt real bad. I had no idea what I was doing," he said.

The relationship eventually ended when she was no longer able to handle his violent nighttime dreams and the unresolved emotions he came back home with. "She tried to tough it out, but at the end it was too much for her to handle," he said. He paused for a moment of silence as if to mourn the end of a relationship that had once meant a lot to him and said, "I was looking forward to a future with her."

Chris's diagnosis of PTSD (Post Traumatic Stress Disorder) followed his turbulent course of hypervigilance and anxiety about routine sounds and noises of everyday life that reminded him of combat. "I was always on the alert, ducking for cover and reaching for my weapon whenever I heard a sudden loud noise or bang," he explained.

"How are you feeling now, Chris?"

"I've been going to the VA hospital for medicine and counseling and feel better now. I want to get my life back together. I feel better now," he said confidently.

Chris's journey of healing took him onto a new life path of serving others instead of constantly focusing on himself and his needs, developing in the process an outwardly focused perspective on life instead of being inwardly focused on his issues. He began to find great satisfaction and a deep inner peace as he reached out to other soldiers facing their own emotional battles and scars.

"I am now helping some of our soldiers who are suffering from PTSD," he said with a firm voice like a field commander on a mission, albeit a different one—helping brave soldiers like himself with wounded hearts to heal, just like he had.

After he left, I thought about his short but powerful story. Chris's days of combat were behind him, but in essence he was still a soldier in battle against a totally different enemy. To him and his battle buddies whose fight was now against PTSD, victory was no longer measured in captured enemy grounds, but in the renewal and healing of their minds, souls, and spirits.

Chris's journey of healing began when he admitted his need for help. Instead of living his life playing the role of a victim, blaming his girlfriend or others for his inner turmoil, anger, and anxiety, he boldly chose to face them all by talking about his feelings and seeking help. He didn't stay down in chains as a PTSD casualty but chose to break his chains, rise up to talk, get help, and begin to experience true freedom and liberty, that of a peaceful soul free from control, anger, and fear.

> He who dwells in the shelter of the Most High will rest in the shadow of the Almighty. I will say to the LORD, "He is my refuge and my fortress, my God, in whom I trust." He will cover you with his feathers, and under his wings you will find refuge; his faithfulness will be your shield and rampart. You will not fear the terror of night, nor the arrow that flies by day.
> —Ps. 91:1-2, 4-5

The journey

> He makes me lie down in green pastures, he leads me beside quiet waters.
> —Ps. 23:2

"So how was your experience in Iraq?" I asked Private First Class Tina moments after I'd finished her demobilization medical exam.

For the next fifteen minutes, Tina shared with me the hard times she endured during her deployment as her unit's medic and her journey of recovery since coming back home.

"Many of the wounded soldiers were sent to the trauma center where I worked. I treated a lot of gunshot wounds as a medic and once retrieved the body of a killed soldier from my unit," she said, looking slightly distraught.

At the young age of twenty-four, Tina had already seen and experienced the ravages and destructiveness of war. My hope was that she would find some peace and comfort in talking about what was in her heart.

"Tina, are you okay talking about that?" I asked.

"Yes." She nodded and proceeded to talk. "One of the worst things I've ever experienced was on that day I was sent to a scene where one of our soldiers had shot himself. He died of self-inflicted gunshot wounds. But why? I just don't understand…he only had two more days before coming back home. I don't know what could have been so overwhelming in his life that he decided to take his life in Iraq rather than come home. I can't understand it," she said, her eyes beginning to tear.

The effect this one moment had left in her heart and mind were obvious to me. I knew she would soon walk on a new journey of healing, surrounded by friends and loved ones. Fully aware of the healing power found in redirecting our thoughts and hence our emotions to serving others instead of dwelling and constantly reminiscing on our past trauma and wounds, I asked Tina one more question before she left.

"What's your advice, Tina, to the new soldiers heading to Iraq and Afghanistan who end up facing traumas? What helps you get better?" I asked.

"Open yourself to others. Thinking all the time about problems back home when you're in the middle of combat is not good. I'm glad to be going back home with my family and friends. I'm planning to take a cruise with other soldiers from my unit. I don't plan to live my life thinking about the past. That's what I tell them, Doctor," she said, looking at me with her fighter's eyes.

I could tell by her, "Thank you, Doctor, for listening," and the peaceful look in her eyes that the time invested behind the exam room's closed doors had been well worth it. I thanked Private First Class Tina for her service in Iraq, signed her medical exam form, and handed it to her.

"Welcome home, Tina," I said.

He restores my soul.

—Ps. 23:3

PTSD, LIGHT AT THE END OF THE TUNNEL

Walking in the dark valley of PTSD

> Even though I walk through the valley of the shadow of death, I will fear no evil.
> —Ps. 23:4

"Dr. Hanna, Dr. Hanna, hurry up. Come quickly to the waiting area. You want to talk to this platoon sergeant. He just came from combat," said Major Sandra as I was heading out of the Troop Medical Clinic for my lunch break. *This is not the time for food*, I thought, as I thanked the major and rushed back to meet the platoon sergeant.

"Good morning, sir. I'm Platoon Sergeant Jerry. The major told me you're writing stories to help the soldiers. I'm glad to talk to you," he said, standing up to shake my hand. He looked very friendly; he was a man of stocky frame and one heck of a powerful hand grip.

"I'm Dr. Hanna. Thanks for taking time to talk to me. I'm working on a book of different soldiers' stories to help encourage the troops."

He invited me to sit on the seat next to his in the middle of the empty waiting area and began to talk about his platoon's most gruesome moments of the war and the ensuing battle with PTSD.

"Eight of my platoon soldiers suffered from PTSD, and four others needed the CST (Combat Stress Team). I asked them (CST) to stay. I felt it was important that they hear from my soldiers. I knew that made some of them uncomfortable but as their commander I wanted them to face the demons inside because I know how it feels to be ripped on the inside," he said, recalling his platoon's worst days of the war.

For the next few moments I listened quietly as he recounted with a hoarse voice and a distinct southern drawl the deadliest and most graphic sights and sounds of the war he just had come from.

"My soldiers were handing candies to children in a busy marketplace. The little boys and girls were happy and loved it. Then suddenly, insurgents attacked with high-power explosives. It was the worst attack in the marketplace and when it all ended, the children were no longer there...all blown away...all dead," he said in a choked voice.

Platoon Sergeant Jerry was no stranger to tragedy. As a civilian policeman patrolling one of the roughest neighborhoods in his state, he had seen and experienced his share of trauma and tragedies and had a bout with PTSD before deploying to Iraq.

"There were gunshot wounds, fatal motor vehicle accidents, rape...I knew what PTSD felt like," he said.

Witnessing the shattering effect of the deadly battles on his platoon brought back the memory of his own walk in the dark valley of PTSD and the lessons he had learned along the way. "One of my soldiers was going through divorce and needed CST to help him deal with it, another one said he hated his life and started to get violent. I got him out of there and saw to it that another soldier who put a gun in his mouth was sent back to the States."

Months after the worst marketplace bombing in Iraq, the memory of that day still lingered in Jerry's mind. He talked about it as if it had just happened. It was as if I was there witnessing the dark images of death and utter destruction as he began to paint the horrible picture, with his husky, strong voice and his illustrative facial expressions, of what had happened to his platoon on that gruesome day of carnage.

"A suicide bomber blew up himself, children, men, and women in the market square— literally off their shoes. There were pieces of human flesh all over; you could see some hanging on barbed wires. The smell of burned, dead bodies was everywhere. Fifty police officers perished on that day. Even Sergeant Keith, a tough man, threw up that day."

He continued his chilling account of the deadly massacre with more gruesome details, including his emotional shock and reaction to that unexpected attack.

"One of the policemen's prayer beads were hanging on a steel fence.... His body parts were scattered around it.... I kept thinking, *One of these body parts belonged to someone who once prayed with those prayer beads.*"

I could see in his misty eyes and hear in the near whisper of his voice the sheer terror of that moment.

"I know our religion is different from theirs, but that was evil. As a police officer your heart just breaks. I felt guilty, guilty that I wasn't there to help these men. The poor Iraqis—they need all the help they can get," he said, pausing briefly in solemn silence. His graphic description of what had happened in that market square took me momentarily from the empty waiting area of the Troop Medical Clinic to the heat of that deadly day in Baghdad. I was writing as fast as I could, barely looking at my notepad as I kept my eyes totally focused on him.

"I felt numb looking at the small, shredded pieces of a police officer's body on the fence. But then I quickly realized we were under attack, and I was in a kill zone. I opened fire and moved all my soldiers away from enemy gunfire, and kept on firing. It was nothing personal, I saved my buddies. My only regret was I didn't empty the magazine of my M16. I get angry every time I remember that day…angry at the insurgents whose deadly attack put me in that position…to open fire."

As a caring commander, Jerry's concern for his troops went beyond their physical safety. With his platoon constantly under attack, and death always close by, he reached out to his troops, encouraging them to talk and share their feelings.

"I wanted them to band together, especially after coming from a big battle. We would bring our chairs out, start a campfire, and pass snacks as we sat around the burning wood listening to Squad Leader Sergeant Keith playing his 'geetar' (guitar)," he said with his melodic southern drawl.

Ultimately, it was that camaraderie and the soul bond between them that enabled Jerry's platoon to survive.

"We were all brothers and sisters—thirty of us, guys and gals from nineteen to fifty-five. After you spend 347 days sharing meals and barbequing three or four times a week, fighting and facing death and blood together, you become just that—brothers and sisters.

"They are back home now with their families, but I still care and cry every time I remember them. I will never forget their faces that still looked happy even when they faced enemy fire, katyusha rockets, or RPGs, and dealt with mortar attacks, roadside bombs, and IEDs.

"The soldiers should be proud of what they endured. I'm just thankful I was one of them," he said, his voice reflecting the depth of his genuine emotions.

For you are with me, your rod and your staff, they comfort me.
—Ps. 23:4

The journey of healing—light at the end of the tunnel

You will surely forget your trouble, recalling it only as waters gone by.
—Job 11:16

After listening intensely to Jerry's heroic story of survival, I was for a moment without words as I wondered about the best way to approach the next phase of my interview—his journey of healing now that he was back home.

"How do you feel now, Jerry? Do you still have a lot of anger?"

"I'll tell you, Doc, what makes me angry now—it's when I hear people fussing and complaining 'bout no ice in their Coke, their steak not being well done, or when they are told to wait and they start complaining about waiting too long. I remember my soldiers—they never complained about going to battle. You know, we trained Iraqi policemen to take over their country...we wanted them to have pride in their country. These poor Iraqis were attacked, hit, and many of them died, but nothing...nothing came out of their mouths. They didn't complain!

"You see, there is a difference between those who fight for liberty and those who just don't know what liberty really means. When you look in the eyes of a soldier, you see different feelings and emotions—fear and anger, but also happiness and excitement when his buddy is saved. You don't see fussing. You don't hear complaining," he said, his voice full of emotion.

"Jerry, you said many soldiers in your platoon and you yourself have suffered from PTSD. How are you doing now?" I asked.

"Right after I came back home, I used to wake up at night, screaming. I had nightmares that felt so real. I still do—the last few nights I saw a coffin draped with a flag. I woke up.

"I'm so thankful for my wife. She knows I killed people...but she understands that I had to do what I had to do. My wife, I can't thank her enough. I'm still struggling with survivor's guilt, but we all had to do what we had to do. The best thing that helps us soldiers get back to a normal life is support, support from our loved ones. God bless her, my wife," he said.

"Jerry, the Iraqi children really meant a lot to you. Am I right?" I asked as I pondered briefly on the eerie scene of death and carnage on that day in the marketplace.

"There were children with crutches who couldn't walk. I have four children of my own. I hope the Iraqi children will remember the American soldier one day, what we did to protect them," he said, struggling to hold back his tears.

"What was the most helpful thing to you in dealing with PTSD?" I asked.

"My wife. Thank You, Jesus, for her love and support. You know, I knew I needed help when I was there and didn't want to wait until I got back home. I went ahead and admitted to my troops that I had PTSD. I stood up in front of all of them and told them 'I have a problem and will be going to the CST (Combat Stress Team) to get help.' I told them, 'Don't be afraid…come with me.' I wanted them to get help," he said with his deep, throaty voice.

"And how did your soldiers take it?"

"When I stood up to tell them about my own struggle with PTSD, I wanted them to throw away all that crap about being tough, brave men who shouldn't have problems. I wanted them to say 'Damn it, I got problems—can't sleep, don't eat, I hate the world—I need help.' I told them they must get this stuff out in the open so that they can manage it."

"You mean the feelings stuffed inside?"

"Right, when that starts to come out, you can learn how to manage it…how to relax. You know, their minds and bodies had just gone through s---. They've got to know how to relax. Some of us just like to sit down and take it easy. I like to walk, swim, and be outdoors. That helps me a lot, you know."

"Is there anything else, Jerry, that you want me to tell the soldiers?" I asked as I continued to write his words on my yellow pad as fast as I humanly could.

"Yeah, talk to somebody who cares. I've got a journal that I keep. I find that helpful. Some of us have a tendency to go to alcohol and drugs; I almost got into that. They need to air their feelings and not let them stay in and grow. Go ahead and tell them that, Doc. You can use my name if you want. All my soldiers know me by the name RC07. They know I care about them and want them to get help," he said with his strong southern drawl.

His love and caring for his soldiers touched me. Jerry's zeal and passion to answer every one of my questions was his way of helping the soldiers and leading his platoon, now nestled in the safety of their homes in America, through the difficult emotional war of PTSD.

I thanked him for his courage and sacrifices and asked him one parting question about his faith story and spiritual beliefs. "Jerry, did your faith help you in Iraq? Is it helping you now?"

"I was once a devout Christian," he said, "but then things in my life blew apart. God…you know, everyone knows He is there…always there. I believe in Jesus Christ. He is the only reason I'm here, back home. My wife prayed for me…my family prayed for me."

I could tell by the eagerness of his voice the depth of his spiritual roots.

"You know something about God, Doc? A lot of people say 'How can he be here, there, and everywhere?' But when we see a tree moving, no one can say he sees the winds that move those leaves. I know that in our battles in Iraq, God was like the wind no one could see. He saved us and brought us back home," he said.

"Was it easy for you, Jerry, to talk about your faith with the soldiers when you were there?"

"There were plenty of Bibles there but many soldiers didn't want to talk about their faith because they were afraid of what others would think about them. They worried about being seen as weak soldiers who can't handle pressure. But you know what? That didn't bother me. My platoon soldiers heard me talk openly about my feelings and hurts. They were probably thinking, *Here he is—so ornery, always pushing us to have a battle victory, but still willing to talk about his faith, feelings, and now pushing us on to get well, and feel better.* That's what my soldiers saw in me," he said, his voice coming to a rest.

The lunch break was almost over, and it was time for him to reunite with his family in the safety and comfort of his "Home, Sweet Home." "Mid pleasures and palaces though we may roam, Be it ever so humble, there's no place like home," as American John Howard

Payne's song goes. Jerry's journey was certainly not in palaces or through pleasures but in fierce combat, and in the dark valley of PTSD, which made his yearning for home even sweeter.

"You've really made a big impact and difference in people's lives. Thank you, Jerry, for your service and for sharing your story with me," I said, extending my hand to him.

"You know, Doctor, if there is a chance of having a free Iraq, then it would all be worth it. I want to see these precious Iraqi children grow up one day in a free Iraq. My son tells me, 'Dad, I want to be part of that,' and will be deploying to Iraq too," he said as we shook hands.

"Does that worry you?" I asked, wrapping up my interview.

"I still remember this twenty-four-year-old man who many years ago took the same challenge. Now it's my son doing the same. Yes, Doc, I worry. But he is a young man who wants to make a difference. He knows he can get hurt, but if he suffers he knows it's for a good cause," he said in a fatherly, warm, quiet southern voice.

A few days after our interview, Jerry left to reunite with his wife and children—a dad, a husband, a soldier who won't let PTSD defeat him, and a man of faith going back home for a well-deserved hero's welcome.

For many months after the interview with Jerry, I reflected on his story and that of many patients who shared with me their own stories and those of their loved ones. I will never forget the anguish of a wife who once shared with me her worries about her husband of many years who after multiple deployments began to show signs of PTSD.

"He looks so well on the outside, Doctor, but whenever he faces added stress in life such as when he is preparing for deployment, he starts having nightmares. He wakes up at night, stands up ready to fight, and shouts at me, 'Stay away, don't touch me,' and begins to push me away with his hands. This scares me, Doctor. I tell him, 'What if you think I'm one of them?' I tell him he needs help and that he is keeping things to himself, but he is afraid of the repercussions to his military career if someone knows he has PTSD. I'm afraid," she said.

One of my dear elderly patients shared with me her forty-five-year war with alcoholism. She was finally able to quit after she decided to get help and joined a twelve-step program. She quoted a sentence she heard repeatedly in her AA meetings, "It's not enough to have will power, but you must have the willingness to quit."

Jerry did indeed show such willingness to help himself and his platoon soldiers overcome the menace of PTSD.

Jerry's story also reminded me of another quote I have heard from many of my patients, some with complicated diseases, terminal illness, or undergoing a long series of endless life crises, "Always be thankful because someone else has it worse than you."

Jerry seemed to be that kind of man. Even as he struggled with PTSD, he decided to humbly share his inner hurts, pain, and wounds with those who cared about him, reaching out simultaneously with love and compassion to his soldiers. He faithfully encouraged the men and women of his platoon and showed tender kindness to the Iraqi children, even as he traveled steadily through his own dark tunnel and began his journey of healing.

He, like many of my patients who are suffering from the worst diagnosis and prognosis, chose to have a thankful heart, no matter what he was going through. He never stopped thanking God, his wife, and his platoon soldiers and showing mercy and concern for the Iraqi children and his buddies who were seriously wounded or nearly killed—those who "had it worse" than he did.

After much reflection on Jerry's story, I now feel certain that his wise choice to walk on the path of humility—talking and sharing about his heart wounds, his thankfulness, and his passion for serving and helping others—is what will ultimately, with God's divine strength, take him on this journey of healing towards the light awaiting him and many others at the end of their hellish tunnel.

I can do everything through him who gives me strength.
—Phil. 4:13

Be joyful always; pray continually; give thanks in all cirumstances, for this is God's will for you in Christ Jesus.
—1 Thess. 16-18

PTSD, finding help for the journey

Definition and diagnosis

PTSD, previously known by various names, including "shell shock," is defined by the National Institute of Mental Health as "an anxiety disorder that can develop after exposure to a terrifying event or ordeal in which grave physical harm occurred or was threatened." An example of such a traumatic experience, which can be actual or threatened, in the medical literature includes violent physical and sexual assaults such as rape and child abuse, injuries, disasters (natural and human-caused), accidents, combat, war, and other forms of trauma and violence that threaten one's physical integrity, including those that are witnessed.

As mentioned in the diagnostic manual of the American Psychiatric Association, to be diagnosed with PTSD one has to meet specific criteria that currently include exposure to one of the traumatic events mentioned above and experiencing intense fear, helplessness, or horror in response to the experience. Additionally, one has to have one or more re-experiencing symptoms related to the event, e.g., recurrent images, daytime memories, frightening thoughts, distressing dreams/nightmares, flashback episodes that bring back the intense combat zone or the event's anxieties/fears. These flashbacks can be triggered by situations reminiscent of the event: a person's thoughts and feelings related to the event, sounds, smells, words, places, reunions, etc.

In addition to the above criteria, the person has to also exhibit three or more of the following: avoidance behaviors (avoiding places, events, feelings, thoughts, certain memories, and things that are reminders of the event), emotional numbness (manifesting itself as loss of interest in previously enjoyable activities), feelings of detachment (feeling unloved, loss of intimacy with loved ones, and difficulty being happy), and loss of hope in the future ("What's the point, anyway?"). And finally, the person has to have, in addition to the above criteria, two or more hyperarousal symptoms (sleeping difficulties, being easily startled, feeling tense/on edge, angry outbursts, loss of concentration, and hypervigilance), all lasting more than a month and causing impairment in relationships, jobs, and other important areas.

Who gets it?

Within the first month of experiencing a traumatic event and possibly up to three months after the tragedy, one can develop the previously mentioned symptoms as a potentially normal human stress response (Acute Stress Disorder) that will gradually resolve over time. If the symptoms last less than three months, this is called Acute PTSD, but if the PTSD-type symptoms last over three months and a person is having problems with normal functioning, it is labeled Chronic PTSD. Delayed PTSD is when the symptoms occur six months after the tragic event.

Not everyone who experiences a traumatic event develops PTSD. Instead of, or in addition to PTSD, a combat veteran or someone who experienced trauma could experience depression and probably other diagnoses in addition to PTSD that would require support and treatment: bipolar depression, attention deficit hyperactivity disorder, substance abuse disorders, traumatic brain injury, and bereavement over loss of a friend or other loved one.

According to the Detroit Area Survey of Trauma (1991) 11.3 percent of women and six percent of men experience lifetime risk of PTSD, i.e., women have twice as much risk of developing PTSD after a trauma than men, with sexual violence being associated with the highest risk of PTSD. The condition can also affect children and adolescents whose initial response to a tragic event might manifest itself as agitation in their behavior and disorganization.

PTSD and relationships

One of the greatly affected areas when someone experiences PTSD is the area of relationships. Some experience big problems with family, friends, and other significant relationships as they struggle with intense anger and impulses or the fear of letting their guard down, thus becoming overly critical to avoid closeness. But others have less severe problems as they develop honest and respectful communication that allows for safe sharing of thoughts and feelings.

Unfortunately, episodes of verbal and physical abuse can occur, and a PTSD sufferer can be very dependent or overprotective of partners or those close to him or her, which can rip through the foundation of any relationship.

On a more positive note, treatment and emotional support from counseling, family, friends, and the strength and comfort found in believing in God and being part of a spiritual community will help bring peace into a troubled household.

Treatment options for PTSD

Fortunately, there are very effective treatments for PTSD. The sooner one starts the treatment, the greater the rate of remission of symptoms (as high as sixty percent within weeks of therapy). Many medications are recommended for PTSD, and they play an important role in conjunction with the psychotherapy known as Cognitive Behavioral Therapy (CBT).

The VA offers for its PTSD patients these two forms of CBT: Cognitive Processing Therapy (CPT) and Prolonged Exposure therapy (PE). The former, in addition to breathing, relaxation, and other skills, involves changing the way a patient feels about the trauma by changing the way he or she thinks about it. The goal is to no longer let the traumatic event define the person or to limit his or her future. The latter involves the gradual approach and repeated recounting of the trauma until it no longer brings the same emotions. Another popular cognitive therapy with documented success, often used by well-trained psychologists, is called Eye Movement Desensitization and Reprocessing (EMDR) Therapy. It has similarities with the Prolonged Exposure Therapy and its objective is to help change how one reacts to the vivid memories of the trauma.

Additionally, Family Therapy is available for the whole family and can help with better communication and good, respectful relationships—a cornerstone for every household.

Sgt. Jerry's home was that kind of safe haven, a shelter, where he found security, peace, and healing for his emotions and a place of rest where he began to walk again in love, hope, and confidence.

We will never fully understand on this side of heaven why would God allow for something tragic to happen, but we can rest assured that He is always in control, that He loves us and will faithfully work out and orchestrate even the worst of our life story into a new plan and a better future.

> "For I know the plans I have for you," declares the LORD, "plans to prosper you and not to harm you, plans to give you hope and a future."
>
> —Jer. 29:11

Resources

National Center for PTSD: www.ncptsd.va.gov

The PTSD information line: (802) 296-6300

Other helpful, and comforting resources

The Healing Path: How the Hurts in Your Past Can Lead You to a More Abundant Life by Dan B. Allender. Colorado Springs: WaterBrook Press, 1999.

The Healing Word of God: Comfort, Peace & Hope. Connie Wetzell (Audio CD. "Audio Scriptures to soothe the soul")

Trauma and Recovery: The Aftermath of violence-from Domestic Abuse to Political Terror by Judith Lewis Hehrman, M.D. New York: Basic Books, 1997.

Psalm 91: God's Shield of Protection by Peggy Joyce Ruth. Lake Mary: Creation House, 2007.

Comfort from above

> The LORD is my strength and my shield; my heart trusts in him, and I am helped. My heart leaps for joy and I will give thanks to him in song.
>
> —Ps. 28:7

The LORD is my rock, my fortress and my deliverer; my God is my rock, in whom I take refuge. He is my shield and the horn of my salvation, my stronghold.
—Ps. 18:2

Though you have made me see troubles, many and bitter, you will restore my life again; from the depths of the earth you will again bring me up. You will increase my honor and comfort me once again. I will praise you with the harp for your faithfulness, O my God; I will sing praise to you with the lyre, O Holy One of Israel.
—Ps. 71:20-22

Praise be to the God and Father of our Lord Jesus Christ, the Father of compassion and the God of all comfort, who comforts us in all our troubles, so that we can comfort those in any trouble with the comfort we ourselves have received from God.
—2 Cor. 1:3-4

CHAPTER 22

RACE AND PREJUDICE

Race and Prejudice

They dress the wound of my people as though it were not
serious. Peace, peace, they say when there is no peace.
—Jer. 6:14

Politically incorrect views on greed, corruption, and race

SGT. JOSEPH COULDN'T wait to talk to me about his views on race, politics, and religion—topics he had raised during his last visit but was too sick to finish. Born in one of the Caribbean islands of black parents who are descendants of Africans forced into slavery and heavy labor in the sugarcane plantations, Joseph had no hesitation sharing with me what could easily be deemed as politically incorrect views.

Political and economic corruption

"Doctor, do you think corruption is only in third world countries? Of course not! It's also right here in the West. Right here in the developed countries of the West, big wealthy, corrupt, and greedy CEOs and companies steal from the middle class and do shady things using every loophole they can find in the law," he said. I could tell how passionate he was about the subject by his voice as he began to compare the corruption here to that in poorer nations in the world.

"The only difference between the corruption in the West and, say, African and other developing countries is in what they do with the money they loot. In the West, a lot of the obscene profits and money the companies steal using the loopholes in the law and corruption goes to the greedy CEOs and investors. But a lot of it is also invested in their own countries to create jobs for the common people, which generate taxes and income that allow us to buy our homes, health insurance, and food to feed our families. That's why, Doctor, a poor man in the West doesn't starve," he explained.

After a brief pause as if to gauge my interest, he began to describe what he considered the main difference between this type of corruption and the type found in third world countries. "My ancestors were brought as slaves from Africa to the Caribbean. I'm not trying to put my African heritage or race down, but this is what I think: corruption in Africa and other third world countries is different in this way: there the corrupt government officials, dictators, and greedy companies and people steal money, but instead of investing some of it back in their own countries to help the poor people, they choose instead, out of fear and greed, to send it out of their countries to Swiss bank accounts and other overseas investments. That's why the common man there starves and lives in poverty without a job, home, or benefits."

Religious corruption

Joseph's frustration spilled from the political realm into the spiritual realm. He shared with me his discontent with the priests who were caught in scandalous situations and found guilty of sexually abusing children. "The corruption in the Roman Catholic Church makes it hard for everybody to know Who God is. People tend to stay away from the church and God with so much corruption," he said.

Heated racial comparisons: blacks versus whites

Joseph's great passion and views on many diverse issues made conversing with him very interesting. After stating his brief view on religion, he shifted his topic to the mother of all controversial topics: black versus white race comparisons. He began to highlight what he considered as the main difference between the two races.

"As a black man, I can say that my people have no unity. We don't work together, but everyone works for his own interest only and those with knowledge and know-how don't care to educate those without it. Take for example Haiti's deposed dictator, Duvalier. He was applauded and treated like a god by the media, but look at what happened after he was no longer in power. The media suddenly went silent and didn't care to reeducate the masses of angry people or to help rebuild their destroyed self-esteem after years of being brainwashed, controlled, and suppressed. The result was that people exploded with anger and went on a rampage, unleashing their frustration and destroying all the infrastructure of the country that reminded them of Duvalier. And after all the damage was done, they looked around and realized that there was no money in the country to replace what was destroyed and fix what they had damaged."

Joseph continued with his analysis of race and differences between whites and "my own race" with more controversial statements.

"We get angry when we see someone doing better than us and if someone disagrees with us or is doing better than us we choose to fight with him or kill him. Why can't we just try to succeed like him instead of being envious and end up destroying him? But if someone is doing better than you here in the West, you just learn from him and then use this knowledge to better your life."

After a brief pause to gather his thoughts, he summarized his understanding of what he believed was the root of the problem, drawing from his own pre-army experience as a taxicab driver in the busy streets of Los Angeles.

"I believe my black race is suffering from a loss of sense of pride and self-esteem. I think this explains our lack of unity and the destruction and crime we commit against each other. The first day I started driving a cab, my friend from Africa told me not to pick up black passengers because they won't pay their cab fare at the end of the ride. He told me about this black man wearing a three-piece suit and carrying a Samsonite suitcase that he picked up from the airport. The man started shouting and screaming at him when the cab meter was running during a routine stop at the red traffic light. He then became very angry and got out of the cab at the red light and left without paying his cab fare.

"I didn't believe my friend until I picked up a black man from the hospital. I knew it was bad news and that I wasn't going to be paid the moment he started to strike up a long conversation with me. He only gave me a portion of the fare at the end of the ride and told me to wait for him outside his high-rise apartment complex for the rest, but he never showed up.

"Look, for example, at tips. White people tip, but growing up I was never taught to tip a waitress or a cab driver," he said in frustration.

He then looked directly at me and offered his firm belief as to what the remedy ought to be. "We black people must be honest with ourselves. We must get rid of our ghetto and poverty mentally, especially after we finish our college degrees and begin to make money. Our low self-esteem, anger, and pride must go. You can't have success with these kinds of attitudes," he said, resting his case.

It was the end of the lunch break and time for Joseph to go. He picked up his Kevlar, adjusted his body armor, and parted with these powerful words of hope: "We must be united and start to care for one

RACE AND PREJUDICE

another, to forgive, to let go of the past. I agree with what you said about God; we can't change on our own. We need someone bigger than us to help us change. We need God. "

After he left, a thought crossed my mind, *Every skin color is so beautiful and shows God's great workmanship. Every different shade is painted miraculously on each one of our bodies by the very hand of the Creator.*

Like a master painter, He created a spectacular array of colors on our bodies that can't be naturally changed and He left it to us to choose the color we want for our hearts. To God, real beauty lies within—in a heart colored with His divine brush in shades of compassion, love, and goodness.

In God's eyes, no skin color is better or superior to others, for all are special and equal in His sight. To God, what separates us and makes us "the apple of His eye" is nothing but the color of our hearts.

> Hope deferred makes the heart sick, but a longing fulfilled is a tree of life.
> —Prov. 13:12

Dealing with prejudice

> "And who is my neighbor?"
> —Luke 6:29

Soon after giving Sgt. Mohammed the medical instructions for his severe allergic reaction, we briefly exchanged views on race and culture. Given his Middle Eastern origin, I was very curious to know more about his personal experience as a US soldier.

"I joined the army soon after I became an American citizen," he said. "I got tired of working for big companies after working years without getting promoted."

Mohammed's journey as a civilian in the workforce was marred by tense moments of uncertainty about his job security and "always keeping two eyes open for other jobs." Leaving one job to go to a more secure one when he could no longer tolerate the intensity of prejudice and opposition became a routine part of his career experience until he joined the military.

"There are people who won't like you because of your color, race, or religion. I learned how to smile when I leave a job I don't like to start a new one; it's not good to burn any bridges," he explained.

"So Mohammed, how do you deal with prejudice?" I asked.

"It's always hard for me to know when I'm being discriminated against. My first reaction is to want to run away from the environment as soon as possible. But then I wait and try my best to be a team player. When the pressure becomes too much for me, I start to quietly look for another job. I also make sure to get support from family and friends who care about me," he said.

Fortunately, Mohammed's views about the attitude in the military when it comes to racial issues were quite similar to those I had routinely heard from other soldiers—it was a much welcome change for him.

"Things are much better in the service. In the military, the system is set up in such a way where you can go up the chain of command, as high as the commander-in-chief, to appeal your case if you're discriminated against," he said, confidently. "That's why, Doctor, I've decided to make the military my career," he said as he walked confidently out of the exam room.

After he left, I reflected on his unique story. There he was, a man preparing to go to a war that will require his total commitment to a nation that had recently opened her arms wide, much like in the old days of Ellis Island where the Statue of Liberty still stands strong, to him, to me, and to people of every creed, culture, color, and religion. This once-in-a-lifetime opportunity is given to foreigners from across the globe in multiple citizenship ceremonies throughout America, in exchange for one single thing—a pledge of loyalty and allegiance to America, the flag that stands for the Republic, and the strong foundation the founding fathers built it on: "One nation under God, indivisible, with Liberty and Justice for all." Generations of Americans, both born here and naturalized, have paid with the precious blood of their children on many battlefields to guard and protect America and to preserve the solid foundation laid down by her wise founding fathers.

Mohammed, as a US soldier, is joining that long line of Americans from generations past, who were willing to be loyal to her even unto death. Like all the early Ellis Island immigrants to America, their children, and their children's children, he too has individually found the great wisdom and joy that comes from America's fair exchange—the blessing of dreams accomplished and freedom and liberty in America in exchange for his uncompromising loyalty and allegiance. This is great wisdom that I pray each man and woman reciting the pledge of allegiance in naturalization ceremonies across America will live by.

As immigrants who are now US citizens with full privileges and voting power, we need to remember that we're not here to change or to weaken the very foundation that America's founding fathers have built. In the first place, it is this great foundation that has given us the opportunity to find freedom and liberty in this great land. Instead, we should always be thankful for this "one nation under God," respect, and fulfill our pledge to America—upholding and strengthening the godly foundation upon which it was built.

> "Which of these three do you think was a neighbor to the man who fell into the hands of robbers?" The expert in the law replied, "The one who had mercy on him." Jesus told him, "Go and do likewise."
> —Luke 10:36-37

I'll die for my friend

> No man is an island unto himself; every man is a part of the whole. Therefore never send to know for whom the bell tolls it tolls for thee.
> —John Donne 1572-1631

Soon after listening to Sgt. Isaac's lungs and assuring him that he didn't have pneumonia, I asked him about whether he has had experience with prejudice in America. Twenty-eight years ago, Isaac moved from his birthplace in one of the Caribbean islands and settled down with his family in New York. He talked proudly about his family's African heritage, his life journey in America, leading to being a US soldier on his way to combat, and about race relations in America.

"It's America, Doc. You see problems with race everywhere, even in the military. We're in America, right?"

For the next few minutes, he talked about his three hundred-soldier unit with "only eleven blacks from Eritrea, Sudan, Haiti, and other ethnic minorities" and the prejudices that some of them have experienced from their fellow soldiers.

"Don't take me wrong, Doc. You can't get away with prejudice in the military like in civilian life. There is always someone higher in the chain of command that you can go to if someone discriminates against you. But you occasionally find a redneck from a small town who has never seen a black face before and has never been exposed to other races. My Eritrean buddy got mad at a commander last week because he showed favoritism to a white soldier. He can't get away with that here," he said.

"What about you, Isaac? How do you deal with prejudice?"

"My best friend, John, is white. We all have the same blood color and feel the same pain when we get hurt. I know my friend will cover my back when we go to combat, and he knows that I'll cover his," he said as he walked towards the exam room door, body armor and Kevlar in hands.

I saw Isaac two other times before he mobilized with his unit. He left me with simple yet profound words that reminded me of how a human mind filled with prejudice becomes sadly blind to what is most important—the great joy and rewards found in walking in unity and love.

Two thousand years ago, Jesus Christ said to a generation like ours needing a life direction, "A great command I leave you, love one another," and when asked He summarized the whole commandments with this sentence, "Love God from the bottom of your heart, and love your neighbor." He said that our neighbor can be a Samaritan, a stranger, or someone of a different faith, culture, or ethnic background that might be viewed as inferior by others.

It's only with such genuine, color-blind love and compassion towards others that prejudice ceases, withers, and dies.

You shall love your neighbor as yourself.

—Matt. 22:39

I'm just American

> Make every effort to live in peace with all men and to be holy.
> —Heb. 12:14

Soon after I finished Sgt. Bridgette's physical exam, she thanked me and began to answer my questions about her views on racial relationships in America. She was born in western Europe—her mother was from the Philippines and her father was an African American. Bridgette's first encounter with prejudice in America occurred when she was ten.

"I was born in Germany and spent the first part of my childhood there. I was color-blind and didn't see any distinction between the races. That ended when I came to the United States and heard for the first time a girl calling another one a 'white b----.' That was a shock to me," she said.

"How did your concept of race change after that incident?" I asked.

"This color is brown, brown, not black," she said, her voice full of passion. "The type of hair I have should not define my race. I'm tired, Doctor, of being called African American. Dad has also been called African American. Why not just American? We are all Americans."

Unfortunately, Bridgette's childhood experience was marred by the confusion she experienced dealing with the new reality in her life—prejudice.

"I never thought of myself as less because my color was different. I never paid attention to skin colors. I still remember the day I asked Mom about the meaning of all of that. I was shocked and hurt to know that some people look down at me because of my skin color. It took me years to try to understand that and I still don't."

"So Bridgette, as an adult, how do you see this whole thing?"

"You know what, Doctor? I really like people. I don't care where they come from or what color they are. We should treat everyone equally, not based on their skin color. Some people just don't know how to use their hearts."

Yet despite the sad reality of racial discrimination Bridgett discovered when she first came to America, she "used her heart" to forgive those who offended her and to not dwell on bitterness.

"You know, the same person you don't care about because of his skin color may be the only one who offers you help when you desperately need it. No one should judge others because of the color of their skin. Only God should judge us," she said.

Right before she left, she said these memorable words. "We should all let go of the past; whatever happened in the past has already passed. You know, Doctor, it takes me more muscles to frown at someone than to smile. I want to keep smiling."

> From one man he made every nation of men that they should inhabit the whole earth; and he determined the times set for them and the exact places where they should live.
> —Acts 17:26

Jaffar: a Pakistani-American soldier

> If it is possible, as far as it depends on you, live at peace with everyone.
> —Rom. 12:18

"It was hard, Doctor, to convince my family of my decision to join the US army," said twenty-one-year-old private Jaffar. He, his parents, and two brothers moved from their birthplace in Pakistan to America seventeen years ago. Despite the extensive culture changes, the family remained committed to its religious and cultural roots.

"My decision shocked them, but I'm very independent, and they finally accepted my choice," he said with a distinct New York accent. To Jaffar, joining the military was one of the best life decisions he ever made. After experiencing his share of prejudices, setbacks, and lost promotions in the civilian world, joining the army was a God-sent direction that has changed his life and exponentially increased his self-confidence.

"It's not that you don't sometimes run into prejudice, but in the military it's hard to get away with it the way you can in the civilian world. Joining the army made me so much more confident and sure of myself," he said with a strong voice.

Jaffar came to see me a few other times before his mobilization to Afghanistan. He always carried a Kevlar in his hand and a thankful, appreciative attitude in his heart. We talked about his family, his dream of finishing his higher education, the emotions that result from experiencing prejudice and injustice in his American journey, and his pride of being an American soldier.

After my last encounter with Jaffar, I thought about his emotional journey through the minefield of discrimination and prejudice he had shared with me—a journey shared by many others. The heartless, dark, and unloving experiences of prejudice that he experienced temporarily shook his self-esteem and sense of value, but thankfully, his military experience restored his self-confidence and renewed his sense of self-worth.

His story reminded me that prejudice, cruelty, and all forms of injustice against any man or woman, boy or girl because of color, race, faith, age, looks—or for being different or disabled—are like a deadly poison. The antidote is not anger, hate, or rage. But it is found in a growing faith in the fundamental truth that we are created in God's image. In God's love, acceptance, and forgiveness we find the only antidote to our souls for injustices suffered.

It's only with such magnitude of divine love and assurance to our wounded hearts that the deleterious long-term effects of prejudice and injustice can be neutralized and reversed. And this is not only in our lives, but also in the lives of our innocent children and vulnerable adolescents who are in desperate need of freedom from its spiritual, mental, and emotional chains.

> Dear children, let us not love with words…but with actions and in truth.
> —1 John 3:18

Race is *not* the problem

> There is neither Jew nor Greek, slave nor free, male nor female, for you are all one in Christ Jesus.
> —Gal. 3:28

In an era where a number of unethical, corrupt business leaders have almost brought the giant US economy to its knees and at a time when America surprised the world by choosing its first African American president, much of what Sgt. Joseph said about the hot topics of business corruption and race in one of the previous stories titled, "Politically incorrect views" seems very pertinent.

Shortly after Joseph's visit, I had the opportunity to talk to Sgt. Adam, who was also featured in a previous story titled, "Leadership from the inside out." Adam, an exceptionally caring and talented commander of his big combat-bound unit, was in my opinion the best candidate to answer more of my questions about race relationships. Without mentioning any names, I shared with him Sgt. Joseph's views and asked for his own point of view. Adam, with his pleasant personality, was very enthusiastic about sharing his opinion with me at the end of his physical exam.

"Any person of any color or race can behave badly, refuse to pay his cab fare, or get out angrily from it at a red traffic light. A man doesn't behave badly because of his skin color. This has to do with the kind of home environment he grew up in. A person of any color—black or white—will do wrong things if he didn't grow up in a good home that teaches about God and doing the right things," he said.

His words were so simple but yet so profound. Sadly, it's so common and spontaneous to attribute bad behaviors to someone's skin color or ethnicity instead of his or her childhood home and background that lacked discipline and the wisdom of God-fearing teaching.

"Dr. Hanna, I'm a black man who was brought up in a home founded on the teaching of the Bible. My siblings and I were disciplined and taught to be honest, to love and respect others, and to pay my cab fare," he said, displaying his characteristic friendly smile.

Adam and his wife decided to apply the same moral principles to their home and family. Together they transformed it into a safe haven for children of multiple ethnicities and backgrounds, who regularly come to play with their own children.

"We take turns watching the children and we take them with our children to church. Our hope is to see them grow up to do the right things in life," he said, his voice filled with passion.

Soon after Adam left to join his unit, a thought crossed my mind—what about those who never had the opportunity of growing up in a good home and those who grew up in a moral and godly home but strayed from their roots and strong foundations?

The only hopeful, and I believe truthful, answer I could think of was that it is never, ever too late to start building a new home on the solid foundation of God's reality and love. A home built on the reverential fear of Almighty God. Nor it is too late to come back home to the good, solid foundation you might've wandered far away from and start anew.

> In the beginning was the Word, and the Word was with God, and the Word was God. He was with God in the beginning. Through him all things were made; without him nothing was made that has been made. In him was life and that life was the light of men. The light shines in the darkness, but the darkness has not understood it.
> —John 1:1-3

> Therefore, if anyone is in Christ, he is a new creation; old things have passed away; behold, all things have become new.
> —2 Cor. 5:17 NKJV

Soldiers, ambassadors in military uniforms

> My name will be great among the nations, from the rising to the setting of the sun.
> —Mal. 1:11

How a midwestern soldier from the small Ohio town of Lima (aka Lost In Middle America) or from Appalachia or a small scantily populated suburban city survives the cultural shock of a foreign country with its different spicy foods, language, and customs always intrigued me. Somehow, someway soldiers from across America end up sharing gladly a dish of pita bread, falafel and fava beans with people they can barely understand in places they've never seen before. In essence, they become ambassadors and bridge builders, succeeding where politics and politicians often fail.

Sgt. First Class Ernie was one of those "ambassadors," who represented his country well. "I trained Iraqi soldiers so they can defend their country. In essence, I was training them to take over my job," he said and then added, "Iraq is a beautiful country with rich history and culture. I made a lot of friends there and would love to go back there, maybe in ten years, not as a soldier but a tourist."

Other soldiers like Major Allen, who had just returned from his tour of duty to Iraq, shared with me the same sentiment. "They cooked and brought me traditional meals, and I ate from the same plate with my Iraqi friends. As an American, I felt it was important that I respect their habits and customs. I plan to finish a degree in international studies one of these days and go back there," he said.

Another soldier shared his excitement about his upcoming deployment to Kosovo. "What a great opportunity to meet people of all cultures. I'm planning to invite many of the international soldiers working with our unit for pot-luck dinners so we can get to know each other," he said.

These soldiers and many others from all across rural, urban, and suburban America seem to enthusiastically bring the heart of America, with its Judeo-Christian ethics, Thanksgiving, Christmas, baseball, hot dogs, and the Fourth of July, to nations and peoples of different religions and traditions. They endure hardships of all kinds in their soldiers-ambassadors' role. In one hand, they carry loaded ready-to-fire M16s, and in the other, a green olive branch—bringing war to some and peace to others.

> Endure hardship with us like a good soldier of Christ Jesus.
> —2 Tim. 2:3

CHAPTER 23

RAPE

Rape

Blessed are those who mourn, for they will be comforted.
—Matt. 5:4

Dark, lingering memories and living again

AS THE SOUND of Mozart's classical piano concerto from my CD player filled the exam room, Sgt. First Class Stephanie, a short-haired, beautiful brunette on her final training days before mobilizing to Afghanistan, seemed to be deeply lost in her thoughts. Soon after the medical exam, we began to talk.

"You like Mozart?" I asked, wondering whether the richness of his music has triggered in her an old cherished memory.

She took a deep breath, and what she said next took me totally by surprise.

"I still remember that cold night twenty years ago when four men took turns raping me in a bar while a loud song played on the juke box over and over and over again. I went to the bar that night with one of them—they were all supposed to be my friends. All I remember from that night was that song. I listened to it again and again, the whole night," she said, holding back her tears.

After that tragic night, Stephanie was in a state of shock as she found herself engulfed in a dark abyss of utter shame and despair. And much like many rape victims, she decided to keep what had happened a deeply hidden secret. But a few weeks later, her life got more complicated and entangled. "I found out I was pregnant," she explained.

The news of her pregnancy was devastating to her in more ways than one and brought into the open another dark secret she could no longer hide. "I was only fifteen at the time and my stepfather had been molesting me for some time before the rape. I felt so lost. I didn't know who was the father—one of the four or my stepfather," she said, closing her eyes.

The baby's father turned out to be one of the four "friends," none of whom were brought to justice. It was almost fourteen years after the birth of her daughter, Amber, that Stephanie finally agreed to let her meet with him for the very first time.

"He was married with children and wanted to meet her. He was very remorseful, and she desperately wanted to meet her biological father," she explained.

Stephanie eventually decided to move forward with her life and to forgive him, her stepfather, and her ex-husband who had subjected her to many years of ruthlessness and abuse. Yet despite her years of abuse and tragedy, she vowed to remain positive, to live and not die. She finished college, fought for a peaceful home environment for her daughter, and got remarried to the "most loving man," who treated her well and her daughter as his own.

Years later, the memories of that tragic night and the abuse by her stepfather have slowly faded, except for the silent and dormant memory of a loud song that reminds her today of the long walk of survival, healing, and her victory over the worst of life adversities.

In her full military gear, carrying a Kevlar in one hand and goggles in the other, she was now looking forward with eyes of hope to her new mission in Afghanistan and to coming back home soon to her "most loving man" and her precious daughter.

To me, how she overcame those adversities and lived to talk about them was nothing short of a miracle. Her decision to forgive and not to dwell on her past painful experiences made me pause and wonder. "Stephanie, you've been through a living hell. What helped you to get through it?" I asked, looking at her light brown eyes.

"You know, Doctor, a lot of women choose to keep these things a secret they keep buried for the rest of their lives. But I believe the hell I had to go through has helped me to be a wiser and a better person."

Her words reminded me of one of my favorite verses, Romans 8:28, "And we know that in all things God works for the good of those who love him, who have been called according to his purpose."

She told me that the turbulent journey of her life from the dark pit of despair to a new life of hope is indeed described by the words of this verse. As I repeated the words to her, I could see a smile on her face. The comfort that many a soul throughout the ages has found in them, she herself seemed to find as she reflected with me on their deeper meaning. God remains in control and with us even in the worst of our suffering. He will "work out for our good" every tear and every hurt we have gone through when we seek Him and determine to live "according to His purposes" for us.

It was time for Stephanie to go and join the rest of her unit. "Thanks, Dr. Hanna, for listening," she said and gave me a big hug.

That was the last time I saw her. She left for Afghanistan with her unit few days after the visit.

The Spirit of the Lord GOD is upon Me,
Because the LORD has anointed Me
To preach good tidings to the poor;
He has sent Me to heal the brokenhearted,
To proclaim liberty to the captives,
And the opening of the prison to those who are bound;
To proclaim the acceptable year of the LORD,
And the day of vengeance of our God;
To comfort all who mourn,
To console those who mourn in Zion,
To give them beauty for ashes,
The oil of joy for mourning,
The garment of praise for the spirit of heaviness;
That they may be called trees of righteousness,
The planting of the LORD, that He may be glorified.
—Isa. 61:1-3 NKJV

The LORD is a refuge for the oppressed, a stronghold in times of trouble.
—Ps. 9:9

Life in the pit, the escape

I am feeble and utterly crushed; I groan in anguish of heart.
—Ps. 38:8

She entered the exam room with her eyes covered with large, dark glasses and quietly sat on the examination table. I wondered if she purposely wanted her eyes hidden behind those shades.

She had come to the Troop Medical Clinic with emotional and physical complaints, but soon after the physical exam Sgt. Tracy began to share the memory of a most traumatic event in her life.

"We worked together in the past, at the same base. I was really glad to see him when I was reassigned to go back. I thought we were good friends," she said as she shared how a friendly visit with an old friend turned into a vicious rape.

Tracy shared with me how he led her deceptively to his off base hotel room, asking her to wait for him in the room as he claimed that he was getting ready in the bathroom. "I never thought he would do that. I ran to the medical center at the base after he raped me and asked the doctor to test me for every STD, but I was too scared to tell anyone about what had happened. I wasn't supposed to be off base in the first place," she said, securing her dark glasses on her face.

The impact of that crime shattered Tracy's sense of self-worth and brought flashbacks of old, bottled, painful feelings and an avalanche of long-forgotten memories. "A lot of old memories that I thought were all but forgotten came back to me—my brother molesting me, Dad wanting to sexually assault me and then claiming he was drunk when I pushed him back, being raped when I was sixteen, and then having an abortion," she said, her voice nearly a whisper.

She removed her shades for a brief moment and began to wipe away the tears from her red, swollen eyes. Choosing to share those dark memories must have been very hard for her, but for some reason she wanted to and seemed to find comfort in my listening and undivided attention.

"After the, assault, I stopped caring. I was in so much pain and felt like nothing in this life matters any more. I stopped caring," she repeated.

Life in general had never been the same for Tracy since that dark night at the hotel. She never told anyone, including her husband, of the assault and began to suffer emotionally, including having an overwhelming feeling of burnout in her marriage. She saw herself becoming increasingly impatient with her husband, separating from him and falling into a slimy, endless pit of infidelity and a succession of relational unfaithfulness in search of her bruised sense of value and her lost sense of worth and significance.

"Some of the men I went out with said they were in love with me, many others just wanted to have fun once in a while away from their wives, and some others wanted to leave their wives for me. But I could care less for any one of them, Doctor. I just feel so lost, confused," she said in desperation.

Then, like a determined soldier fighting a just and righteous battle, she lifted her head, looked up high, and said with a warrior's voice, "It's not fair...not fair. So many women who were raped feel so much shame and are scared to death to talk about it. They keep it to themselves and never tell anybody about their feelings. My neighbor did that and ended up in a mental hospital. You know what questions women get asked? 'What clothes were you wearing? What did you say or do to cause it?' This is like blaming the woman for being raped. It's just not easy being a woman. It's a man's world…it's a man's world."

Tracy's powerful words made me ponder on the iceberg of deeply buried and painful scars and sense of shame that each of the women she referred to silently endure. *Could I be the first and only one that Tracy felt safe enough emotionally to remove the dark shades and the thick walls surrounding her bruised heart and talk to*, I silently wondered.

"Tracy, I believe love heals. God's love can heal our wounds and your scars," I said, overcome by a sense of compassion and praying to find the right words to comfort her.

With tears flowing from her beautiful eyes, she said, "Thank you, Doctor Hanna, thank you," and began to share a story I will forever remember.

"A friend of mine once told me this story: A father once gave his son, who was always doing bad things and saying hurtful words to others, a hammer and many nails. He told him to go and nail each one of them completely on a wooden fence. After the son did what he was told to do, his father told him to pull each one of the nails out of the fence. He wanted to teach him that hurting others with words and deeds is like those nails going through the wood; they hurt the feelings as they go in, and leave a scar in the heart that will need to heal just like the nail on that wooden fence.

"I believe that too," she said. "My scars can only heal with love. I need God's love to heal."

That was the first and last time I saw Tracy. She left the camp soon after this visit to start her next military assignment. I wonder at times if she has finally found healing for her bruised heart and healing for her soul's scars with the power of love, God's love.

"A bruised reed He will not break, and a smoldering wick He will not snuff out. In faithfulness he will bring forth justice" (Isa. 42:3). "The LORD is close to the brokenhearted and saves those who are crushed in spirit" (Ps. 34:18).

> He will wipe every tear from their eyes. There will be no more death or mourning or crying or pain, for the old order of things has passed away.
>
> —Rev. 21:4

CHAPTER 24

ROMANCE

Romance

But one thing I do: Forgetting what is behind and straining toward what is ahead.
—Phil. 3:13

Mistakes

"I FOUND THE last two months here at the base my best opportunity ever to just rest and reflect on my life," said Sgt. Brian, answering my question about how much his life had changed since his deployment.

"Doctor, I am just glad to get away from so many relationships and commitments that are doing me no good. I plan to move to Indiana after returning from Iraq. I like it here, and it's going to be for the best if I stay away from my ex-wife."

"She must be a controlling woman," I said, guessing.

"Very controlling," he immediately responded. "My seven- and eleven-year-old boys have lived through all of this and saw me working three jobs for two and half years just to afford my child support and pay for my rent, car, and food. For many years she made it impossible for me to see them. Now that I'm deploying, she has finally decided to allow me more time with them."

"I have heard plenty of stories like this," I said, acknowledging his plight.

At that moment his cell phone rang. "Sorry, Doc. Excuse me," he said as he reached for his pocket, checking the caller ID before answering it. "Oh, no, what the hell does she want now?" he said in frustration as he turned off the phone.

"Oops! Must be the ex-wife," I remarked.

"No, Doc. That was my second wife calling. We've been married for one and half years and we're going through divorce now."

"Do you guys have any children? So what happened?"

"No children. She was controlling too. She wanted me to quit my eleven-year military career. I told her no, and so she decided to leave," he said, reflecting on his second broken marriage.

He then added, with a survivor's smile on his face, "I have finally found someone new in my life who is also military. She understands me and what I go through and prays before meals! I can't believe it! Where was she all this time in my life?"

Brian's journey through many mistakes and misery in pursuit of a Mrs. Right in his life made me wonder about whether he has learned something from his painful experiences that can be helpful to others. I asked him about that.

"I have learned a lot from my mistakes. I would tell anyone to be careful and judge the other person very well before making the next major move. My best advice is to forget the past and to move on. The past is past and you've got to judge the person by what he or she is today," he said as he began to walk towards the door.

Truly wise words from a man who has survived his falls and learned from his mistakes, I thought.

Indeed, just like Brian we can all grow and mature from our failures and brokenness if we dwell on the hope of the future instead of the hurts of the dead, old past.

Like a skillful conductor, God allows strategic suffering and hardships to come to our lives. Some are the consequences of our own choices and others are not from a fault of our own, to help us know Him, grow in faith and character, and begin to hope in Him and not in a vanishing world with its fleeting relationships, positions, possessions, and obsessions.

> Not only so but we also rejoice in our sufferings because we know that suffering produces perseverance, perseverance, character; and character, hope. And hope does not disappoint us.
> —Rom. 3:3-5

The "wicked ring" story

> How beautiful you are my darling!
> —Song of Songs 1:15

Twenty-two-year-old Private Steven looked very embarrassed as I proceeded to examine the bruised tip of his penis.

"I just came last night from Iraq, sir. I got hurt in the plane."

"So what happened?" I smiled, wondering about what kind of story I was about to hear.

He started to laugh and explained how air turbulence during the plane ride bumped his organ against the front of the toilet seat as he was sitting comfortably on it (the small toilet seat).

That explained the minor trauma and after assuring him that it was only a minor bruise that would heal, we began to talk about his coming home after a long deployment.

"I bet you can't wait to go back home," I said.

"Can't wait to see my fiancée. We're getting married next year," he said, hardly containing his excitement.

"Man, you must really miss her," I said.

For the next few minutes, Steven forgot about his bruised body part and began talking about his love story and one of his dearest memories—the night he proposed to his bride to be.

"I got her this wicked, shiny ring with a wicked price tag, a wicked good ring," he said proudly.

Armed with his wicked ring, Steven decided to do the right thing and ask for his girlfriend's hand in marriage the old-fashioned way. "I took her father to the jewelry store to see the ring and then asked for his permission to marry his daughter. I asked her mom too."

"You did that! Good job. That was cool, really good," I said as I thought about the high standard that he was setting for his bachelor friends around him.

"That was about showing him respect, Doc. He is part of her life, and I needed his permission. It just makes things much easier for our relationship."

After securing their permission, Steven surprised his woman with the wicked ring.

"I took her to Portsmouth to a very fancy restaurant on the waterfront. I ordered a big vanilla ice cream bowl and hid the ring inside it. It was so wicked shiny and as soon as she found it she said, yes."

A beautiful story of love and chivalry that I never thought would end on such a romantic note, considering his presenting complaint, I thought.

Before leaving the exam room, I reminded him to apply antibiotic cream to the bruised tip of his private part as I reached out to the small medication tubes in the top drawer of the medical supplies closet. To my amusement, next to the antibiotics was a handful of similarly sized two percent lidocaine lubricating anesthetic gel tubes.

"Hey, Steven, I am definitely giving you a couple of the antibiotic cream tubes and not the lidocaine anesthetic; you definitely don't want to numb it up," I said, smiling, as I pushed the lidocaine gel tubes away.

"Oh, thanks! You are a funny doctor," he said as he shook my hand and began to laugh. The ride about to take him and few soldiers from his unit to home sweet home was leaving soon and he was not going to miss it.

My lover is mine and I am his.
—Song of Songs 2:16

CHAPTER 25

SHINING LIKE A DIAMOND

Shining Like a Diamond
Hunter and Prey

Charm is deceptive, and beauty is fleeting; but a woman who fears the LORD is to be praised.
—Prov. 31:30

Hunter and prey

> Do not be misled: Bad company corrupts good character.
> —1 Cor. 15:33

TWENTY-SEVEN-YEAR-OLD SGT. BRUCE entered the room and pointed at his groin as soon as he sat on the exam table.

"I've a rash here, Doctor," he said, pointing at a few small red spots.

After examining the area, I assured him that it was a bacterial skin infection, folliculitis, and not genital herpes, to his great relief.

Soon after I assured him of the diagnosis, he began to tell me about his busy sexual history with a very long exposé of his previous conquests and his own personal analytical view of women. As a physician who needs a good sexual history when diagnosing a potential STD, I got way more information than I bargained for.

"Women are morally easy, Doc. I can't begin to count the number of women I hunted. It's all about the hunt, Doc," he declared.

"What makes you think they are?" I asked, puzzled by his statement.

He responded with more of the jungle imagery depicting himself as a hunter and the women he hunted as his prey, much like a hungry, roaring lion, hiding and patiently waiting to devour unsuspecting prey.

"Getting a woman in bed is easy. I always felt like kicking a woman out of my bed in the morning. I never wanted to be close to them after sex, and so I just went to a different room. I lose all interest in them."

Fortunately, my day was quiet and with all the sick soldiers who had come in the morning seen and released, I had plenty of time on my hands to ask, listen, and probe a little more into his thinking.

With his easygoing and charming personality, he began to tell me the "secret of the trade," the tools and tactics he has repeatedly used in the past to conduct his hunts.

"I divide women into different groups. First, there are those who grew up not experiencing the love of a father and looking desperately for someone to love them, and then there are those women who just want to have fun and sleep around. There are also those women who will do it with anyone for drugs and alcohol. I've always been careful with this last bunch," he said.

He noticed the puzzled look on my face and with a big smile began to explain how he executed his predatory strategy on the unsuspecting women.

"I used to go out with three women at the same time. None of them knew of the others. One was easy and loved to drink. The other one wanted me to take her to nice, classy places. The third one was Jewish and was deeply in love with me. All of them wanted commitment, but I was just there for the hunt."

Bruce's explanation of how he conducted the hunt sounded again to me like that hungry jungle lion hiding in thick bushes and swiftly devouring its victims before they ever have an inkling of what happened to them.

"I would find out first what a woman likes, what's interesting to her, and what she wants to hear. I then make sure to say the things she wants to hear and do the things she likes. I did my bad boy act with the girls who like bad boys and my intellectual, smart college kid talk with the college girls. I always made sure my women friends introduce me and say a good word about me to their female friends. That usually worked the best for me because the girls tend to trust their female friends and I usually ended up taking them out," he said.

As I listened to him, I began to wonder about how many women who had trusted him ended up being his sexual prey. How many had fallen to his suave style and manipulative skills, and how many suffered emotionally, physically, and spiritually when they realized they were reduced to objects of pleasure, left to face pregnancy alone, led to abortions, used, hurt, and left spiritually confused about their value and life purpose by the time he completed his hunting.

"Bruce, a lot of the women who were 'easy' to you were probably wounded or molested, or raped, abandoned, and abused when they were children and teenagers. Many might've never experienced the love, acceptance, and security of having a father who cares for them. Every one of them dreams of having a home and a family one day and of finding true love. All that can also make them vulnerable and an easy prey for someone whose intention is just to have sex. Don't you think so?" I asked, wondering about his answer.

To my surprise, Bruce nodded his head in agreement and began to list the negative consequences of the very lifestyle he had once actively led.

"You're right doctor. I worried a lot about catching STDs and about the jail baits who swear they're eighteen but they aren't. Getting a woman pregnant and taking her for an abortion didn't feel good. I also hated when a woman rejected me after trying everything to go out with her."

"Bruce, let me ask a question: what if someone does the same thing to your sister or one of your female relatives?"

My question surprised him and changed the whole course of our conversation as he suddenly adopted a more serious tone and a caring attitude.

"Doctor, I've two nieces who go to private schools and are quite disciplined. I tell them, 'Don't be like Uncle Bruce. Don't follow his footsteps and do what he did before.' I'm teaching them how to recognize a predator when they see one. I'll kick in the face anyone who wants to mess with them," he said. "I tell them, 'The party life ain't for girls like you' and that they better stay away from men who cuss a lot, use the F word, drink, and smoke pot because these men won't be bringing money back home," he continued.

Talking about his nieces seemed to bring out the nicer and gentler side of Bruce. He began to talk about his girlfriend, whom he "cheated on a few times" but finally decided to marry after his return from his current deployment, and his dream of starting a family.

"She will be waiting for me when I get back," he said.

Witnessing his transformation from a hunter and predator to a lover was a bit of a surprise to me. For the next few minutes, I asked him about his childhood, his family, and lessons learned from his experiences.

"I grew up in the streets, Doc. I learned there how to fight to protect myself and how to say the right words to get out of trouble. It upsets me to see how in our society the role of a father is not respected. I had no father to look up to and, you know, kids whose parents no longer care but start to baby them and stop asking where she was and who're his friends end up in the streets, like me," he said.

"Bruce, you took advantage of a lot of women who were hurt and looking for love. Now that you are not doing that, what advice do you have for women to avoid getting themselves involved with the wrong men?" I asked.

"You're right, a lot of the women I knew were feeling lonely and desperate for love. Even the ones who seem to only want sex want to be loved.

"I'm now telling young girls "Wait. The longer you wait, the more men will wait for you. The more sex you have when you're young, the more men will stop respecting you. Your body will be unhealthy and messed up, and the time you spend messing around will be lost from your life forever."

He paused for a few minutes and added a few more words, showing the paradigm shift in his thinking.

"I tell them if they want to marry a doctor or a lawyer or someone else with education, they need to wait because if they don't, they will end up being single women raising four children by themselves. How many doctors or lawyers will want to marry them? Doctor, who is going to take a single mom with four children on vacation? Not a doctor. Not a lawyer," he said.

"What about the guys? What do you tell the young men who major in hunting women for fun?"

"What I tell them is, 'Stop sleeping around if you don't want to pay child support for the rest of your lives. That pretty much scares a lot of them. Many years of paying child support really sucks; I know how that feels."

I was still curious about Bruce's major transformation from that of a hunter to a mentor. I wondered if he had found religion along the way as he actively engaged in his old lifestyle. I shared with him my view of God as the Creator of all things, including sex, and asked for his opinion.

"You know, Bruce, I believe God created the miracle of sex. He intended for us to enjoy it with the right person, at the right time, and in the safety and security of a committed and loving marriage relationship," I said and waited, expecting some protest from him.

To my surprise, he didn't disagree but offered instead a passionate defense of his own faith.

"You know, Doctor, I've my own issues with the Catholic Church—the priests' scandals and all the other stuff. But the real problem with our society is taking religion out of the classroom and teaching stuff like homosexuality is okay. School kids need to be taught from an early age about the church, religion, morality, and what's right and wrong and the consequences of their behavior," he said.

It was time for him to join his unit for more late-morning training. "Thanks, Doc. I enjoyed the conversation," he said, smiling, and left me wondering about his colorful personality, the like of which I'd never seen before—a hunter turned mentor.

Bruce's story opened my eyes to the reality of how vitally important is parental guidance to a child and how destructive is its lack. His parents' absence, specifically his father's, drastically altered the course of his life. Miraculously, after a long journey in the wilderness, he finally settled down with a woman he loved and found the beauty of true love and commitment, virtues that escaped him for so long. The seed of confusion, personal sins, and sins against others that once grew and mushroomed in the soil of his heart died and gave way to a new seed of passion and spiritual zeal to help others as lost today as he once was.

Two weeks after his visit, Bruce came to see me before leaving for combat. He looked very upbeat and ready for the biggest challenge and fight of his life.

> Do not be deceived, God is not mocked; for whatever a man sows, that he will also reap.
>
> —Gal. 6:7 NKJV

Abstinence war

After repeatedly assuring nineteen-year-old Private Brooke, who had just returned from the theater of operations, that the bump on her vaginal area was an infected hair follicle, she thanked me and began to tell about her reasons for choosing to remain a virgin.

"I want to be in love before having sex. A lot of girls I know felt pressured to do it but not me," she said proudly.

"How're you going to know that the guy you finally decide to get sexually active with really loves you?" I asked as I thought about the constant pressure and temptations a beautiful woman like her probably faces every day from the predominantly male soldiers around her.

"Well, I plan to wait a year before I get involved, just to be sure," she answered confidently.

"Okay, but what if he passes the one-year probation period very well, only to leave you for someone else after you get involved," I asked, thinking about the many brokenhearted and unexpectedly pregnant, alone, and confused young patients I've routinely seen in my medical career.

Interestingly, my question took her by surprise, and for a moment she was silent, as if pondering for the first time the painful possibility of the breakup of a future love affair that she hoped would include "living happily ever after."

"You know, my best friend is also a virgin. She told me that she wants to wait till she gets married. She is a Christian," she said, comparing her friend's spiritual motive of preserving her virginity to her own motive.

For the next few minutes, she talked with great admiration about her friend, whom she viewed as role model. It was easy for me to see how this friend's decision to remain celibate until her wedding day had influenced Brooke's life and challenged her to newer, harder, and higher standards.

"I enjoyed our conversation," she said with a big smile as she left the exam room.

Will she continue to resist the peer pressure she will face, and will she one day subscribe to her Christian friend's spiritual motives for remaining celibate? I wondered.

I could see how both of them were faced with a big challenge they wanted to accomplish—to not go with the flow but to chart their own courses in life. In our society where young girls are pressured to behave and play the role of grownup women before fully enjoying the best of their childhood and teenage years, it was refreshing to see how Brooke's friend had taken the narrow road of purity.

For that, I thought, she deserves a standing ovation as she perseveres in her character on the path of being a lasting role model for beautiful Brooke, who is in turn beginning to follow in her footsteps, swimming against the current amid the blowing waves of sexual temptations and in desperate need of a guiding hand.

> Like a gold ring in a pig's snout is a beautiful woman who shows no discretion.
> —Prov. 11:22

Like a diamond, no more sex before marriage

> Create in me a pure heart O God and renew a steadfast spirit within me.
> —Ps. 51:10

Somehow, I expected Private Michelle, an attractive blonde in her mid-twenties, to be angry and start crying when I told her that the blisters on her vaginal area were indeed genital herpes. But to my surprise, she calmly accepted her diagnosis without venting any anger at her herself or her partner, whom she had met shortly before her deployment.

"I'm breaking up with him when I get back. I just wish we never had sex," she said.

For the next few minutes, I talked to her about a topic that gripped her full attention: sex as God's divine creation and His special gift to us. It was a novel idea to her to hear that God created us with unique custom-made bodies equipped to enjoy His miracle of lovemaking, and that His only wish, when it comes to that, is that we enjoy it within the sacred confines and security of a marriage relationship.

"Doing it God's way is meant to not only give us physical pleasure and the satisfaction of our deepest longings for love and acceptance that we experience when we 'become one' with another human being. But it also gives us a strong sense of assurance and security backed up by the married couple's public commitment and vow to honor their covenant and 'to love and to cherish…until death do us part' before God and man," I said.

It has always intrigued me that it's not only by the romantic sentiment of, "I love you forever, baby," that the married couple and their marriage home will be glued together. But it is in the deep, foundational accountability to God, to each other, and to those around them to honor their marriage vows and live up to the spirit and obligations of the covenant they have entered into that the greatness and magnetic appeal of marriage is found. The magnitude of the commitment, the marriage covenant, between a man and a woman, is so fascinating, powerful, and beyond comprehension. To add to the intrigue and amazement of the marriage covenant is the fact that God Himself created, ordained, and elevated it to the equivalence of the divine, deep, intimate, and loving relationship between Jesus Christ and those who believe in Him.

But as in everything else, there is a vast ocean between what God commands and what man and woman can deliver. Sadly, in our human hands, marriage has often become a license to be cruel, use, abuse, betray, destroy, and even kill someone's body, mind, and spirit. Divorce, which God hates and that was never intended to end the covenant relationship of marriage, has become the only escape route, the Underground Railroad if you will, for many betrayed, used, bruised, and abused spouses. It has become the fire escape that some, with God's direction, are left no option but to take, yet many choose to unwisely take on their own.

But on the other hand, there is the reality of our human experience where sex is traded, sold, bought, and reduced to an animalistic pleasurable instinct. Some use it to manipulate, abuse, control, and degrade others. Those who voluntarily, without the safety net of a healthy marriage, decide to give and enjoy sex to receive love, and those who give it away and trade it for power, position, money, and pleasure will all one day face the same emotional uphill battle when the relationship is no longer desired by the partner and is brought to an abrupt, unexpected end. Long after the temporary emotional and physical highs of the sexual pleasure, and the sense of power and control, dissipate, the feelings of being used, controlled, taken advantage of, and treated "like a third world toilet" (as a woman tearfully told me recalling her story) will still remain.

A person, in the majority of cases, a woman, who has been reduced to a subhuman level of being an object of pleasure or used like a controlled sexual slave will need time to heal from her sense of shame, guilt, hurt, and the anger bound to happen. She will need a healing time, not only for her body that might be suffering from herpes, genital warts, or the aftermath of an abortion, but also time to restore the truth of her God-given value, worth, and self-esteem. Thankfully, with a supportive circle of family and friends, good chaplains, pastors, counselors, and caring doctors who become God's hands and mouthpieces of healing, peace, love, and comfort, her restoration and healing *will* take place if she decides to take this path.

And then, there is also a new path of change, healing, and a new beginning for anyone who chooses to love instead of lust, to care instead of use, to comfort instead of abuse, to help instead of hunt. We men can all learn one day to treat a woman with respect, especially the lost souls who can no longer find any beauty, value, or worth in themselves. We can all learn to treat every woman with the respect we owe a mother, a sister, or a daughter, and not as objects to prey on for our pleasure and enjoyment. What we choose to enjoy and do today we will pay for with physical, mental, emotional, and spiritual consequences later. It makes sense to change the old bad ways quickly and start to do the things that will renew us and bring good and positive future consequences that we can live with and be proud of.

As I was wrapped in my thoughts and reflections, she suddenly asked me a question I wasn't expecting. "Dr. Hanna, do you think a guy will look down at me and feel I'm easy if I have sex with him?" she asked in a serious tone of voice.

It almost sounded like she was at a crossroads of decision in her life. *Could the sobering reality of a lifetime of an STD become her turning point into a deeper appreciation and understanding of her sexuality? Was she on a new path of self-control in this very pivotal area of her life?* I wondered.

"Do you really want me to tell you? Okay, this is what I really think. It's our human nature, Michelle, to crave and desperately want what is hard for us to get. And so the harder it is for us to get something, the harder we try to get it, and the more we want it. It's like the person suddenly becomes so valuable and precious in our eyes, like a diamond that's so amazing and precious because it's so hard to find. Does that make any sense to you, Michelle?" I asked, wondering if she had any clue what I was talking about.

She eagerly nodded her head. "Ya, I know exactly what you mean, Doctor. It's really my choice to be like that precious diamond."

For the next few minutes, I answered more questions about herpes, treatment options, chances of recurrence, and the precautions her obstetrician would follow when she gets pregnant in the future. She listened to me intensely, absorbing every word I said like a living sponge as I encouraged her.

"Thank you so much for your time. I know I'll have more questions about my disease in the future, but I have to learn how to live with it. I just feel bad for the right man when he comes to my life. It's not going to be fair to him," she said as she looked at me with her big blue eyes.

"You know, Doctor, I've made up my mind to wait for sex until I get married. I want to be like that hard-to-find, precious diamond," she said with a tender smile as she opened the exam room door.

> Your beauty...should be that of your inner self, the unfading beauty of a gentle and quiet spirit which is of great worth in God's sight.
> —1 Peter 3:3-4

Repentance

> Blessed are the pure in heart, for they will see God.
> —Matt. 5:8

"My girlfriend saw her doctor some time ago. He told her she had genital warts," said twenty-three-year-old Corporal David soon after sitting down on the exam table and showing me a warty growth in his genital area.

I asked all the medically relevant questions, poked, probed, examined, and confirmed to him what he already suspected. "It is a genital wart, David."

After explaining to him more about the disease, answering a barrage of questions about it, and prescribing him a medicated gel, we began to talk.

"So what's going to happen between you guys? Do you plan to be together after your deployment?" I asked.

"I care a lot about her, Doctor. I dated her before I got married, and we just started dating again after my divorce."

"What happened? What broke up your marriage?" The question seemed to draw David's interest, and he began to talk about the day his marriage shattered.

"We met in a Christian college and fell in love. We couldn't wait to get married. The marriage started great until that day, three months after our wedding day, when she came to visit me during basic training. She told me she was three months pregnant and the baby wasn't mine. She said the father was her ex-boyfriend!"

"What? You're kidding. And you had no idea!"

"No idea. I had no clue she was pregnant with his baby on our wedding night," he said, shaking his head.

What a big mess, I thought. *Your bride pregnant with someone else's child on your wedding day and you have no clue! A memory that's probably too painful to probe.* I quickly decided to change the subject back to his girlfriend.

"Tell me about your girlfriend, David. She must be a very special person."

"She is! We dated two years before my marriage and parted ways until my divorce. You know, Doctor, getting this STD was a wakeup call for both of us. After ten months of dating, we decided to stay celibate till we get married. Both of us are Christians, and we decided it was time to follow our Christian faith."

"Was that a hard decision to make?" I asked.

"It was really her idea first. She decided to recommit her life to Jesus Christ and remain pure until marriage. I decided to do the same," he answered, confidently.

I was curious at that moment to know how he managed to finally reign in his sexual desires and exert self-control in an area that many can't or don't care to.

"How did you manage to do it?" I asked.

After a brief pause, David recalled his Christian journey of "growing up in a Christian home, attending Christian camps, and regularly attending church until he 'got hold of porn.'"

"I started looking at dirty magazines. All I could think about was sex. After looking at the dirty pictures, all I wanted from women was just one thing."

But David's long, rocky road, of what sounded like sexual addiction suddenly came to an end with his girlfriend's sobering diagnosis of genital warts. He recalled how his pastor's words had given him the strength and freedom to no longer be controlled by his sexual desires and encouraged him to start a new page of his life.

"My pastor in Nebraska said to me that when sexual thoughts fill my mind, I need to change my thoughts and focus. He told me I shouldn't let any sexual thoughts advance to images, but I must get rid of them as soon as they come to my mind."

It was time for David to go. Before he left, I asked him one last question. "Are you planning to marry her?"

"I love her. She's the most wonderful person I've ever met in my life. I trust her fully. I know for sure God gave us a strong physical desire for each other, but He doesn't want us to act on it until we get married. We plan to get married when I come back home," he said, his voice filled with passion and excitement.

David left a few days after this visit to start his long deployment in Iraq. But the story of his survival after the betrayal of his ex-wife and his walk of freedom from the darkness of sexual addiction into the light of a genuine, pure relationship with God and side by side with a Christian woman who deeply loves him, I will always remember.

> I know, O LORD, that a man's life is not his own; it is not for man to direct his steps.
> —Jer. 10:23

Sexual battles

> Flee from sexual immorality. All other sins a man commits are outside his body, but he who sins sexually sins against his own body.
> —1 Cor. 6:18

As I stepped into the exam room, I could almost hear twenty-five-year-old Private First Class Victoria singing softly the words of the hymn playing on my CD player. She seemed quite familiar with the song and absorbed by its words.

"I used to be in my church choir," she said, singing one more note.

"So Victoria, what brings you here to our humble dwelling?" I asked, welcoming her using one of my silly greetings.

"I want to make sure I don't have any STDs, Dr. Hanna," she said in a whispering voice and pointing to a small bump close to her privates.

After a thorough history-taking and a chaperoned physical exam, I handed her a blood work lab order for further testing.

"Your exam is normal, Victoria, and hopefully the blood work will be okay too," I said, hoping to calm her fears.

She sat up and began to share with me some of her deepest worries, fears, and regrets. "I just feel real bad, getting involved with someone else. My fiancé is back in Tennessee. He loves me and wants to get married to me," she said, regretting her decision.

Realizing her confusion and how much she cared for her fiancé, I decided to dig further into her story.

"Thanks for trusting me with your story. You know, Victoria, I will do my part as a physician to give you the best treatment if this turns out to be an STD and of course I really hope all your tests will be normal. But you know what? It's going to be up to you to get to the cause and root of the problem that made you unfaithful to your fiancé in the first place. It sounds to me that you really love him. Am I right?"

She nodded her head in agreement as tears began flowing from her eyes.

"Dad is a pastor. He and mom pray every day for me. I'm afraid God won't accept me…I'm afraid of sinning again after I come back to Him, you know what I mean?" she said, wiping away her tears.

I could see in her face and tell by her voice a genuine sorrow for her sexual tryst and the depth of her inner conflict: a strong desire to be forgiven by God and welcomed into His presence on one hand, and the fear of messing up, falling, and failing God after being forgiven and accepted on the other.

Sensing the depth of her soul struggle, I decided to share with her a well-known, life-changing Bible story in Luke 15:11-32, commonly known as the parable of the prodigal son. I had shared it with a couple of other soldiers who felt very encouraged by it, and I knew Victoria would find a blessing in it as well.

"Victoria, Jesus once told a story to a big crowd about this guy who came to his father one day and asked him for his share of the inheritance money. That was a very disrespectful and cruel thing to do to the father, but still he gave him what he wanted.

"But then the son took the money and wasted it away on very bad things. And when he had no money left for food or a place to stay, he decided to go back to his father's home, asking him for forgiveness and for a place in his servants' quarters to sleep in. But the father, who was waiting daily for his son to come back home, hugged him, welcomed him back, restored him fully to the family, and to top it all threw a welcoming party on his behalf!

What Jesus was saying in that story is that God is exactly like this loving father and no matter how terrible the things we've done in the past, we'll always be forgiven and welcomed back home when we come back to Him in genuine repentance. This is much like your dad, Victoria, who will always welcome you back home."

"Dad always talked about this story. That really makes sense, it does," she said in a tender, quiet voice as her eyes welled with tears. The angelic voice of the choir was still echoing from the CD as if celebrating with the heavens her homecoming.

"Thank you so much, Dr. Hanna. I believe in divine appointments; this was one of them. I plan to go to chapel with my friend this Sunday," she said with a beautiful smile on her face.

As she was getting ready to leave, I offered her my untouched breakfast plate with eggs and two pieces of French toast that she gladly accepted and immediately began to eat. "You're sure? I missed going to the chow hall this morning. This is so delicious," she said and gave me a big good-bye hug.

Witnessing how God used an old Christian hymn to help transform Victoria's heart was a humbling experience to me. Her tears of guilt for betraying her fiancé's trust gradually gave way to tears of repentance as the sacred words of a hymn and a story told by Jesus over two thousand years ago reminded her of her father's teaching and God's never-failing fatherly love and forgiveness.

Victoria left with her unit for Afghanistan soon after this visit.

Do not conform any longer to the pattern of this world, but be transformed by the renewing of your mind.

—Rom. 12:2

Torn apart by two men

"Jesus, Take the Wheel"

—Song by Singer Carrie Underwood

Even at the young age of twenty-five, Private Tammy's life had become increasingly complicated. She was simultaneously dating two men and torn between "Tom, a playboy who just wants to have fun," and "Jack, who is considerate, believes in God, and is moral." Her years of friendship with Jack had just recently evolved into a steady dating relationship that she had high hopes for.

But to complicate her life a little, she had gotten herself into an intimate sexual relationship with the seemingly "bad boy" Tom, whom she keeps on going back to.

"Tammy, you're telling me one guy is with you for your body, and the other one respects you. But obviously you're finding it very hard to break a relationship that you know is just based on sex. Do you feel like it's meeting some deep emotional need in you?" I asked, reflecting on the tangled emotional and physical web she had gotten herself into.

"It's probably not the same for men, but I feel wanted, loved, and attractive when someone wants to be intimate with me, I mean sexually. That's why I find it hard to break up with Tom," she said, her eyes wandering to the walls. "I know what I'm doing is wrong. I want to be loved by a man who thinks I'm beautiful and special to him, not just wants me for the sex. I should've listened to my mother."

What a messy triangular web of confusion this young soul found herself immersed in. With so many young women facing dilemmas like hers, I wonder how many of their dreams and life plans are derailed and sidelined before they ever begin.

"I have a strong feeling, Tammy, that you and your mom are very close. I bet you guys talk on the phone every day, and she probably prays for you and tells you 'I love you' all the time. Right?"

"She really does! She always prays for me and tells me how much she loves me. You're right, Doctor," she said, eagerly agreeing with me.

"Tammy, you know whom your mom reminds me of? Of God in the story of the prodigal son in the Bible. Do you know the story?" I asked.

"I think I heard of it before. Can you remind me of it?" she asked.

It was time again for me to tell my favorite, life-changing, eye-opening Bible story to yet another soldier, and I couldn't wait to start.

"It's about this guy who came to his dad and asked him for his share of the inheritance money. That was really bad because he wanted to take the money his dad was planning to leave him after he died. He didn't want to wait. So anyway, he got the money and took off to a land very far away and spent it all on bad stuff—prostitutes, getting drunk, and stuff like that. This guy kept on wasting the money until he lost it all and lost his friends when nothing was left.

"Then the Bible says he ended up working in a pigsty, feeding them and cleaning their mess. The guy had no food to eat because there was a famine. He even wished to eat what the pigs were eating, but he wasn't allowed to do that. Anyway, he was in a very bad shape with no food to eat, working with the messy pigs, without any money or friends. And by the way, working with pigs in the Jewish culture was a very shameful thing. He decided to go back home to his dad. He prepared a short speech, basically saying, 'I'm sorry. Please let me stay in the servants' quarters because I don't deserve anything better. I'm hungry and I really want to eat.'

"As the son got closer to home, and before he even made it, he saw his father running towards him with his arms open wide. It looked like he was waiting every day for him on the same road that his son had taken when he wandered far away, and he couldn't contain his happiness when he saw him. He quickly covered him with a robe and put the family ring on his finger, a sign of totally restoring him back to the home and family he once left behind. Then on top of that, the happy father decided to throw a big party to celebrate his son's safe return home. That made no sense to the father's other son, who complained bitterly to his dad about why he would have such a festival for a son who sinned big time and not for him, given the fact that he hadn't done the bad things his brother did. But to the loving joyful father, that celebration was heartfelt and important. He told the disgruntled brother, 'Your brother was lost but know is found, was dead but now is alive. I am so happy he is back home, come on and join the party.'"

I paused briefly and then told her what the story really means to me. "You know, Tammy, Jesus said that the father in the story represents God. God is our Father, our Daddy, Who loves us and is always ready and waiting with open arms to take us back home to a relationship with Him, no matter what we have done and how lost in sin we've been. Just like in the story, He will celebrate with the angels when we come back to Him, abandoning our old ways and asking Him to forgive us. Jesus Himself assures us of this forgiveness."

I stopped briefly to gauge her reaction and see if she was with me or if I'd lost her somewhere at the beginning of my mini talk. She looked totally captivated and like a sponge absorbing every word I said. So I continued with these last few words.

"You know, Tammy, your mom is much like the father in this story. She cries when you leave home to go to faraway places that might be risky and dangerous for you. She worries about you and prays for your safe return home, always waiting for you to come back so that she can hold you and protect you from any predator…and to encourage you, love you, no matter what mess you find yourself in. She probably can't wait for you to come back home so she can hug you and tell you how much she missed you. This is just like God, our Father, Who always waits for us to come to His love and safety when we wander away from Him, lost in our depression, anxiety, loneliness and in desperate need of love, mercy, and healing. This is why, Tammy, I say your mom is like God waiting for her daughter to come back home."

Tammy's eyes began to well with tears. I could tell that her heart was deeply touched. "Mom," she said, her tears gently flowing down her young face, "always tells me to be safe. She doesn't want me to be hurt or taken advantage of. She worries about me and waits for me just like the father in the story."

She wiped her tears, then looked at me and said, "You sure know how to make me cry. You have really touched my heart."

Tammy returned to see me a few other times for follow-up medical care after this visit. She was always appreciative and thankful.

It still amazes me how a simple story told by Jesus over two thousand years ago has assured generations throughout history, as it assured Tammy during her visit, that God is not a destructive, indifferent cosmic force, but a Father. He's a loving Dad Who sheds tears of grief when we wander away in life like lost sheep and patiently waits for us to come back home.

The parable of the prodigal son has indeed been a beacon of light throughout the ages to many souls lost and confused in the darkness of our world. For at its heart is the good news that God calls us all into a new beginning with Him. It is a call to walk away from the many pigsty-like, shameful and hurtful places where predators devour us, and we live in emotional turmoil in desperate need for love, peace, rest, and a place to call home.

It's ultimately about coming back home to God, crying, "God, my Father, I can't figure out what to do with this situation. I got myself into it, and now I don't know what else I can do. I'm lost. So I come back to you to give you my worries, my fears, and my impossible situation. I come home so that you can take over, and I can finally find rest and peace for my weary soul."

> In the same way, I tell you there is rejoicing in the presence of the angels of God over one sinner who repents.
> —Luke 15:10

Torn apart by two women

> Out of the heart come evil thoughts, murder, adultery, sexual immorality.
> —Matthew 15:19-20

Soon after Private Aaron's medical exam, the topic of our conversation quickly shifted to an issue that weighted heavily on him. Apparently, his life had become quite complicated since he had gotten himself simultaneously involved with two women. Aaron's life had become so hectic that his war zone deployment had become a sort of respite and a break from the many demands of his two relationships.

"It's getting pretty hard deciding between them, Doc. It's more complicated than I thought," he said.

Poor Aaron, it must be taking plenty of precious time and energy to keep his two women happy, and each one of them totally clueless of the other, I thought. He did look older than his age, probably worn out from their combined weight that seemed heavier on his mind than the bulky body armor on his body. *No wonder the rigorous training in the heat with his heavy Kevlar and body armor on was a welcome relief to him.*

"I've been with Courtney for five years. She really gets on my nerves—overeating, gaining weight, annoying habits, and she won't change," he said, justifying his decision to get involved with Brittany.

"Brittany is something else, hot, thin, exciting, and the sex is great. The problem is that she goes out partying with her girlfriends in bars all the time," said Aaron, comparing his two women.

It seemed to me at that moment that Aaron was holding tightly to both of them—one for her inner beauty, and the other for her outer looks. On one hand, he saw Courtney as loyal, dependable, and boring. On the other hand, Brittany was a hottie—wild, exciting, and hard to trust with her drinking and troubling bar-hopping habits.

"I think you must make up your mind quickly before your life spins out of control. You might end up with an STD, getting one of them pregnant, and paying child support to both of them for eighteen years. And what do you think is going to happen to you when they finally find out that they are both sharing you? This might mess up your life pretty fast," I said, offering him an outsider's view.

I had Aaron's full attention. His eyes wandered briefly to the window, then he looked directly at me and asked for my opinion about what I think he should do.

"I think what's most important is who truly loves you. Which one of them is loyal, compassionate, and cares about you? One good way to look at it is to ask yourself, 'Who would make a caring, faithful wife whom you can trust to watch your back?' You might want to start praying to God for wisdom and guidance to help you make a good decision.

But don't rely on your feelings and emotions to make this decision. They can be like a yo-yo and can lead you the wrong way," I said.

"Does that help at all? I hope I'm not confusing you."

"No, not at all. What you said makes a whole lot of sense, doctor. I'll be thinking hard about it. Thank you," he said, reaching out to shake my hand.

As he walked down the hallway in Kevlar and full body armor, I thought about how much heavier is the weight of worry, guilt, and fear on a soul and mind than all his military gear combined. The burden of invisible negative emotions is too much for any one of us to bear alone. I was glad that Aaron had decided to share his burden with me, and perhaps begin the process of unloading it before its emotional weight destroyed his peace and disrupted his sanity, as it most certainly can.

But then I wondered, *What is Aaron looking for by having two relationships side by side? Could it be that his thirst for love, acceptance, and intimacy is so deep, like the rest of us except perhaps a notch deeper, that he is drawn to risky behavior and decisions that can cost him dearly?* How many of us live in such deep thirst that we're willing to trade our most precious gifts, talents, time, and safety of our bodies, minds, and spirits for that drink of love even if it is temporary and counterfeit, and no matter how dearly it's costing us.

It usually takes a few drinks of the water of love relationships before few of us get the message that no relationship will ever fully satisfy the thirst of our souls for love, healing, acceptance, and belonging. Many of us are in, or are repeatedly in and out of, lousy, unsafe, destructive, or abusive relationships that temporarily give us a sense of belonging and unpredictably. Like a rollercoaster, they make us temporarily feel wanted, loved, and accepted.

But that temporary comfort quickly fades and gives way to intervals of neglect, uncaring, control, and physical, mental, emotional, or spiritual abuse characteristic of such relationships. We end up with a deeper sense of letdown and abandonment, and we're thirstier, angrier, hungrier for love, and more afraid, ashamed, and depressed than when we started at the onset of our pursuit of love. What started as a search for tasty waters to satisfy our souls ends up with drinking from a well that only satisfies for a brief time, leaving a bitter taste in our souls. Our hearts become thirstier than ever.

This dilemma that we all face in pursuit of love, value, and a sense of belonging was well addressed by Jesus at an old well on the outskirts of a village inhabited by people called the Samaritans. At the time of day when women usually didn't go to that well to get their daily supply of water, there she was—a Samaritan woman who went secretly, hoping not to be noticed. She was a woman whom the village people gossiped about, a woman who was like many of us today, migrating from one failed relationship to another in hopes of finding a source of lasting love that will forever satisfy our souls. Her earthly pilgrimage took her to a series of five men whom she married and a sixth one whom she was living with. That was when she was ambushed by Jesus at that well.

Jesus knew her story and her lifelong search for a source of water that would calm and satisfy her soul and the lifetime of let downs and shame on a heartbreaking road of relationships that never quenched her inner thirst. He asked her for water to her surprise as men back then in that part of town would not talk to a woman, let alone a woman from the Samaritans, a tribe of people despised by the Jews of that time.

After she expressed her surprise that a Jewish man would ask her for a cup of water, He surprised her again with what would eventually bring a radical change in her spiritual life.

> Jesus answered her, "All who drink of this water will be thirsty again.
>
> "But whoever takes a drink of the water that I will give him shall never, no never, be thirsty any more. But the water that I will give him shall become a spring of water welling up (flowing, bubbling) [continually] within him unto (into, for) eternal life."
>
> The woman said to Him, "Sir, give me this water, so that I may never get thirsty nor have to come [continually all the way] here to draw."
>
> At this, Jesus said to her, "Go, call your husband and come back here."

> The woman answered, "I have no husband." Jesus said to her, "You have spoken truly in saying, 'I have no husband.'
>
> "For you have had five husbands, and the man you are now living with is not your husband. In this you have spoken truly."
> —John 4:13-18 AB

The woman thought she had discreetly come to draw water from the well. Shock waves traveled through her when her secret life was divinely exposed and Jesus declared that He was the Living Water that would satisfy her soul and every human soul on earth back then and now.

> The woman said to Him, "I know that Messiah is coming, He Who is called the Christ (the Anointed One); and when He arrives, He will tell us everything we need to know and make it clear to us."
>
> Jesus said to her, "I Who now speak with you am He."
> —John 4:25-26 AB

In her life back then and in our modern world today where many give their bodies and hearts to others in relationships to receive back love and satisfaction to their souls, Jesus said to the Samaritan woman that relationships she meant to be like water to her thirsty soul never satisfied her and never would. He tells us today there is no relationship, no matter how lousy, abusive, destructive, amazing, caring, or safe, that can ever fully satisfy our inner thirst, for just as he declared to the woman drawing water at the well, He declares to us today:

> Everyone who drinks this water will be thirsty again, but whoever drinks the water I give him will never thirst.
> —John 4:13-14

Ultimately, none of Aaron's relationships could fully satisfy him even though one of them seemed safer than the other. He and all of us ultimately need to find true contentment, value, peace, and satisfaction within our hearts and not from human relationships that will always lack and are bound to fail in one way or the other.

The same inner peace and contentment offered by Jesus to a weary, wounded, and thirsty woman at a village well two thousand years ago is available to us today.

Relationships that we're in or those we're pursuing, no matter how great and wonderful, or bad and dreadful, are never meant to replace God in our hearts and souls. For like Jesus told the Samaritan woman, we will never find inner peace, unconditional love, and true satisfaction apart from Him.

And it is with this very peace and satisfaction within that we can say no to any abuse in our relationships and have the courage to flee dangerous ones. With the same peace and inner satisfaction, we can begin to appreciate safe and loving relationships and finally learn to stop complaining about every little thing and being too selfish and demanding instead of serving one another and being content and thankful. It is when we see ourselves and others through God's lens of love and forgiveness that we finally start to see the beauty and treasure He sees in us and in others.

Aaron's life and ours change forever the moment we finally realize that we'll never find satisfaction in outer things such as relationships or any material thing—money, beauty, pleasures, and possessions, power, or position—until we find inner satisfaction within our hearts. A satisfied heart is a treasure to have because it sees life with an eye of contentment. It is rich without having any material things because it is peaceful, satisfied, and content from within.

Until we fully comprehend and embrace that, our life walk will be an endless rat race, never finding real joy or fulfillment. We become like lost sheep in the wilderness of life in a perpetual destructive path. We hop from one lousy relationship to another and from a promising one to another, bringing havoc and pain to ourselves and to many along the way, until we, desperately thirsty, meet Jesus by one of our water wells and receive the same living water He offered a lost, wounded woman two thousand years ago.

> Above all else, guard your heart, for it is the wellspring of life.
> —Prov. 4:23

CHAPTER 26

SOLDIERS' SURVIVAL SKILLS

Soldiers' Survival Skills: Photo provided by Camp Atterbury Public Affairs

Be strong and courageous. Do not be afraid or terrified
because of them, for the LORD your God goes with you;
he will never leave you nor forsake you.
—Deut. 31:6

Life-saving advice

WITH FOURTEEN YEARS of extensive worldwide military experiences, lots of courage, caring, a radiant personality, and solid character, Major Morgan was to me the prime example of a true soldier with a compassionate heart.

She was about done with a few last-minute instructions to soldiers under her command when I approached her with a laundry list of questions about her military life, deployments, and words of wisdom to the deploying soldiers. She knew I was interested in encouraging the mobilizing and demobilizing soldiers during their medical visits. As always, she was ready to help.

She welcomed me warmly in her office with her typical friendly smile, and we started talking during her lunch break. What followed were stories of heroism, compassion, and most of all wisdom and guidance to the young and inexperienced soldiers who were so near and dear to her heart.

On the toll of frequent deployments

"How did your family deal with your constant deployments, Major?" I asked.

"I still remember how when I first joined the army, my husband also received his orders to deploy to Iraq, and my son was also deployed to Kosovo, all at the same time! I remember how overwhelmed I felt. I prayed to God and tried to make a deal with Him. I said to Him, 'I promise to treat every soldier under my command the same way I want my husband and son to be treated during their deployments.' I know you can't make deals with God, but that was my way to deal with my fears."

Then she explained how dual deployments are hard on the whole family. "Everyone becomes very stressed out…children, grandparents, everyone."

On deploying with other military family members to combat

"Have you ever been deployed to combat with your son and husband before?"

"Yes, in Kosovo with my son. I used to be so worried about him every time he went out for a mission. I was the medic at the Troop Medical Clinic over there, and I remember how terrified I felt when his unit was ambushed and took some casualties. I was so worried during the helicopter ride to the site to treat and medvac the casualties. I kept wondering if my son was one of them and couldn't focus. 'Was my son one of the casualties?' was all I could think about."

Miraculously, her son wasn't one of those killed or wounded whom she ended up triaging and treating in the field.

On loneliness in the war zone

"Civilians have no idea what it means to be lonely, without your loved ones. I still remember how hard my unit's soldiers tried to create a sense of family with each other on Christmas day the best we knew how. We made Christmas stockings from webril (cotton material used for padding under a cast) and gauze and stuffed them with presents for each other. On the outside we looked happy. I looked happy, but I cried so much on the inside because I missed my family."

On getting married before deployment

"Major, do you think it's wise for young soldiers to get married before deployment? A lot of them do that," I asked.

"I see many young soldiers nowadays rushing to get married and have a baby before their deployment. Many of these marriages don't work. There at the theater of operations they are dirty, tired, afraid, and feel lonely and miss being hugged. Every time I heard one of them yelling on the phone at his partner in the States and then hanging up feeling so angry, I could tell how lonely he felt and what was coming next for some of them—getting involved with someone else closer to him."

On being a woman among many men in the military

"Major, any words of wisdom for women in the military?"

"As a woman, I tell the girls who end up having sex, especially with married soldiers, 'You're ruining it for the rest of us by sleeping around.' Some of the married men totally change their behavior during AT (annual training) and you find them acting like singles, taking off their rings and sleeping around. Port-a-potty sex, getting pregnant, and then having abortions on 'pass.' 'Girls, you're really ruining it for the rest of us.'"

On the hardest thing experienced during combat

"That was in Kosovo, you know, the war between Albanians and Serbs. I was the pediatric trauma nurse medic at the army hospital. I had a total of twenty-four children who died in my arms as I held them. There was nothing we could do to save their lives. Poor children, some of them came in with head traumas, accidents, and many of them were just playing and picked up land mines and explosives that looked colorful like toys. They were so innocent and trusted no one but our soldiers in BDUs (Battle Dress Uniform). I remember how angry I was feeling but somehow I felt God wanted me to be there to help those I was able to help, and comfort the twenty-four I held in my arms before they died. I felt so sad watching a small child dying in my arms. We took turns holding them until they died. We would then walk around the blocks of tents five to six times. We prayed and cried before going back to our tents to sleep. That's the kind of stress that families back home can't understand," she said, holding back her tears.

On the difference between emotional stress in combat and back home

"What, in your view, is the difference between the emotional stress you faced there and the stress back home in America?"

"It's higher here in America than the time I was rocking the children in my arms in Kosovo before they died," she answered without hesitation.

On learning thankfulness, gratitude, and appreciation from overseas deployments

"I see a lot of people in America who no longer appreciate what they have. My deployments to El Salvador and many poor countries helped me to see how much I really have and to be thankful. I once saw a woman holding her ten-year-old child by the hand and desperately looking for food. She could hardly afford even one meal a day. Her leg had had a big, infected ulcer on it for years but all she could afford to put on it was some topical cream. She had no money to see a doctor or for antibiotics, yet she was always smiling.

"I saw people who could only afford a hole in the ground for a toilet with scorpions crawling in and out of it. Many had no access to medical care or health insurance to pay for their medical needs like an elderly woman who had been limping for years from a hip fracture. This stays with you forever; you feel blessed and become thankful for all what you have.

"After one of my overseas deployments, I was working in the ER and heard a woman complaining loudly about having to wait too long. I couldn't take it anymore. I told her, 'Why don't you go to a country where there is no medical care and no toilets to sit on?' I have no more patience with ungrateful, unappreciative people. Even rich folks aren't thankful for what they have. There is a Native American proverb that says the bigger the tree, the more the winds. We have so much...so much in our society, but we still don't feel blessed. We don't feel peace."

Her words are so right, I thought. It's so easy to forget our abundance and blessings in this land of plenty as we turn our focus on the empty half of the glass of our lives, what we don't have or the pain of life's trials we're going through. We become totally blind to the other half full of God's abundant goodness and blessings: a loving family, and caring friends, health, physical provisions, and a roof over our heads. Constantly dwelling on the flaws of others and the empty half of our glass instead of the full half turns us into unthankful, selfish, never-content or satisfied individuals. We become unhappy, continually angry naggers and complainers, who see nothing good in ourselves or in others. That's when we're no longer able to see God's goodness and love, peace and joy that can only be seen and fully experienced by a content, thankful heart.

On surviving PTSD

"I used to think PTSD is bulls– until I saw what happened to my friend. She used to take turns with me taking care of the dying children in Kosovo. The whole experience affected her so much that she began to sleep walk.

"I was like a mother to these children. I felt their mother's pain as I held them tightly in my arms as they slowly died. Soon after coming back home from my tour of duty, I began to feel startled and look for cover when I heard street noises like a speeding car or something that reminded me of the sound of explosives. That was the time I realized I was dealing, like my friend, with PTSD."

Her admission of her past battle with PTSD took me by surprise. For a moment, I thought about the dark and stormy path she must have endured to be the strong, inspiring leader she has become today.

"What's your advice, major, to the young soldiers who return from war?" I asked.

"Imagine! A seventeen-year-old soldier who just came back from combat. He just experienced killing, blood, losing his buddies, and death, and now he is back home and we're expecting him to smile and have a great life. But these young men and women have changed. They are now different and will need time to heal. They need to talk, talk, talk, talk. I tell them, 'Your parents and friends might not understand your feelings of emptiness, anger, and pain. So go talk to someone who understands what you're going through—your chaplain, your closest friend who listens, or to another soldier.' I tell them they will learn to live with it even if it's hard to forget it. I tell them, 'Don't let it worry you when someone is mean to you. Don't do drugs to get over your pain. A lot of what you feel might be confusing to you, and might make no sense to you but just talk…talk about it.'"

On having any regrets about becoming a soldier

"Do you ever regret joining the army?"

"I've traveled to so many places and experienced so many cultures. I know this: I'd never trade my experience with anything else in the world."

Her words were powerful and straight from the heart. I didn't want her to stop but soldiers were starting to gather for their afternoon meetings with her. It was time to go but there was yet one last question to ask her.

On fear of death

"What do you say, major, to a soldier deploying to Iraq or Afghanistan who is afraid of dying?"

She took a deep breath and said these wise words that we all can learn from, "This is what I tell them, Dr. Hanna: all of our days are numbered by God. Death is going to happen…in the back of a Humvee in Iraq…or here in America."

I rested the stethoscope on my shoulders as I walked towards the exam room to see my next patient. I knew that somehow I was a better doctor after listening to her and eager to share the life-saving advice of a wise, caring, brave heart to those who would listen.

> The fear of the Lord is the beginning of knowledge, but fools despise wisdom and discipline.
> —Prov. 1:7

CHAPTER 27

SURVIVING WORDS THAT KILL

Surviving Words: Photo provided by Camp Atterbury Public Affairs

Reckless words pierce like a sword, but the tongue
of the wise brings healing.
—Prov. 12:18

Enslaved by words, freed by the truth

"THE SCAR ON your face...how did you get it?" I asked twenty-four-year old Sgt. Jared as I started to place an air cast on his sprained ankle.

"That was from my stepmom. There're a lot more of those," he said, pointing to his back, and began to tell me about his rough childhood.

"I heard you're from Ohio, Doc. I was born there and moved from my stepmom's home to the East Coast when I was eleven to be with my biological mom. Dad has been in and out of jail all my life and is now locked up for selling drugs. I haven't seen him since I was eleven," he said.

Jared eventually finished high school, joined the army, and adopted his two half brothers, who were themselves abused by his stepmom.

His story made me ponder on the living hell that this young man must've endured—a drug addict father in and out of jail, a broken home, and a childhood marred by physical and emotional abuse.

"You're a survivor! How did you deal with all of that?"

"I remember the first year I moved to the East Coast. I had a lot of problems at school, and my grades started to slip. My mother decided to take me to her doctor. He knew all about my family's background and decided to lecture me. I'll never forget how he looked right at me and told me 'You'll never finish high school. You'll be exactly like your father and uncle, an alcoholic and a drug addict.' He sounded so sure I'd end up like them," he said with uneasiness.

His doctor's words must have had a massive effect on him since even over a decade later he still remembered them so vividly with such depth of emotions.

"The words he said made me angry, very angry. They were so negative and discouraging, but you know they eventually became to me like a negative encouragement. When I first heard what he said, I got so mad but then I became so determined to finish high school, stay away from drugs and alcohol no matter what, make it in life, and not end up being like my dad and uncle."

At that moment, I thought we'd arrived at the end of his inspiring story of survival, but then, with a distressed look on his face, he looked at me as if appealing for help and said, to my surprise, "I don't want to believe that I'm destined to be an addict like my dad. The doctor who told me that died recently. I'm still struggling with what he told me. What if he was right? What if no matter what I do I'll end up like him? Is that possible, Doctor? Is it in my genes?"

If I have ever had any doubts about the potency and power of a spoken word to free or enslave a soul, what Jared had just said removed all my doubts. Those long-gone spoken words from his deceased physician seemed to still haunt his soul from the grave, despite his amazing survival and escaping his dad's legacy. The power of words spoken by someone, dead or alive, do indeed take on a life of their own, imprisoning, tearing down, wounding, and destroying, or blessing, building up, healing, and uplifting one's soul. They do indeed become a blessing or a curse.

"Jared, your physician was wrong! Your genetic makeup will never force you to do what you choose not to do. Your family history puts you at a higher risk of alcoholism than the average population if you start drinking heavily. So it's ultimately your choice, and you have already chosen time and time again to stay away from alcohol and drugs," I explained to him.

I could see a sense of relief on his face. I knew I had his full attention, and so I finished with words that I hoped would help renew his mind and offer him freedom from his late physician's enslaving words, which I labeled as a curse, not to suggest a magical power to them but based on the fact that they were not true and they have inflicted long-term harm on him.

"Jared, see if this makes sense to you. Many years ago your old physician said words that still affect you. He placed something not true like a curse on you and it made you feel bad for years. But now as your new physician, I'm hoping the truthful words I told you will replace that old curse with a new blessing that will bless your life," I said. He agreed with me as we both started laughing.

He thanked me and walked slowly towards the door for a day of leg elevation and icing at the barracks before returning to his combat training. "I need luck in my life, Doctor. Wish me luck," he said as we shook hands for the last time.

Your word is a lamp to my feet and a light for my path.
—Ps. 119:105

Wounded by the tongue

Like a model gracing a runway, Isabella walked briskly, with her slim, tall figure, to the exam table. My initial guess was right on target: twenty-two-year-old Private First Class Isabella, on her first deployment to the combat zone, was indeed a highly acclaimed model in her state.

"Isabella, what made you join the army?" I asked curiously.

"I know for sure it's not the money. I probably make in a couple of months walking a runway in Paris or New York more than I'll make the whole year in the military. It's more important for me to be a soldier than be on modeling assignments I didn't care about," she answered with a big smile, revealing her perfectly aligned, pearly white teeth.

"Wow! You must be a famous model. So what brings you here today?" I asked.

"I'm worried about my cervical cancer recurring, Doctor. I'm waiting for the test results to come back and just wanted to talk to you about it," she said.

For the next few minutes, we talked extensively about her diagnosis, treatment, and worries about the recurrence of her cancer.

"Seems like you've a lot to think about on top of your deployment. How are you dealing with all of this?" I asked and prepared myself to listen to what was in her heart.

"At times, I feel like I have too many things on my plate, Doctor. But I've learned to live to the fullest every day of my life as if it's my last one."

What could be so overwhelming in such a beautiful young life? I wondered.

"So what's on your plate, Isabella? Does it help to talk about it?" I asked quietly.

With a gentle voice, she began to talk about her three-year-old Ann, who gives her hope and whom she missed terribly, and the uneasy feeling of leaving her with an ex-fiancé, the biological father, who verbally and emotionally abused Isabella for over three years before she decided to leave him.

"He made me feel shameful and worthless with his words. I felt like nothing. It took me a long time to feel confident about myself," she said.

Unfortunately for her, Isabella had experienced both physical and verbal abuse and learned the hard way the difference between them. After years of suffering emotional and mental abuse from Ann's dad, she decided not to marry him. She gathered all her strength and left him only to fall into the snare of another new abusive relationship, a physically abusive one this time. After suffering through a period of pushing, shoving, and punching she had wised up and decided to leave her new abuser for good.

"You know, Doctor, it took me less time to get over the physical abuse and the scars than it took me to forget the words and the emotional abuse of Ann's dad," she said, choking back her tears.

Her words reminded me of those of a seventy-three-year-old patient who once summarized to me the many years of abuse she suffered during her previous marriage with this sentence, "A slap on the face stings for a while and then goes away, but words stay with you."

Isabella's two bad relationships nearly destroyed her body, mind, and spirit but she was able to survive and grow from her adversity.

"I learned to value the more important things in life and be able to see beyond the physical attractiveness of a man. I'm now attracted by kindness and humor in a man like my boyfriend, who is very nice and funny. He is a marine! A marine! I've never dated a marine in my life, Doctor," she said with a giggle.

Her escape from brokenness and the destructiveness of her two abusive relationships made me wonder about the source of hope that kept her going when her life seemed so bleak and hopeless.

"Isabella, how did you deal with all of your problems? Do you believe in God?" I asked, probing into her spiritual world, which turned out to be just as rocky as her relationships with men.

She told me about the pain of rejection she has felt in her parish church when the priest found out that she was pregnant out of wedlock.

"I was about six months pregnant when some of the women told me I could no longer attend mass, and at the same time the priest started to avoid me and stopped talking to me," she recalled.

To be rejected by the very people whom God meant to hold her hand in love and acceptance at a time of her deepest need must have been a painful spiritual blow, I thought.

To her credit, the rejection by the very people who failed to show Jesus' unconditional love failed to extinguish the flame of her faith and her pursuit of God. "I was so disappointed, but I never gave up on God. I still pray and read the Bible and was able to find many other good churches that made me feel welcome," she said.

I thanked Isabella for trusting me with her story. *The beauty of her inner faith, love, and maturity has certainly outshone her external physical beauty*, I thought.

She gracefully stepped down from the exam table, reached out to me, and hugged me. "Thank you, Dr. Hanna, for listening," she said.

Isabella left with her unit shortly after this visit to start her tour of duty. A few years after she had boldly walked away from two abusive relationships, it was again her own courageous decision to volunteer as a soldier to walk the dangerous, sandy desert of Iraq rather than gracing the smooth, shiny runways of Paris and New York as a model.

> With the same tongue we praise our LORD and Father, and with it we curse men who have been made in God's likeness. Out of the same mouth come praise and cursing. My brothers, this should not be.
> —James 3:9-10

Escaping the dark valley of abuse

Isabella's history of three years of abuse saddened me and reminded me of the soldier, Diana, who had also suffered from emotional abuse by her dad when she was just a child. Both of them were made into scapegoats and punching bags by people in their lives they fully trusted. They were intimidated verbally and at times physically abused by the very people they loved and cherished. Sadly, those men (women can also be perpetrators of abuse as I found out in some of the other stories I have heard) treated Isabella and Diana like human targets. They waited, like roaring lions awaiting their prey, for the opportune time and unleashed their fury of pathological, bottled, raging anger, insecurity, fear, and flaming arrows of pride, selfishness, and sick obsession with dominance and control on the two defenseless souls.

The dark, destructive cruelty that those souls inflicted on Isabella and Diana became in a distorted way like a temporary calming medicine and therapy to those abusers' out-of-control raging emotions and sick, angry minds. And in the heat of their never-ending cycle and barrage of abuse—their self-medicating pills—they never dared to face their own inner darkness and turmoil, their inner rage against the injustices, abandonment, control, and abuses they themselves suffered in their lives. They chose abuse as their medicine instead of seeking the right medical, psychological, and spiritual help for their deeply troubled souls.

By the time their cycle of abuse ended and they were no longer under their abusers' sphere of anger and control, both Isabella and Diana were left emotionally bruised (hopefully, and assuredly with God's help, a bruise that will one day heal, making them inwardly stronger) and struggling with inner doubts about their sense of value, security, and whether they are worthy of being accepted, liked, or loved.

My prayer is that both of these women's stories of abuse will serve as a warning to every abuser or anyone tempted to be one, of the wrong and grievous damage done in using a human being with value, hopes, and dreams, as a human punching bag upon which they release their emotional illnesses, rage, and selfish desires. Perhaps their stories will also serve first, as a reminder that no human should ever be subjected to such evil and second, as a strong cry of freedom that says, "I'm your scapegoat no more," shouted from the hearts of two free souls who were once abused to every abused person's heart—woman or man.

It's also my hope that whoever reads these lines will know that accepting abuse *is not* the Christian thing to do, but saying a clear no and separating immediately from a dangerous, raging abuser or an emotionally abusive person who continuously refuses to stop crossing your God-given boundaries *is*.

Even though Diana was too young and Isabella was too dependent to shout loudly, "I'm your scapegoat no more" early and fast enough, they nevertheless decided to escape when their abusers turned their homes into prison cells. And as they found healing for their wounds and were able to rebuild their brokenness with God's help through caring family, friends, counselors, and doctors, they themselves became beacons of light to many held captive in the dark valley of abuse.

> The LORD is my shepherd, I shall not want.
> —Ps. 23:1 KJV

> Because of the LORD'S great love we are not consumed, for his compassion never fails.
> —Lam. 3:22

CHAPTER 28

THANK YOU, SOLDIER

Thank You, Soldier: Photo provided by Camp Atterbury Public Affairs

> In everything give thanks.
> —1 Thess. 5:18 NKJV

Angela's tears

I NOTICED TEARS streaming gently down Private Angela's face when I asked her my favorite, "How did your four-day pass go?"

question. The twenty-three-year old had just returned from visiting her family for the last time before mobilizing with her unit to Iraq.

As I saw the tears in her beautiful eyes, I began to wonder, *Did someone hurt her feelings? Did she break up with her boyfriend? Is she gripped by fear now that she is only two days away from departure?*

"Are you okay, Angela?" I asked.

"Yesterday, my last day of pass, I went to the VA hospital. I was wearing my military uniform. I was walking down the hallway when a veteran sitting in a wheelchair stopped me. He lifted himself slowly from the wheelchair, barely able to stand up, and reached out to me. He didn't say a word. He just stood up, leaning on his chair and gave me a hug. That was his way of saying thank you. I felt…appreciated," she said, wiping her tears.

Her story was so short and simple, but it touched my heart in many ways. It reminded me of many a soldier who had passed by my exam room and felt so appreciated and at times tearful, every time I uttered this simple phrase, "Thank you, soldier" at the end of every medical office visit.

I will always remember the many selfless responses I've so often heard from them, "It's my job, sir." "Someone's got to do it, sir; I would rather that someone be me, sir."

"Thank you, sir, for taking care of us."

Thank you said from a genuine heart to those among us who are always ready to lay aside their riches, comfort, and security for the sake of others always has a way of bringing tears from the hardest and toughest of people. For much like a hardworking, faithful, and dedicated mother, father, husband, wife, son, daughter, family member, friend, worker, or total stranger deserves and feels comforted by a simple Thank you, a soldier needs and deserves that too.

Thank you is said not just in words but in deeds. Easing the financial burden by offering jobs and education, and lifting the emotional and spiritual burden by accepting, praying, and showing kindness, love, and compassion from country, community, family, and friends are ways to say thank you. After all, we're all created special and beautiful in God's image as the Bible says and are reminded that even God loves to be thanked and praised for His love, faithfulness, goodness, and mercy towards each one of us.

If a wheelchair-bound veteran, dependent on an oxygen tank and too weak to say a single word, takes the risk of a serious fall by standing to hug Angela in an act of appreciation and thankfulness, I wonder what then is stopping me and America from doing even more.

I got out of my comfortable chair quickly, reached out to Angela, and hugged her.

"Thank you for all your sacrifices," I said, barely holding back my tears as I looked deeply into her misty blue eyes.

P.S.

Soon after I finished the last sentence of this story, while waiting for my Southwest flight from Orlando to Columbus, a middle-aged female passenger noticed the army pants and jacket that I happened to be wearing and approached me. She smiled at me and with the warmest voice said, "Excuse me, are you in the military?" Before I could finish telling her about my history of offering medical services to the troops, she said with the most appreciative, sweet voice, "I just want to tell you thank you for what you're doing…what you did for the country. I try to tell every soldier I see thank you.'"

"Hearing thank you means a lot to every one of them. It really does," I said, hardly able to contain my appreciation as I boarded the plane. I thanked God for this miraculous confirmation and for every thankful heart, like this woman's, in this great country of ours—America, the land of dreams—my dreams, our dreams.

> Dear friend, I pray that you may enjoy good health and that all may go well with you, even as your soul is getting along well.
> —3 John 2

> For God, who said, "Let light shine out of darkness," made his light shine in our hearts to give us the light of the knowledge of the glory of God in the face of Christ.
> —2 Cor. 4:6

> When Jesus spoke again to the people, he said, "I am the light of the world. Whoever follows me will never walk in darkness, but will have the light of life."
> —John 8:12

CONCLUSION: THE LIBERTY OF REDEMPTION

A CONCLUDING REMARK BY PASTOR DARREL GABBARD

ONE OF OUR nation's most cherished values is liberty. The Declaration of Independence says, "We hold these truths to be self-evident, that all men are created equal, that they are endowed by their Creator with certain unalienable rights that among these are life, liberty and the pursuit of happiness."

Patrick Henry, one of our nation's early patriots, famously cried out, "Give me liberty or give me death!"

The young men and women you have read about in this inspiring book risked their lives to preserve the liberty of our great nation and of other nations as well. How wonderful it is to live in a nation where we are politically free from an oppressive, tyrannical government. This freedom was attained and has been preserved through many great sacrifices.

As wonderful as it is to live in a nation where individuals are politically free, there is another kind of freedom that is even more wonderful. The Bible teaches that all people need a spiritual liberation. Why is this so? When God created us, He created us in His image, which meant that we are persons with minds, emotions, and free will. We are not puppets or machines. God wanted us to willingly worship Him out of love, not out of coercion. He wants us to enjoy His abundant life.

But we humans, from the beginning, chose to disobey God and exalt ourselves. The Bible says, "For all have sinned and fall short of the glory of God" (Rom. 3:23).

The "glory of God" refers to God's moral perfection and righteousness. The results of our sin are spiritual bondage and death. Sin has an enslaving power over our souls and separates us from God and the abundant life He wants to give us. The Bible says that we have become "slaves to sin" (Rom. 6:16) and that "The wages of sin is death" (Rom. 6:23). This death is a spiritual death. Physical death is the soul separated from the body, but spiritual death is the soul separated from God. The Bible calls this "the second death" or "eternal death." And so there is a great gap between God and people due to our sin.

But there is good news. This is what the word *gospel* means. The gospel is that God did not abandon us to face the consequences of our sin without hope. Out of His love for us, God took the initiative to redeem us from our bondage to sin and spiritual death. The word *redemption* means liberation through the payment of a price. In biblical times, a slave could be set free when a free man entered the slave market and paid a ransom. The free man who paid the ransom was called a redeemer. This term became a metaphor picturing how God intervened into human history to redeem our souls.

How did He make our redemption possible? God the Father sent His divine Son to this earth as a man, with the mission to be our redeemer. He was given the name Jesus which means *the Lord saves*. Jesus retained His full deity, but He was also fully man. He was the infinite God-Man. Jesus said He came "to give his life as a ransom" (Matt. 20:28).

You see, God is full of grace and mercy. He loves us and He doesn't want to punish us, but He is also holy and just, and He must punish our sin. So Jesus came to this earth to ultimately take upon Himself the judgment we deserve and make it possible for God to liberate us from the spiritual bondage of sin and its consequences. He did this by dying on the cross for our sins. The shedding of His blood was the ransom price that was paid. He became our substitute, paying the penalty for our sins and meeting the requirements of God's moral law.

CONCLUSION: THE LIBERTY OF REDEMPTION

The Bible says, "But God demonstrates his own love for us in this: while we were still sinners, Christ died for us" (Rom. 5:8). The Bible also says, "For you know that it was not with perishable things such as silver and gold that you were redeemed...but with the precious blood of Christ..." (1 Peter 1:18a, 19a).

Consider this passage: "For Christ died for sins once for all, the righteous for the unrighteous, to bring you to God" (2 Peter 3:18).

Now our redemption would not be possible if Christ had remained dead. On the third day, He rose from the dead having conquered the enslaving power of sin and death. He is a living redeemer Who has returned to heaven to bridge the gap between God and people. The Bible says, "For there is one God and one mediator between God and man, the man Christ Jesus, who gave himself as a ransom for all men..." (1 Tim. 2:5-6a).

Christ, the Redeemer, has done for us what we cannot do for ourselves. We are incapable of redeeming ourselves. But through Christ, God, in His grace, offers us redemption as a gift. This gift includes the forgiveness of sin, a right relationship with God, and a new spiritual life that is eternal. This means liberation from our old lives of bondage and separation from God and a new freedom to enter into a love relationship with God and enjoy Him and His abundant life now and forever in the kingdom of heaven.

How does one receive this gift? You must, first of all, repent. This biblical word means to change your mind. It means that you are no longer content to live the old life of sin and separation, and you choose, with genuine remorse, to confess you are a sinner and turn away from your life without Christ. Then you must turn to Christ, trust in Him as Lord and Savior, and receive Him and His gift of redemption by personal invitation.

Look at several verses in the Bible that give various descriptions of this personal commitment to Christ.

> For the wages of sin is death, but the gift of God is eternal life in Christ Jesus our Lord.
> —Rom. 6:23

For it is by grace you have been saved through faith – and this is not from yourselves, it is the gift of God – not of works, so that no one can boast.
—Eph. 2:8-9

Everyone who calls on the name of the Lord will be saved.
—Rom. 10:15

Here I am. I stand at the door and knock. If anyone hears my voice and opens the door, I will come in.
—Rev. 3:20

For God so loved the world that He gave His one and only Son, that whoever believes in Him shall not perish but have eternal life.
—John 3:16

These verses make it clear that the liberty of redemption through Christ involves a faith commitment. The Redeemer will not force Himself and His liberation upon you. You are free to choose. Will you choose to receive Jesus Christ right now? If the answer is yes, here is a suggested prayer you could use to express what is in your heart:

Dear Lord Jesus,
 I know that I am a sinner and that I need to be set free from sin and its consequences. I believe You died for my sins and rose from the dead. I turn away from my sins, and I ask for Your forgiveness. I invite You to come into my heart and life. I choose to trust in You alone for my redemption and to follow You as my Lord and Savior. Thank You.
 Amen

If you prayed this prayer with sincerity, you have been redeemed. Congratulations! You have just made the greatest decision a person can ever make. Jesus described this experience as being "born again" (John 3:3). When you receive Christ, the Spirit of God comes to indwell you and imparts to you new life. You must then begin to

CONCLUSION: THE LIBERTY OF REDEMPTION

grow spiritually. This is just the beginning of a wonderful new life in Christ. To enable you to continue to grow, you must:

- Read and study the Bible on a regular basis.
- Communicate with God through prayer every day.
- Find a church that faithfully teaches the Bible where you can worship, learn, and fellowship with other believers.
- Get involved in active Christian service sharing the love and truth of Christ with others.

Pastor Darrel Gabbard
Retired Senior Pastor:
Dublin Baptist Church
Dublin, Ohio

RESOURCES FOR YOUR SPIRITUAL PILGRIMAGE

GROWING SPIRITUALLY IS a lifetime journey that God never meant for us to take alone. Here is my personal list of resources, teachers, and mentors God has brought my way to help me grow and know Him in a more intimate way. This is only a small personal list that doesn't include countless other wonderful teachers and God-loving preachers, but it is a list of solid, powerful spiritual leaders who will lead you by their teaching into a relationship with a real, powerful, and loving God. I pray you too might find help and guidance from their zeal for God in your own spiritual journey.

The Bible, the Word of God

Billy Graham Evangelistic Association: www.billygraham.org 1-877-247-2426

St. Francis of Assisi: Peace Prayer of St. Francis, "Lord, make me an instrument of your peace"

Charles Stanley: www.intouch.org 1-800-789-1473

Joyce Meyers: www.joycemeyer.org 1-800-727-9673

Pastor David Johnson, Church of the Open Door, Maple Grove, MN: www.thedoor.org 763-416-5887

Pastor Dave Workman, Vineyard Community Church, Cincinnati Ohio: www.cincyvineyard.com, 513-671-0422

Pastor Rich Nathan, Vineyard Columbus: www.vineyardcolumbus.org 614-890-0000

Retired Senior Pastor Darrel Gabbard, Dublin Baptist Church, Dublin Ohio: www.dublinbaptist.com, 614-889-2307

Pastor David Uth, First Baptist Church of Orlando: www.firstorlando.com 407-425-2555

Brennan Manning, author of *Abba's Child*, *The Ragamuffin Gospel*: www.brennanmanning.com

Michael W. Smith, contemporary Christian singer, songwriter: www.michaelwsmith.com

Dr. Rick Warren, author of *The Purpose Driven Life* and devotions: www.purposedrivenlife.com

C. S. Lewis, author of *Mere Christianity*, one of the clearest and best introductions to Christianity

OM Ships International, Operated the Logos ship, and current ships that carry educational and inspirational books to millions around the world, including a book I read about an American medical missionary that changed my life: www.omships.org

To order additional copies of this book and
the e-book version:
please visit our website at
www.hopeforsoldiers.org
Blog: www.adelhanna.com
or
www.Amazon.com
www.BarnesandNoble.com

www.ingramcontent.com/pod-product-compliance
Lightning Source LLC
Chambersburg PA
CBHW051937290426
44110CB00015B/2016